ONE TO ONE

ONE TO ONE

Resources for Conference-Centered Writing

CHARLES W. DAWE
Orange Coast College

EDWARD A. DORNAN
Orange Coast College

LITTLE, BROWN AND COMPANY Boston   Toronto

Library of Congress Catalog Card No. 80-83746

ISBN 0-316-177245

9 8 7 6 5 4 3 2

HAL

Published simultaneously in Canada
by Little, Brown·& Company (Canada) Limited

Printed in the United States of America

Credits

Pages 46, 49–50, Jane van Lawick-Goodall. From *In the Shadow of Man* by Jane van Lawick-Goodall. Reprinted by permission of Houghton Mifflin Company and Collins Publishers. Copyright © 1971 by Hugo and Jane van Lawick-Goodall.

Page 59. Reprinted by permission from *Time, The Weekly Newsmagazine*; Copyright Time Inc. 1978.

Pages 60–62, Edward Abbey. Copyright 1968 by Edward Abbey. Reprinted by permission of the Harold Matson Company, Inc.

Pages 75–77. Reprinted by permission of Lisa M. Beckley.

Pages 82, 340–341, Richard Selzer. Copyright © 1974, 1975, 1976 by Richard Selzer. Reprinted by permission of Simon & Schuster, a Division of Gulf & Western Corporation.

Page 85, Donald Hall. © 1969/75 by The New York Times Company. Reprinted by permission.

Page 119. Copyright 1977–78 by Newsweek, Inc. All rights reserved. Reprinted by permission.

Pages 123–124, 279, Joan Didion. Copyright © 1979 by Joan Didion. Reprinted by permission of Simon & Schuster, a Division of Gulf and Western Corporation.

Pages 155–157, Delia Ephron. Reprinted by permission of Delia Ephron, c/o Clarke Literary Agency, Inc. Copyright © 1976 by *Esquire*.

Page 159–163, Roberta Ridgely. From Roberta Ridgely, *The Tijuana, Mexicali, Ensenada Shopping, Restaurant. and Entertainment Guide, Ole!* Reprinted by permission of J. P. Tarcher, Inc., Los Angeles. Copyright © 1975.

Pages 237–239, Arnold Bennett. Excerpts from *The Journal of Arnold Bennett*. Copyright 1932, 1933 by the Viking Press Inc. Reprinted by permission of Doubleday & Company, Inc.

Page 262, E. E. Cummings. From "anyone lived in a pretty how town," in *Poems, 1923–1954* by E. E. Cummings. Reprinted by permission of Harcourt Brace Jovanovich, Inc.

Pages 280–281, Isaac Asimov. Copyright © 1972, by The Review of the Arts, Inc. Included with the permission of the author.

Page 297, Emily Dickinson. Reprinted by permission of the publishers and the Trustees of Amherst College from *The Poems of Emily Dickinson*, edited by Thomas H. Johnson. Cambridge, Mass.: The Belknap Press of Harvard University Press, Copyright 1951, © 1955, 1979 by the President and Fellows of Harvard College.

Page 328, Jules Henry. From *Culture Against Man* by Jules Henry. Copyright © 1963 by Random House, Inc. Reprinted by permission of Random House, Inc.

Page 344, Joyce Maynard. © 1969/75 by The New York Times Company. Reprinted by permission.

To Patti, Hugh, and Aaron Dornan
and to Sandy Lee Woon Ho

TO THE STUDENT

Two activities are important to learn to write well. First is to write, and to write a lot. Second is to get sound advice about your writing from someone who knows how to write. The class you're in will bring these two activities together.

Your teacher has probably selected *One to One* in order to support conferenced-centered instruction. Although *conference-centered instruction* might sound a little fancy, the concept behind the phrase is quite simple. It involves nothing more than you and your teacher sitting side-by-side and talking about each paper you write. The conference will last from three to fifteen minutes, depending on the length of the assignment. But no matter how long the conference lasts, the major activities will be the same — the teacher will read your work, listen to your comments, and offer advice and directions to help you develop your writing strengths and weaknesses. Simple enough, but to make it work takes some effort. We want to give you a few suggestions that will make that effort easier.

First, we suggest you become an active participant in the conference. Don't just put yourself in the teacher's hands and wait for your fate. Instead, identify and talk about the problems you faced in the assignment. Ask specific questions about solving the problems. Take some brief notes that capture your teacher's responses and recheck them when the conference ends.

We also suggest you try to see your instructor as a writing coach rather than as a judge. Just as a coach wants an athlete to win in competition, your teacher wants you to succeed at writing. If you don't agree with a particular comment about your work, say so and present your view as clearly as you can without arguing or being defensive. Then let your teacher explain the reasons behind the comment. This way the two of you will be building a working relationship that fosters success.

Third, make an effort to treat your papers as works in progress. If you follow the advice of many successful writers who claim that to learn to write well, the beginning writer must learn to rewrite, then you'll have no difficulty improving your writing. But if you come to a conference convinced that you've attained perfection in your writing, you'll have some trouble because a conference will often end with an assignment that requires you either to revise or rewrite a paper. Our best advice is to relax and keep in mind that the purpose of the conference is not just to get your work accepted but to improve your skills. View each assignment as a stage in the process of mastering different kinds of writing. Sometimes that mastery comes faster by rewriting a flawed paper rather than by starting a new one.

Finally, you can help make your conferences work by carefully studying the material your instructor assigns. Read the explanations, analyze the illustrations, review the marginal notes — do all this before you start to write. If you work in this way, you'll save valuable conference time by keeping the focus on your writing and not on explanations of the assignments you didn't read thoroughly.

A quick glance at the book will show you it's divided into four main parts and that the first three are subdivided into several sections, each identified by number or week. (The fourth part is arranged alphabetically.) Since the book teaches writing by getting you to write, each subsection ends with an assignment called a "Writing Task" that's designed to help you learn the information presented in the section. In Part One, Getting Started, you'll learn to write for a reader, how to work through a four-step composing process, and how to combine the particulars of an experience with your reactions to it. In Part Two, Writing Tasks, you'll learn different ways to develop paragraphs and several ways to develop essays. In Part Three, Daily Writing, you'll go through nine weeks of writing practice that will help you overcome the fears you might have when facing a blank page. By working through daily writing tasks you'll also generate subjects and material for the more formal assignments in the course. In Part Four, Index for Writers, you'll find help with common problems beginning writers face: how to get sentences to flow together; where to put commas, semicolons, and apostrophes; when to use quotation marks, and so on.

In closing we'd like to offer one last thought. Soon after completing Part One, Getting Started, you may discover that you are doing writing tasks that are different from the ones your neighbor is doing. Don't be concerned about that. In one-to-one instruction individual students work on what they need at the moment. Our advice is to take advantage of the flexibility in one-to-one instruction and use this text to help you find your own path to the common goal — good writing.

ACKNOWLEDGMENTS

We wish to express our gratitude to Roger Garrison for helping us adapt the conference method of composition instruction to our classrooms and for encouraging us throughout the writing of this text. We'd also like to thank Charles Christensen, Elizabeth Philipps, Joan Feinberg, and Elizabeth Schaaf of Little, Brown for their trust, patience, and guidance and express our appreciation to Richard Andrews, Clackamas Community College; Peter Brunette, George Mason University; Judi Burken, Kellogg Community College; Judith R. Hert, San Bernardino Valley College; Robert G. Lesman, Northern Virginia Community College, Annandale Campus; and Harvey S. Wiener, LaGuardia Community College, for reviewing the manuscript in its early stages.

We owe a special debt to Richard Beal of Boston University whose cogent comments and suggestions helped us establish the final form of the manuscript.

We received indispensable assistance from our colleagues at Orange Coast College, especially those who listened to our ideas and shared with us their one-to-one teaching experiences over five years of lunches and coffee breaks: John Coates, Margaret Callanan, Robert Dees, Michael Finnegan, Judith Jernigan, Patricia Kubis, Richard Linder, Margaret Langhans, and Thomas O'Keeffe.

Finally, any acknowledgment would be incomplete that fails to thank those teachers who attended seminars, conferences, and workshops and shared with us their responses to our materials. The list is too long to include here, but certain names come immediately to mind: Patricia Barney, Citrus College; Edith Conn, Ventura College; Don Heidt, College of the Canyons; Sevia Kaye, Nassau Community College; Jan Lawson, College of the Desert; Nancy Roediger, Tarrant County Junior College; James Roman, Delaware County Community College; Ellery Sedgwick, Longwood College; Michael Seeley, Ventura College; Jo An Simmons, Los Angeles City College; Gayle Smith, Pennsylvania State University; Norman Williamson, Mendocino College.

CONTENTS

PART THREE

DAILY WRITING   191

PART FOUR

INDEX FOR WRITERS   249

PART ONE

GETTING STARTED

This section will introduce you — in four phases, with a writing task at the end of each phase — to the process of putting your thoughts on paper. You will base the writing you do in this section on your own observation and experience, not on your ability to collect material from other writers' thoughts. In other words, you will not be researching but will be collecting, recording, and organizing your personal experiences.

Besides the primary question that plagues most beginning writers — "What should I write about?" — there is a second question usually linked to it: "And how should I get started?" A third question, probably as fundamental as the other two, seldom gets consciously asked yet is important for the success of any written communication: "For whom am I writing?"

As for the first question, for every writing task you do in this part of the book, we will guide you to something to write about. So for now that problem is solved. Our main goals in this section are to give you a simple way to start writing and to make you aware of your reader.

1 LISTING AND WRITING FOR A READER

Getting started on a written project may be the most critical point in the entire enterprise. Perhaps the difficulty has something to do with facing a blank page and knowing that within an hour, a day, or even a week that page, and most likely many others as blank, will have to be filled with words. Of course, the problem is more complex than that. The words must be nudged into sentences. The sentences must link logically together and be fitted into paragraphs. The paragraphs must be assembled into a coherent essay, report, or letter. Besides all the nudging, fitting, and assembling, you must put in the squiggles called punctuation. And then there is spelling — the mind shudders. The part of the brain that sends energy to the arm freezes. Writer's elbow sets in. It's too painful to shape the words with a pen. You're blocked.

There is a way to overcome the block. Instead of worrying about all the meticulous arranging you have to do to finish a piece of writing, begin by randomly collecting the raw material that will make up the content. One way to do the collecting is to draw up a list.

Everyone is familiar with grocery lists. Consumer advocates often advise shoppers to make grocery lists before going on shopping expeditions. With a list in hand, the expedition won't turn into a spending spree. Well, the advice is equally valid for a writer setting out on a journey.

A list works as an ordering system through which you may quickly gather the material you want to communicate to a reader. By writing a list you can rapidly capture fleeting details. A list can also fire your imagination and guide your direction. No doubt you can see how a piece of writing could easily form around a list of joyful or frightening experiences. Or around a list of dreams, fears, or memories.

3

So whenever you start a piece of writing, tear a page from the home-maker's manual and draw up your own grocery list. Now let's see how a list works.

Our homemaker is planning an Italian supper. After surveying the cupboard, she realizes she needs a few items to complete the menu and sees she's also short of juice and coffee. She quickly makes a list to remind herself to get what she needs.

juice
tomatoes
coffee
bread
onions

Five simple items. About a ten-minute trip with the written reminder keeping her on target. Of course, the plan may change — she may rear-range it as she goes. For instance, she would probably pick up the to-matoes and onions at the same time because they would be in the produce section, then go to the nearby frozen food compartment before stopping for coffee located somewhere near the market center, and end up at the bread rack near the check-out counter. The list makes her shopping a breeze.

Unfortunately, writing is not as simple as jotting down a grocery list and collecting the items. The writer must communicate with an audi-ence — a reader. Somehow, in order to make the communication clear, the writer must anticipate the reader's mind.

Audience

The reader's mind. Some distant space impossible to touch in order to feel out its boundaries. It's a mystery. To anticipate it is guesswork. And a writer must always guess, try to figure out its moves, its questions, its blind spots.

Consider our homemaker's grocery list again:

juice
tomatoes
coffee
bread
onions

Could she give this to her teenage son and expect him to gather what she wanted?

If she were naive enough to do so, he might return with freshly squeezed guava juice when she wanted frozen orange juice. He might buy two green tomatoes when she wanted four ripe ones; instant coffee when she wanted regular grind; wheat bread when she wanted French; white onions when she had (purple) in mind. The confusion could deepen. Her teenager might even go to the wrong market — you know, the exclusive one where the goods cost a nickel or dime more.

For our homemaker to avoid the confusion, she would have to recast the list in note form, anticipating her teenager's mind, thus making her thought as clear as necessary in order to get what she wanted. The finished note might look something like this:

> Darren, I need some items from the market for tonight's dinner and tomorrow's breakfast. Please get them at Safeway.
> 1. four ripe tomatoes
> 2. two purple onions
> 3. a six-oz. can of frozen orange juice
> 4. regular grind coffee — whatever brand is on sale
> 5. French bread — the long kind, not the presliced

You can see how composing even a simple grocery list for a particular reader puts demands on the writer. The homemaker needs to include specifics, such as *four ripe* tomatoes, *two purple* onions, a *six-ounce can* of *orange* juice, and so on. Otherwise her teenager will interpret the note according to the characteristics of his own mind.

If the homemaker were writing for someone else, she might need to include more information. If she were writing the note for out-of-town guests or a grandparent or a child, what information would she have to give? Let's see.

Suppose our homemaker wants to leave a shopping note for her ten-year-old child. The list she has begun will start the process of writing the note, but for a ten-year-old the list needs more detailing in anticipation of the child's thinking. The homemaker, therefore, adds more information. The fleshed-out list will then serve as a rough guide for writing the final note.

1. four ripe tomatoes — deep red, not orange; squeeze them for softness
2. two large purple onions, at least as big as your fist
3. a small can of orange juice, the kind you've helped me make for breakfast
4. a small can of coffee with "regular grind" written at the top. Buy the one that costs the least
5. French bread, the kind your brother says looks like a spyglass.

For her child she has made the list even more specific than for her teenager. Aside from the details, she has made some comparisons: "at least as big as your fist" and "looks like a spyglass." She also recalls previous experience: "the kind you've helped me make for breakfast." She even gives a brief lesson on how to select a ripe tomato. All this information is necessary because she knows it will help her ten-year-old understand her meaning. There will be less confusion in the communication.

With the list before her she can begin to write the note. But while writing, she must continue to anticipate her child's responses. For instance, her teenager would have no trouble with money transactions; her ten-year-old might. More than likely, her teenager would easily find his way around the market; her ten-year-old probably would not think in the neat categories in which most market managers arrange their merchandise. And, finally, it is doubtful that her teenager would get sidetracked on the way home; her ten-year-old might stop to play. So you see, even after developing a detailed list, the writer, when arranging the contents in a final draft, must continue to anticipate the reader's mind.

By this point you may think that anticipating the reader's mind is a tough job. Don't fret. Once you get into the habit of doing it, you do much of the anticipation automatically. The important thought here is that you must keep asking yourself what the reader needs to know in order to understand what you mean and then include the information as you go.

What follows is our homemaker's note to her ten-year-old son, based on the list developed above. Read it and see how she used the list for content and how, as she wrote the note, she added information as she thought of it so that the message would be clear to the child.

> Take this ten-dollar bill and hurry to Safeway to buy some groceries for dinner.
>
> First, go to the vegetable and fruit section on the far side of the market and get four ripe tomatoes. The tomatoes should be deep red — not orange. Be sure to test them with a slight squeeze for softness. Don't buy mushy ones and don't buy hard ones — find some in between hard and mushy. Near the tomatoes, you'll see the onions. I need two purple ones about the size of your fist or bigger.
>
> Next, while you are on that side of the market, go to the frozen food section for a small can of orange juice. A small can is the size you've helped me make for breakfast some mornings.
>
> After getting the orange juice, go to the toy section — you

should have no trouble finding it — and right behind it you'll find the coffee. I need one small can, the pound size, that says regular grind near the top. Check the prices and take the one that costs the least.

And finally, from the rack near the check-out counter, pick up a loaf of French bread, the kind your brother says looks like a spyglass.

After you've done all that, you may buy a treat. Not candy or ice cream, but some dried fruit or nuts.

When you've finished paying for the groceries and your treat, put the change in your pocket and rush home without stopping at the hobby shop to look at models, or at the park to toss the football, or at Jack's to watch "The Munsters" reruns.

"Now scoot!" the homemaker might have put at the close, sending her ten-year-old off in a swirl of uncombed hair and baggy clothes.

The note might have been more effective if put in a different format. For instance, the homemaker could have begun with a general statement, then numbered each item with its additional comments, and ended with the reminder not to stop to play. A diagram of this format might look something like this:

General opening statement

Individual items with   1.
descriptive directions   2.
                       3.
                       4.
                       5.

Closing reminder

But to illustrate our purpose in this section — that is, showing the importance of anticipating the reader and building a piece of writing from a list — the note works well. After drawing up the details, our homemaker anticipates her child's mind right down to the distractions he might be drawn to on the way home. She even anticipates how much he would like a treat after facing all the temptations supermarket managers scatter along the aisles to ensnare children; unwilling to have him select a sweet, she guides him to a more healthful choice.

Of course writing from a list and anticipating your reader will not solve all your writing frustrations, but they do give you a way to start working. Perhaps now facing a blank page seems a little easier.

WRITING TASK

Write a note in no more than 250 words. First decide who you're writing for. Second, draw up a "grocery list" that captures the content of your piece. Finally, write the note, using the list as a rough plan.

Choose a reader who represents a challenge: a younger brother or sister, a parent or grandparent, an out-of-town friend, or a complete stranger. Don't select a close friend with whom you talk daily — that's too easy.

Though you are free to select your own subject, you may want to direct your reader to a favorite spot of yours, such as a restaurant, bookstore, record store, or hideaway. You may send someone on a shopping errand to a nearby shopping center. You may give someone instructions on how to focus a camera, drive a car with a manual transmission, fly a kite, set up a tent, light a Coleman stove. If you decide to do a "how to do something" note, try not to sound like a book of directions; instead use a personal tone.

2 THE COMPOSING PROCESS

This section is the beginning of four related assignments. We've assembled them to introduce you to a method of working we hope you'll use whenever you tackle a writing task. They have been built around the idea that writing is a process best done in drafts. Paragraphs, essays, reports, or entire books do not hatch fully formed from the writer's imagination. They are usually nudged and teased into life, sometimes unfolding in elaborate ways. Of course, all writers use their own processes to build their work. Indeed, one of the secrets of becoming a good writer is to discover your personal method of nudging and teasing experience and ideas into words. In the spirit of exploration and as a way to begin the search, we offer the following approach.

In this series of tasks, you will first record the details of a brief experience — this will be called the prewriting phase. Second, we'll ask you to write a rough draft by arranging the details of the prewritten material in an orderly form. Once the rough draft is done, you will go on to edit and revise it by tinkering with the arrangement of words, phrases, and sentences so that the entire piece reads smoothly. After editing and revising, the next step in the method will be to integrate the changes by writing a final draft, thus polishing the whole piece.

When you have completed this series you will have used one observed experience to work through the four main steps of the writing process:

1. prewriting
2. rough draft
3. editing and revising
4. final draft

Prewriting

Prewriting is an extension of making a list. When prewriting, a writer is interested only in gathering the raw material to use later. He need not be concerned with the nitty-gritty of writing — that is, grammar, syntax, punctuation, and spelling. The nitty-gritty is important but not at this inventive stage. For if you consider the writing process, you will easily see that it involves two different kinds of thought: (1) creative thought, which grows from a writer's intuition and has something to do with allowing the mind to connect events and images; and (2) critical thought, which grows from the intellect, allowing the mind to organize the appropriate words into sentence patterns. Creative thought is less self-conscious than critical, yet both are important. Although a writer never wishes to completely sever intuition from intellect, when prewriting it is best to stress the creative side while restraining the more self-conscious critical side. Therefore, as you work to capture raw material in a pre-write, attempt to open yourself to experience and select from it without concern for critical judgments. The reshaping and organizing — that is, the judging — will come later.

Although the prewriting phase works for all kinds of written projects, for learning purposes you'll begin by working with a brief description that draws a bead on an experience you set out to record. A little later — after we've inched through an illustration of prewriting — we'll ask you to stroll around your neighborhood, across campus, through the library, or wherever you may wish in order to start the search for something to describe. Once you find it, like a reporter using a note pad and pencil to capture colorful background for an article, you'll record the details of whatever it is that has caught your interest. These details will come to you through your senses — through sight, sound, taste, touch, and smell. In other words, you will be working to capture the externals or surface experience, as opposed to what you may feel or think about the experience. The task will be to make the reader "see," not to tell the reader what you think. Try to keep in mind that there is a difference between using writing to "think about" or "respond to" an experience and using it to capture the sensory detail of an experience. Each use has an important place and the two cannot be cleanly separated, but for this assignment we'll be asking you to concentrate on gathering sensory detail. A later task will ask you to respond to experience.

Here's how one student prewrote the experience of watching two joggers circle a high school track at sunset. While you read this prewrite, keep in mind that it is a form of listing that the writer uses to collect the details of the events she's experiencing.

> – Dusk at the track. Two joggers. Both wearing white shorts. One shirtless. The other in T-shirt.

- One short-legged, short-necked. Reminds me of a buffalo bull driven too hard, too far.
- The other tall, thin-legged. Reminds me of a stork, but doesn't move like a stork, very smooth, gliding, flowing like a human river or stream. Moving like a deer across an empty meadow (how can a meadow be empty?).
- I hear the buff/bull huffing and puffing. The sound more like a throat rattle as he passes me up in the stands. The wooden bench cold. His feet scrape the track — scuff, scuffing sound. The head bobbing from side to side and down. Tired.
- The tall one moves easily, chatting as they go. He seems to be warming up, his feet dancing.
- Overhead, about a mile away, a jet flying low at an angle, just taking off. The engines loud, thrusting. Rumbling like distant thunder. Nearly sunset, the sky reddish-orange behind the jet.
- The two men still circling, the tall one pulling ahead of the first/short one. Behind them in the distance down the hill the university lights coming on. The air cooling. A silhouette with flashes of light. The sun nearly sunk from sight. The orange sky deepening red. A southern California sunset. Dark blue indigo.
- Check the time. 6:30. Time. The second hand turning luminous. The numbers also. The second hand sweeping over the luminous numbers.
- The joggers still circling. The plane, now just a distant speck arcing north. It will soon circle east. The day coming to an end. The joggers stop — the heavy one sitting on the ground, leaning on his hands. The other does some stretches. Getting dark. I can hardly see them as they walk toward the gate. Feel alone: the sky black. Stars appear like chips of glass sparkling.

Now let's take a closer look at this illustration of a prewritten draft to see what can be learned about writing one.

First, notice how the writer frees herself of critical concerns by paying little if any attention to arranging words into sentences and sentences into paragraphs. She generates an expanded list, gathering the raw material into raw form. Because she relaxes her critical intellect, she sees the external details and connects some of them with images. For instance, she sees that one runner is short and the other is tall and she sees and hears how one breathes with difficulty and the other with ease. In a strict sense she does not see the buffalo and deer; her intuition makes the connections from experience in her memory. That's fine. Often while describing experiences, writers will reach for comparisons of this sort in order to put themselves and readers on common ground. These comparisons help the reader experience what the writer experienced. So if you have associations or make connections like these, good. Put them in the prewritten draft and later you may use them in the rough draft.

Next, notice that the writer begins by focusing on two joggers but that the scene around the track — the sun setting, a jet taking off, the university, her watch — comes into play. The joggers center the prewrite; other details radiate from them. At this point we may disagree with what this writer has recorded. After all, if she started out to describe one thing, she had better stick to it — right? And we may even bring our knowledge of high school tracks to bear in second-guessing the writer. For instance, where is the chalk-lined football field with goal posts at both ends, or where are the sawdust and sand pits and piles of high and low hurdles? But remember that it's important within flexible limits to give the mind free range when prewriting. You want to generate a creative flow; follow your own interest.

Also notice the writer's use of simple words. Simple does not mean simplistic or oversimplified; simple words are basic, not complicated or complex. With the exception of *luminous* and *indigo* you probably carry all the words from this prewrite in your own language pool and can dip for them whenever you need to. Notice too that many of the writer's words, mainly stressing sight and sound, are concrete — words that call up images of what can be seen, heard, touched, smelled, and tasted. Often concrete words are the ones most common in your vocabulary. With them you can build a solid description.

And, finally, notice how the writer sticks to gathering the externals of the experience. She does not slump into recording what she thinks about the experience. For instance, if she had written what she thought about the joggers and jogging, she might have included some comments such as the ones italicized below:

> – Dusk at the track. Two joggers wearing white shorts. One shirtless. The other in T-shirt. *How silly to be out running on a chilly night. Dumb!*
> – One short-legged, short-necked. Reminds me of a buffalo or bull driven too hard, too far. *He's too fat to be jogging. My guess is his heart is about ready to burst. Jogging might be healthy for some people, but it's going to kill the fat guy.*

For this prewrite we'll ask you to stay with collecting the externals and not to make any judgments about the experience.

What does all this add up to? Well, prewriting is building an expanded list to get your writing started. The prewrite represents a first draft: maybe an awkward first draft, but one that will give you enough detail to shape into a rough draft — the second step in the process.

WRITING TASK

Take a walk around your neighborhood, across campus, or through the library, a market, shopping center, or park and look for something to describe. When that something catches your interest, sit down, and record the details. Act like a detached reporter neutrally collecting the raw stuff of the experience. A word of caution: resist the temptation to do this task from memory; it may turn into a something-interesting-happened-to-me-last-week piece. We're asking that you set out to find something fresh. If you record from memory, the chances are you'll end up writing a narrative — a story. The list you make will be the prewrite for a descriptive piece, not a story. So, take our best advice: accept the challenge and take the thirty or forty minutes to do an on-the-spot prewrite.

Rough Draft

Now that you have completed the prewriting phase, it's time to shape your notes into a rough draft. Rough draft stage is when the mind begins to shift from the intuitive into the intellectual. The shift is not sudden, like stepping from land into water, but happens gradually, like a river meeting the sea, where the water is neither completely salt nor completely sweet. To make the shift you will have to face a whole new set of problems.

The first problem has to do with shaping the rough draft. If your prewritten draft is anything like the one about the joggers at sunset, it is streaked with flashes of concrete description and creative inspiration — all scribbled in fragments and ragged sentences. That's fine. Capturing the flow is what prewriting is all about. In contrast, the rough draft is the first step toward bringing order to the random collection of detail. Not complete order — you still need the creative instinct to fill in the gaps — but enough to give the details shape.

We want you to begin shaping the rough draft by setting a limit on the length. Write it in no more than 300 words. If you have pages of notes, meeting this limit may be tough. But it just means that you, like most writers who work from notes, will have to select the outstanding details to include in the rough draft. One way to make this selection is to decide what the purpose of the piece is — in other words, decide what you are trying to communicate to the reader. Once you have the purpose clearly established in your mind, select the details from the prewritten material that will help convey that purpose.

While writing the rough draft try to create a sense of roundness: the rough draft should have a beginning, a middle, and an end. Unfortunately, as with most aspects of writing, there is no magic formula for writing a rounded piece. A sense for it often comes from intuition. But because most writing you do will have deadlines, you can't sit around waiting for a blinding insight. We suggest, therefore, you start by writing a sentence or two that leads readers into the experience without their needing to know anything that came before. The beginning sentence or two will also convey your general purpose. You can then move into the middle of the piece by developing a sequence of sentences that grow from the lead. The middle will be the bulk of the piece. As you write, you will be constantly referring to the prewritten draft to haul in detail you need to build the sentences. Finally, you can close the piece where the middle sequence seems naturally to end. And here's where you have to rely on sensitivity. Endings often have a great deal to do with feelings. Someone once compared a good ending with the feeling one has after hearing a box click shut. On the other hand, an ending may also have the effect of a door slamming. We suggest you try to link the end of your piece with the lead, like a snake biting its tail.

Besides shaping the overall structure of your piece, you must also shape the sentences. When you did your prewrite, you recorded the experience on the fly, in phrases. While writing the rough draft, you should shape the phrases into complete sentences. To write in complete sentences at this point does not mean to fret over the nitty-gritty niceties of grammar, syntax, punctuation, and spelling. It only means that you should be aware of them without getting yourself bogged down. If you remember that in most writing assignments the rough draft will be for your eyes only, you may be able to find the balance between being aware of and getting mired in concerns over writing correctly. Also remember that there are still two more steps in the process: (1) editing and revising and (2) the final draft.

Before showing you an example of a rough draft, we want to bring up two more points. First, when you write your rough draft, try to use simple, concrete language. There's no need to be fancy with words. Second, select part of your prewritten draft to "showcase." Remember that for the prewriting stage we suggested you find an experience and use it for your prewriting. This experience may be the part you wish to showcase. Your descriptive piece will then serve as a showcase to display it. The way to showcase this part of the experience is to write more about it than any other part.

Let's now see how the student who wrote the prewritten draft in the last section shaped it into rough form.

Last night at dusk I took a walk to the high school track at the top of the hill. There I sat alone in the wooden stands and watched the day come to a close. Two joggers were circling the track. Both were wearing shorts. One was shirtless; the other wore a T-shirt. One was heavy and ran huffing and puffing, his feet scuffing along like a tired buffalo's. His head bobbed from side to side. He was tired. The other was tall and thin, built like a stork, but ran like a deer I had seen last summer running through a meadow. I watched them circle the track four, five, or six times. Each time they passed me up in the stands I could hear the thin one chatting, while the heavy one's breath rattled in his throat. Behind them the sky was turning reddish orange as it often does in southern California at sunset. A jet plane no more than one mile or two miles away was climbing in the sky. It had just taken off from the airport. The engines sounded like distant thunder, a low rumble. It started to arc north, becoming a speck. The lights of the university were blinking on. The buildings were becoming a light-spotted silhouette against the darkening skyline. The men still circled, although the thin one was ahead of the heavy one. The one strided away into a curve. The night was getting darker, turning indigo. The stars were coming out and looked like chips of glass. I felt alone and saw the joggers had stopped. They walked toward the gate and faded from sight with the light.

Indeed, this is a very rough draft with many awkward spots. That's okay. The purpose of the rough draft is to shape the material, not to make it perfect.

Let's examine this rough draft by comparing it to the prewritten draft. The writer had to limit her piece to fewer than 300 words; that limitation forced her to be selective. To be selective means to decide not only what to include in a written piece but also what to exclude. Notice, for instance, that the writer excluded the details related to glancing at her watch. She also dropped some details related to the runners: their sitting on the ground and exercising and the comparison of one's running style to a stream.

Why did the writer exclude these details and not others? Since writers make their own choices — often by intuition — the answers may be hard to come by. One reason might have something to do with the purpose of the piece. The writer suggests in the lead sentences that she is going to describe what she saw at the day's close. She reflects that purpose at several points: the sky turning reddish orange, the lights blinking on, the day getting dark, the stars coming out. Certainly the details of the watch — the time of day and the hands and numbers turning luminous

— would fit, but to haul them in might detract from the larger elements that relate to the day's close.

Another reason the writer excluded certain details could have something to do with the overall flow of the piece. For instance, if she had included the details of the exercises, the smooth movement to the end would have been interrupted. After all, she would have had to drop the runners to the ground, describe the one doing stretches and the other sitting, and then get them to their feet to move them toward the gate. All that would have taken several sentences. Better to leave it out to keep the piece moving.

And, finally, the writer might have excluded some details because they seemed inappropriate. For instance, to compare the thin jogger's running style to a stream would be inappropriate under any circumstances: the comparison fails to call to mind either a visual image of the jogger or the way he runs. The idea of "smoothness" is the only link. But if you examine the image, like the writer of this draft, you will realize that streams are not always smooth-flowing things. They gush, pour into pools, and sometimes cascade. When thoughtfully applied to someone running with ease, the comparison doesn't make sense. Would any thoughtful writer want to imply that a runner might gush, pour, or cascade around a track?

It's easy to see that the process of selection is important whether you do it with the general purpose, concern for the overall flow, or appropriateness of the details in mind.

The writer has also kept her language simple. She uses concrete words that create a picture of her experience, such as "one was heavy and ran huffing and puffing, his feet scuffing along like a tired buffalo's." She also transforms the fragments of the prewritten draft into complete sentences, although at times the sentences are ragged and need repair. For instance, the sentence just quoted would read more smoothly and accurately if written "One was heavy and, like a tired buffalo, ran huffing and puffing while his feet scuffed along." But this is still a rough draft. The writer will change much of the raggedness when she edits and revises the whole piece.

The writer has also shaped her material by developing a rough beginning, middle, and end. She opens with sentences that suggest her purpose — to share some observations she's made at sunset. After leading the reader into her description, she develops a sequence of sentences that carry out the purpose. She ends with a sentence that describes the joggers fading from sight as dusk turns into night, thus circling back to the lead sentences.

Finally, within the framework, the writer showcases the runners. She describes them at the beginning, then returns to them at the end. The whole piece seems to be built around the runners.

Now, before you confront your rough draft, we wish to point out three decisions you must make before you start to write.

First, decide what point of view will rule your piece. In the task that involved writing a note, the point of view probably came naturally. Notes tend to be written in the first person singular — "I" — and addressed to the reader in the second person — "you." By using the "I" point of view you wrote as a participant in the process. Whenever writing about first-hand experience, as you will be in these early tasks, the use of first person is appropriate. On the other hand, for some subjects you will need to keep a more impersonal stance by avoiding the first person altogether. You will then be writing as a detached observer who stands some distance away from the reader and the material. The impersonal point of view is appropriate when the subject needs to be treated in a neutral way — in history, for instance, scientific writing, or news reporting. Whether personal or impersonal, the subject usually determines the point of view. The concept to remember here is that the point of view needs to be consistent throughout the piece. For instance, the writer of the rough draft above wrote consistently in the "I" point of view and did not shift. A shifting point of view confuses readers; a consistent one adds to their sense of order.

A second choice you must make before starting the rough draft has to do with tone. Tone is a very complicated part of writing, but if you begin by thinking of it as the voice in which you wish to address a reader, you have started to master its complexity. You might approach a reader in a casual or chatty voice or in a more reserved or formal tone. Either is acceptable. In fact, any tone is acceptable as long as it fits the subject. For instance, to write about the crash of a Boeing 707 in the breezy voice of a sports journalist would be inappropriate. It would also be inappropriate to write about Woody Allen's humor in the deadened tone of a government pamphlet. These voices just would not fit the subjects. Also remember that, as with point of view, you need to keep the tone consistent.

A third conscious choice you must make before starting a rough draft has to do with selecting the principal verb tense. In practice the choice is simple. Most writing is done in the past tense: "I *sat* in the wooden stands and *watched* the men while they *were jogging* around the track." But some writers decide to record experience in the present tense: "I *am* on the bench *watching* the men while they *jog* around the track." Since the present tense sounds awkward when used as the principal tense in a lengthy piece, we suggest you use the past tense. However, the present tense is not necessarily improper. What is improper is to shift from the principal tense to another without having a purpose for the shift. "I *sat* on the bench and *watched* the men while they *jog* around the track. Just *watching* them *makes* me *feel* tired." Notice how the writer shifts the principal tense from past — *sat* and *watched* — to present — *jog, makes,* and *feel.* The shift is awkward. However, it is not always awkward to use a variety of tenses. In fact you must. Verb tenses have to do with showing *time* — past, present, and future. Often you will need to glance backward and forward when writing. "It *had been* four years since I last *visited* my former high school, and after only a few minutes on campus, I *realized* that I *would never be able* to recapture the feeling of my school days." In this sentence the shifts are natural and controlled. The writer is aware of them but keeps the principal tense, *visited* and *realized,* consistent.

WRITING TASK

Using your prewritten draft as a starting point, write a rough draft in no more than 300 words. Before beginning, decide on the point of view, the tone, and the principal tense you'll be using. Then decide on the general purpose of your piece and what part of your experience you wish to showcase. Begin by writing an opening sentence or two to lead the reader into the body and to a conclusion that somehow echoes the beginning. Remember to write in complete sentences and to use simple, concrete language.

We suggest you leave plenty of space between the lines so you'll have room to edit and revise the rough draft without recopying it.

Although we have given you a great deal to consider while writing the rough draft, remember that your goal is not perfection: there are still two more stages in the process.

Editing and Revising

The time to begin the editing and revising phase is when you have a suitable rough draft in hand — a piece drawn from the prewritten draft that you believe adequately covers the experience. At this point, while holding the intuitive part of your mind in check, you must muster all the intellectual skills you can to evaluate your work. Under these circumstances evaluation does not involve deciding whether your work is good or bad. Instead, it involves deciding whether or not your work is as vigorous and concise as you can make it. No sentence should have any unnecessary words; no paragraph any unnecessary sentences. This is not to suggest that all sentences are to be simple or short, but only that the piece is to be as concise as possible.

The way to start is with a pencil in hand and the rough draft before you on the desk. Begin by reading aloud at a much slower pace than normal to see and hear whether any words or phrases can be deleted without loss of meaning or emphasis. Draw a line through the words and phrases you wish to delete; but don't totally obscure them, for later on they may remind you of detail to add when you are working on the final draft.

The first words to delete are the empty, meaningless ones: *lovely, pretty, beautiful, good, great, terrific,* and others that lack specific qualities. Also line out words that you may have added for emphasis: *very, quite, rather, really,* and *so.* Words of this sort tend to carry over into writing from speech habits. When spoken, they add vocal emphasis to intensify a point or feeling. But writing is different from speaking. Writers intensify by being concise and by using concrete detail. For instance, consider what the writer actually expresses in the following sentence:

> The very lovely woman with a rather pretty smile walked down the beautiful lane.

Begin by asking yourself what a "very lovely woman" looks like. Or a "rather pretty smile." Or a "beautiful lane." "Very," "lovely," "pretty," and "beautiful" fail to give a clear picture of what the writer experienced. These words only suggest a good feeling about seeing the woman; they have no content. Like a child's coloring book, they function as blank spaces for readers to fill in their private perceptions.

For the beginning writer, words of this sort can be deceptive. They can deceive him into believing he has said something when he hasn't. By crossing out such words, he can get a better look at the content of the sentence.

> The woman with a smile walked down the lane.

Not much content. And when written more concisely,

> Smiling, the woman walked down the lane.

the sentence seems to say less.

Now there is an advantage to this kind of editing. It gives the writer a chance to revise — to return to the prewritten draft or memory and select more concrete details to add to the work. After revision, the sentence might read like this:

> Smiling, the thin woman with flowing blond hair walked down the lane edged with blooming geraniums.

Now the sentence creates a clearer picture of what the writer experienced. The writer has included details the reader can visualize.

There's more to editing and revising then deleting empty words and rebuilding with concrete details. The writer must also combine loosely arranged sentences, delete words that repeat the contents of other words, and replace weak and general verbs with more accurate ones. As an illustration, let's examine part of a rough draft that sets out to describe an autumn day:

> As soon as I walked outside I knew fall had come. Clouds came in from the west and filled the afternoon with dark shadows. The wind blew around the leaves. They were dead and dry and made a scraping sound against the pavement. Children walking home from school were bundled in heavy coats and many of them had scarves wrapped around their necks.

The opening sentence sets up a clear purpose. It also leads the reader into sentences that detail the writer's sudden awareness that fall has arrived. That's good, for setting purposes and leading readers into passages are what opening sentences should do. But notice how the descriptive flow is interrupted by the fourth sentence:

> They [the leaves] were dead and dry and made a scraping sound against the pavement.

As we all can see, the details relate to the writer's description of fall, but the piece seems to come to a momentary standstill by shifting the focus to the leaves. The sentence could be cut out, but no writer wants to lose good detail. Rather than cutting it, he can combine it with the preceding one. So instead of retaining

> The wind blew around the leaves. They were dead and dry and made a scraping sound against the pavement.

he could revise it to read

> The wind blew around the dead and dry leaves that scraped along the pavement.

The piece is now concise and reads smoothly:

> As soon as I walked outside I knew fall had come. Clouds came in from the west and filled the afternoon with dark shadows. The wind blew around the dead and dry leaves that scraped against the pavement. Children walking home from school were bundled in heavy coats and many of them had scarves wrapped around their necks.

This doesn't end the process of editing and revising, though. It only helps the writer see where other changes need to be made. He might continue by working on the part he just rebuilt:

The wind blew around the dead and dry leaves that scraped against the pavement.

Consider the words *dead* and *dry:* each has within it the idea of the other — a dead leaf is dry and a dry leaf is dead. There is no reason to use both. Now, consider *wind,* the verb *blew,* and the preposition *around* tacked to *blew.* Also consider the phrase *that scraped against the pavement:* a nice image appealing to the reader's sense of sound, but the wording is sloppy. By pausing to examine these words, the writer will realize that wind has the idea of blowing in it. After all, what does wind do if not blow? "Around," which is used to buttress "blew," might even be mis-read. Certainly the wind does blow around leaves, but it also blows around corners, which is not the same thing. A solution to the sloppy wording lies in the phrase "that scraped against the pavement." From it the writer can lift the verb "scraped" and revise the sentence to read

The wind scraped the dead leaves along the pavement.

Keeping in mind the need to delete unnecessary words along with words that repeat the contents of other words, combining weak sentences and substituting accurate verbs for weak or inaccurate ones, an edited and revised version of this piece might look like this:

As soon as I ~~walked~~ stepped outside I knew fall

had come. Clouds ~~came~~ blew in from the west and   *"Blew" is more accurate than "came."*

filled the afternoon with ~~dark~~ shadows. The   *A shadow is dark. No need to say dark.*

wind scraped dead leaves against the pavement.

Children walking home from school ~~were bundled~~ wore   *"Wore" easily replaces the wordy "were bundled in." Also makes the sentence active.*

~~in~~ heavy coats and many ~~of them~~ had scarves

wrapped around their necks.   *"Of them" is unnecessary.*

The edited and revised piece now reads:

As soon as I walked outside I knew fall had come. Clouds blew in from the west and filled the afternoon with shadows.

The wind scraped dead leaves against the pavement. Children walking home from school wore heavy coats and many had scarves wrapped around their necks.

On rereading the revised draft, the writer may think the sentence "The wind scraped dead leaves against the pavement" might be more effective if "against" were changed to "along." The change would give the piece a little more movement:

The wind scraped dead leaves *along* the pavement.

Well, the tinkering has to stop somewhere. Otherwise, papers would never get turned in.

If by this point you are starting to feel that writers need to become familiar with each word, phrase, and sentence they write, you are on target. When editing and revising, you need to examine each aspect of the piece. As an illustration of the importance of examining your work, printed below is the edited and revised joggers piece — the rough draft as changed by the writer. Study it. Also study the brief explanations in the margins, while keeping in mind what has been said above. When all this is done, reread the piece straight through the way the writer has changed it.

~~Last night at dusk I took a walk to the high~~ *yesterday*
~~school track at the top of the hill.~~ ~~There~~ I

The writer trims unnecessary information from the lead sentences. This helps the reader move into the piece faster. Dusk is the time between night and day. More accurate to change "Last night" to "Yesterday." Moreover, if the writer is there at the day's close, no need for "dusk."

high school bleachers
sat alone in the ~~wooden stands~~ and watched the

"Wooden" is an unnecessary detail. Changing "wooden" to "high school" sets the location and gives the reader an important bit of information. "Bleachers" may be more accurate than "stands."

in white shorts
day come to a close. Two joggers were circling

"In white shorts" is integrated from below. "White" is a more effective detail than "wooden" as it was used above because it helps the reader see a more important part of the piece.

the track. ~~Both were wearing shorts.~~ ~~One was~~

~~shirtless; the other wore a tee shirt.~~ One

This detail seems unnecessary. It interrupts the flow of the piece.

Unnecessary detail deleted. Sentences combined and tightened. Often when a writer uses was/were constructions, sentences can be combined.

like a tired buffalo, scuffed was heavy and, ~~ran huffing and puffing,~~ his feet, ~~scuffing along like a tired buffalo.~~ *H*is head bobb*ing*~~ed~~ from side to side. ~~He was tired~~. The	By using "scuffed" instead of "ran . . . scuffing along . . ." the writer gets the same effect with fewer words. By changing "bobbed" to "bobbing" this bit of description can be included in the preceding sentence. No need to devote a whole sentence to it. The details of the preceding sentence show the runner is tired. No need to directly tell the reader.
and reminded me of other was tall and thin/ ~~built like a stork,~~ ~~but ran like~~ a deer ~~I had seen last summer~~ *loping* ~~running~~ through a meadow. I watched them circle *As* the track four, five, or six times. ~~Each time~~ *where I sat* they passed ~~me up in the stands~~ I could hear the thin one chatting, while the heavy one's *wheezed.* ~~breath rattled in his throat.~~ Behind them the	There's no need for the writer to tell the reader when she had last seen a deer. "Loping" is more accurate than "running." This revision clears up some confusion. At first it reads as if the joggers were running through the bleachers. No need to repeat "stands." "Rattled" calls to mind marbles rolling around in a tin can, whereas "wheezed" is associated with labored breath. The use of "wheezed" also has in it the idea that it takes place in the throat.
horizon ~~sky~~ was turning ~~reddish~~ orange. ~~as it often does~~	Words can only approximate an experience; no need to try to do the impossible, such as trying to accurately describe a color. Therefore, reddish is dropped. The clause that begins "as it often does" breaks the tone. Sounds as if it belongs in a travelogue.

about
~~in southern California at sunset.~~ A jet ~~plane~~
~~no more than one mile or~~ two miles away was
climbing, ~~in the sky. It had just taken off from~~
t   *rumbling*
~~the airport.~~ *T*he engines ~~sounded~~ like distant
thunder./ ~~a low rumble. It started to arc north,~~
                    J
~~becoming a speck. The lights of~~ the university
was silhouetted against the sunset, a few lights
~~were blinking on. The buildings were becoming~~
speckling its outline.
~~a light spotted dark silhouette against the~~
                              jogged.
~~darkening skyline~~. The men still ~~circled,~~
	Jets are planes. No need to say jet plane.
	Does the question of one or two miles matter?
	A plane can climb only in the sky. No need to say so.
	"It had just taken . . ." is excess detail.
	More excessive detail that interrupts the flow.
	
	These next sentences needed to be combined. The result is much more precise.
	No need for "dark" since a silhouette is dark. "Speckling" replaces "spotted" in the revised sentence.
	"Silhouette" is changed to a verb.

~~although the thin one was ahead of the heavy~~   *More detail that seems to detract from the flow is deleted.*

~~one. The one strided away into a curve~~. The

light   *almost gone, the horizon*   *This sentence is awkward, assuming that it is already night. The writer sees that it is more effective to stress the fading light.*
~~night~~ was ~~getting darker,~~ turning indigo. ~~The~~

The sky began to fill with stars that
~~stars were coming out and~~ looked like chips of   *The writer revises this sentence and develops the image.*
   tossed on a dark highway.
glass/∧ I felt alone and saw the joggers had   *The writer includes a slight subjective response to the scene — "I felt alone" — but picks up the concrete details immediately. The closing sentence echoes the lead: "Yesterday I sat alone . . . and watched the day come to a close."*
   running and were walking   *fading*
stopped/∧ ~~They walked~~ toward the gate, ~~and faded~~

~~from my sight~~ with the light.

To study a revised draft in this fashion can be misleading. It may seem that these changes were made all at once — that the writer did them while working her way through the rough draft the first time. In practice, editing and revising does not work that way. Writers need to read and reread. They often try out new words and different sentence arrangements before making a final change.

WRITING TASK

Edit and revise your rough draft. With pencil in hand and rough draft before you, begin to reread. Delete words that repeat the content of other words along with empty and meaningless words. Pencil in more concrete details where you need them. Cut out phrases where a single word might be more effective, sharpen the verbs and revise sentences so they flow together.

As you pare away at your piece, you may notice that, like the piece on joggers, it becomes substantially smaller. Don't worry about it. Instead, work toward an edited and revised draft of from 150 to 200 words.

Final Draft

When all the editing and revising is done that can be done on the rough draft, there still remains one step — the final draft. In many respects the final draft is another revision.

At this point you probably have a piece of writing that looks like a Jackson Pollock painting — you know, the kind with dribbles and streaks across the canvas. A scribbled appearance is typical of edited drafts with revisions penciled between lines and in margins. Professional writers have been known to tape or staple additional strips or sheets of paper to the sides of their rough drafts in order to accommodate extensive revisions. You may want to try that technique when you are editing and revising future assignments. In the meantime, you are now ready to start your final draft. The final draft continues the revision process. We suggest you begin it by thinking about your readers.

In this series of tasks we haven't said much about readers. Yet more than likely they have been on your mind. For the final draft you need to include them as part of the revision process. If you have not identified a specific group of readers, as you did when you wrote a note in the first assignment, then you must act as your own readers. This is a neat trick that requires you to separate yourself from your work and examine it as if you had not created it. You begin by reading your edited and revised manuscript aloud. You include all the revisions — by that we mean you drop from the reading all you have crossed out and include all you have added. While reading, ask yourself some simple questions. Do the opening sentences guide readers to what follows? Do the sentences seem connected and flow smoothly from beginning to end? Does the piece end in a satisfying way? And finally, would readers unfamiliar with the information or experience understand the piece? To act like vigilant readers is tough, demanding that you step from your skin into other people's.

Before going on to an illustration of a final draft, we want to mention two concepts that help a writer keep a reader on the right track. One has to do with arranging material; the other with connecting sentences.

There are several common and logical ways to arrange written material so that the reader can follow it. Time arrangement is probably the most common. A writer will often use it in narration to tell a story or to explain a process — that is, to give directions on how to do something. In time arrangement the writer begins with the first event or step and ends with the last one.

For material that does not fall into a clear time scheme, a writer may use a space arrangement, especially in descriptive writing, arranging the visual material from west to east, left to right, high to low, near to far, far to near, or whatever.

A writer can also arrange material in order of climax, selecting the most dramatic part of the piece and holding it back until the end. For this arrangement the writer would begin with the least important details and arrange the rest of the material in increasing importance, and then close the piece by showcasing the most dramatic part.

Other arrangements are possible — such as ordering from the general to the particular or from the particular to the general — or any combination of them. The important part of this concept is that the material be arranged in a clear fashion so readers can follow it.

Besides arranging your material in a consistent pattern that readers can follow, you will also have to make sure your sentences are connected. Although there are many techniques a writer can use to connect sentences, one way to do it is through overt transitions — words and phrases that guide a reader from point to point. Without adequate transitions, papers seem to skip about, letting readers' attention stray somewhere in the spaces. As a writer, your goal is to keep readers with you. You must not allow them to stray, so smooth their way from beginning to end.

Now, before going on let's reread the edited and revised draft of the joggers piece. Remember, this is not the final draft, but the edited and revised version with the penciled notations integrated and the deletions left out. Read it while keeping in mind what we have just said about arrangement and transition.

> Yesterday, I sat alone in the high school bleachers and watched the day come to a close. Two joggers in white shorts were circling the track. One was heavy and, like a tired buffalo, scuffed his feet, his head bobbing from side to side. The other was tall and thin and reminded me of a deer loping through a meadow. I watched them circle the track four, five, or six times. As they passed where I sat, I could hear the thin one chatting, while the heavy one wheezed. Behind them the horizon was turning orange. A jet about two miles away was climbing, the engines rumbling like distant thunder. The university was silhouetted against the sunset, a few lights speckling its outline. The men still jogged. The light was almost gone, the horizon turning indigo. The sky began to fill with stars that looked like chips of glass tossed on a dark highway. I felt alone and saw the joggers had stopped running and were walking toward the gate, fading with the light.

It doesn't take much reader vigilance to see the many flaws in this writer's arrangement. At times the piece seems to lurch forward and heave backward. Notice, for instance, that after the lead sentence the writer focuses the readers' attention on the joggers. The focus becomes even sharper as she describes them in the next four sentences. The description is fine, but the immediate focus on the joggers might seem too abrupt to sensitive readers because the lead sentence prepares them for the close of day, not for two joggers. This part needs to be revised.

After presenting the joggers, the writer shifts to the horizon. This shift seems smooth, because the writer uses a transitional phrase — "Behind them" — thus guiding the reader into another phase. She continues by presenting details of the jet and the university. Then she leaps back to the joggers before pitching forward to the horizon and the sky. This movement is awkward. She then returns to the joggers and closes the piece. In arrangement and transition this whole last section seems clumsy, clearly needing structural repair.

Let's pause for a moment before illustrating one way to repair this piece and complete a final draft. At this point beginning writers might begin to object. They could feel that a final alteration of their work puts them in conflict with their original experience. To answer the objection, we suggest that whatever experience writers try to collect is altered through their very effort to translate it into language and communicate it. To restructure a piece is only a continuation of that altering process.

Take for example the work we've been following. The writer first compiled an extended list that approximated some experiences she observed. She couldn't document everything going on — that would have been impossible — so she had to alter her vision by selecting certain details from the scene. The selecting and rejecting procedure continued right through the rough and revised drafts — in other words, more alteration of the original experience. Now, at the point of the final draft, the writer needs to alter even more by rearranging the entire structure so that it reads smoothly. This is when frustration, a common malaise among beginning writers, gets sharp. If the writer goes ahead with the alteration, she may wonder whether she is still giving a true rendering of the initial experience, whether she is being honest.

If you as a writer consider it absolutely necessary to record the details and sequences of events as you experienced them — and the reader's needs be damned — you would be dishonest to change them. But if you stick to this value of literal accuracy, you will seldom generate anything more than a written crazy quilt that nobody will want to read. Instead of holding to the position of literal honesty, we suggest you see your task as much larger than merely stitching together loose impressions. Your task is to communicate experience so a reader can take it in. You still work with the same details, the same vision; only now you shape a new pattern; one that was already there but that you did not see when you did your prewriting. From this perspective, writing becomes a take-and-give affair — the writer honestly takes in raw experience and then gives it in organized form to a reader.

Now we'll examine the final draft, along with marginal comments, of the joggers piece we've been following. Pay close attention to the way the writer has restructured the material. After the lead sentence, which she has altered to include the joggers as a main element in the piece, she focuses on the distant sunset instead of going immediately to the joggers. She then moves the focus in by describing the jet climbing. Next, she moves still closer by describing the university. Finally, she zeroes in on the school track immediately in the foreground and the two men jogging laps. To this point, the piece has been reshaped into a far-to-near arrangement. Before closing the piece, the writer glances back at the horizon, then returns the focus to the joggers, who, with the light, fade from sight.

As you study this final draft, also notice the writer's use of overt transitions. At critical points she guides the reader's attention from sentence to sentence with phrases such as "About two miles away" and "Not far in the distance." By using overt markings such as these, the writer is doing all she can to smooth the reader's way.

This example also illustrates another element involved in writing a final draft — an element not as clearly seen as rearranging the whole structure of a piece or integrating transitional phrases, but still important. Even though the final revision is mainly an intellectual process, the act of doing it often stirs the creative part of a writer's mind. Forgotten details or new comparisons may appear in your awareness. They shouldn't be shut out. If they fit and add clarity to the description, you may use them. On the other hand, along with rearranging your material and working in transitions, you will often find you need to rework your sentences so that they flow smoothly together. This reworking will sometimes force you to drop some detail. At this point any fresh detail or comparisons may help you flesh out your piece after other details have been dropped. The writer of this final draft has done both — she has dropped some details and added some. She has also included a new comparison at the end.

Before you dig into the final draft, we want to suggest a way for you to proceed. First, reread the writer's edited and revised draft on pp. 22–24. Then read the final version here. As you read, note the changes the writer has made. Then, after the first reading of the final draft, reread it, and as you work through it, study the marginal notes. You should be aware that at a certain point the successful act of writing becomes a mysterious activity. Although we can talk about using concrete language, writing in complete sentences, placing punctuation marks properly, arranging the material in a logical order, and creating consistent point of view, verb tense, and tone, the final work becomes more than the guidelines to set it up. Writers are alchemists of words and images. They shape new realities from base materials. Therefore, at some point explanation fails — the act cannot be defined. But it can be illustrated. We suggest you study the illustrations in detail, while appreciating that there is more to writing than can be said.

`Yesterday, I sat alone in the bleachers`   *Notice that the writer adds the "two joggers" to the lead sentence, thus making*
`and watched two joggers in white as the day came`   *it fit what follows.*

to a close. The horizon was turning a deep	*"Deep"* is added to suggest how low the sun has sunk.
orange while the sun sank behind the ridge of	*"While the sun sank behind . . ."* is added to flesh out the picture.
a hill. About two miles away a jet climbed,	*"About two miles away"* works as a transitional marking that establishes the distance and the movement from far to near.
the engines rumbling like distant thunder. Not	
far in the distance the university was silhou-	*"Not far in the distance"* is another transitional marking that indicates the movement closer.
etted against the orange background, a few lights	*"The orange background"* adds more detail and reminds the reader of the whole scene.
speckling its dark outline. On the track below	*"Dark"* seems to be unnecessary, but serves to remind the reader that night is coming.
the bleachers two men jogged. One was heavy and	*"On the track below"* is a transition that directs the reader's attention and brings the movement nearer the observer.
scuffed along like a tired buffalo, his head	
bobbing from side to side. The other was thin	She begins to display the joggers, focusing the reader's attention on them by the use of descriptive details.
and reminded me of a deer loping through a	
meadow. They circled the track--four, five, six	
laps. As they passed I could hear the thin one	*"As they passed"* locates the joggers near enough to the writer so she can hear them.
chatting and the heavy one wheezing. Soon the	*"Soon"* serves as a transition in time. The whole sentence momentarily guides the reader's attention from the joggers to the horizon.
light was almost gone. The horizon turned indigo	
and the sky began to fill with stars scattered	This shift from the joggers to the horizon and sky reminds the reader of the writer's purpose — to describe the close of day. The stars are coming out; night is near.
like chips of glass tossed on a dark highway.	
I felt alone and glanced back at the track to	*"I felt alone"* is a brief phrase that could be cut but seems important because it adds a deeper dimension to the piece. This closing sentence brings the fading light (the close of day) and the joggers together. It circles back to the lead. The afterthought of comparing the joggers to ghostly figures also connects to the image *"two joggers in white"* in the lead.
see the joggers like two ghosts fade with the	
light.	

WRITING TASK

Write your final draft while acting as your own vigilant reader. Be sure your piece is arranged in a suitable order to be easily followed, add any transitions it needs to guide the reader's attention, and re-structure any sentences that need restructuring, adding and dropping details when you find it appropriate to do so.

Often the final draft is the last version you will have to write before turning in your work. But sometimes you will need to write a polished draft. Preparing the polished draft involves first rereading to check for sentence fragments, run-on sentences or comma splices, misspellings, and errors in punctuation. Also check to see that the principal verb tense, point of view, and tone are consistent. If you spot these kinds of errors, correct them and recopy your paper, integrating your corrections. So a polished draft is just what the term *polished* suggests — a piece that represents your best effort at communicating a point while using correct writing conventions.

3 RESPONDING TO EXPERIENCE

In the last series of tasks you worked with description. You stuck closely to what you observed and avoided writing about what you thought or felt. Though generally you won't write much pure description of this sort — usually you'll explain, argue, analyze, or report — we started with it for several reasons.

First, concrete description is the bedrock of most good writing. Vivid details and images, even if offered only in spoonfuls, make an explanation, argument, analysis, or report more interesting. Second, by beginning with a simple descriptive piece, you avoided the nagging question "What shall I write about?" You only had to plunk yourself in a spot and record. Instead of getting bogged down, you quickly confronted the agonizing process of working in drafts. Besides using description to introduce you to this valuable process, we also hoped tinkering with several written drafts of the same experience would dispel a common misconception: that the first effort that pours from a writer's pen is sacred script. Now you know it isn't. Metaphorically speaking, writing is much like working with clay. Potters who don't like the first shapes they pull from their lumps rework them until they have figures that please them.

We also used this simple descriptive piece to introduce you to several problems every writer, whether professional or beginning, must wrestle with: selection, organization, point of view, tone, voice, transition, and so on. The writer's bout with these problems never ends. Of course, you'll see that more clearly as the semester unfolds. Fortunately, however, the struggle becomes less fierce with practice.

And, finally, there is a very important reason for doing a simple description. To write a brief description you had to record the specifics of the experience you observed. Not your inner responses — your conclusions or feelings about the experiences — but only concrete details. Description riveted you to specific details. Left untended, most beginning writers move in giant steps. They stride from general point to general point without filling in the specific details behind their general conclusions. We want you to focus on the specifics behind your general responses. And we want to keep your attention there while you develop good writing habits.

We must admit, of course, that the urge to generalize from experience is natural to people's thought patterns. And the tendency to write large generalizations is a habit carried over from speaking into writing. After all, in our typical conversations there is little need to specifically describe the details behind our judgments. A listener who wants to hear them will ask. For instance, consider a general statement a friend of yours might make: "It was great at the beach yesterday." You might nod your head and agree, saying, "Wish I'd been there." End of conversation. On the other hand, your curiosity might be aroused enough to start asking questions.

"What do you mean by *great?*" you ask, a frown crossing your brow.

"Hot. The sun was out and there was a lot of action," he answers, his face lighting up with the memory.

"Action? What kind of action?"

"Well," he says, rubbing his chin, "there was a grueling volleyball match between the Daytona Beach and Miami champs. The surf was up — about four feet. And the water was in the sixties."

Depending on the extent of your interest, the questioning might go on. But somewhere you would probably stop and agree that the day was great. The flat assertion might not have convinced you, but the specifics would. Whenever you write, remember nothing so exhausts readers as being led through a bog of general assertions which go unsupported by specifics — like this:

> It was beautiful at the beach yesterday. The weather was terrific. The shore was filled with plenty of action. The waves were great and the water the best it's been in months.

On the other hand, if you keep in mind that readers, unlike listeners, lack the right of cross-examination, and if you mix your responses — your thoughts, feelings, judgments, conclusions, assertions, whatever you wish to call them — with the specific details they're based on, readers will move through your work with ease. To write meaningfully, then, you must give readers specific details behind your general responses so that they can make up their own minds about the experience. If the beach conversation had been put in written form, a final draft fleshed out with more detail might have looked like this:

> Yesterday I went to the beach. By eight the sun, like a huge arc light, had burned through the morning haze. The surf, which had been flat for three days, stayed smooth as glass, and the swells reached four feet before breaking in even lines. The water was in the sixties, so warm I didn't need a wet suit. That afternoon about three, two championship volleyball teams held a playoff. Miami had a six-foot-four giant with a spike that hit the sand like a Nike missile. But one scruffy Daytona player kept digging it out. The game lasted for over an hour until Daytona finally caved in. The day was great.

Except for the first and last lines, which carry the writer's responses, the entire piece is made up of specific details. In writing it's never enough just to state your response to an experience; you must also include the specifics behind it.

For your next writing task we'll be asking you to describe another experience. But unlike the last piece, this one will include any inner responses the experience draws from you. The piece will be mostly composed of specific details, but the responses you sprinkle in will let readers know how you feel about the experience. The abundance of specific detail will allow them to see why you respond as you do.

A key tactic to use for this task is to select details that lead the reader to the same response you had. For instance, in the brief piece above, the writer included only the details that supported his response "It was a great day." He didn't describe the frustration he might have felt while searching for a parking place or standing in line for a hamburger. Instead, he selected details that supported his purpose: the heat, surf, warm water, and volleyball match. There is a specific reason for including these details: to trigger a specific response in a reader.

Not all writing of this sort needs to be as simple as the beach description. Using specific details to reflect an inner response can work in very subtle ways. A writer can use them to suggest a deep personal meaning in an experience that could never be captured by direct statement. Pieces of this kind are rich in implication and require a great deal of concentration on the part of the reader. All the more important for the writer to pay close attention to the arrangement of specifics. Read the following student example and see if you can figure out what responses the writer is leading you to.

> Last week I toured Safari Land. While we were passing through the gate decorated with jungle trimmings, a friend tapped me on the shoulder and pointed to a sign: "Keep your windows rolled up. Don't feed the animals." He laughed and said, "Wait 'til a lion eats your new van," before passing an open

box of chicken to another friend sitting in the back. I took up a camera and looped it around my neck before joining the procession of cars that twisted along the narrow road toward the hills. Soon we came to a herd of elephants prancing and rolling in a muddy pond. Nearby a man in a tattered safari costume stood by a jeep and filled the pond from a hose attached to a hydrant. Some fifty yards beyond, a pride of lions sprawled under a tree, one swishing its tail, others sleeping. And not far from them a lioness gnawed the remains of a side of beef. Within that lioness's easy spring, a herd of zebras grazed on busted bales of hay as if blind to the age-old knowledge that lions lived on zebra flesh. A strange world, where creatures that once filled my exotic dreams are tamed by having their desires met with water hoses, hunks of meat, and bales of hay. Then, through a mouthful of chicken, I heard someone mumble, "Look!" Ahead, circled by a moat, was an island full of apes. Gibbons and chimps swung from rings. Gorillas leaned forward on their knuckles, watching the passing cars. Maneuvering around a Ford, I pulled to one side and stopped. One bull gorilla caught my eye. He lumbered forward, held back by the moat's edge. I raised my camera, my lens tapping against the window glass. My shutter clicked. As if he heard, he lifted a hairy arm and held out a fist filled with carrot bunches. I clicked again, while he curled the fist back to his chest. Was he gesturing me to join him? Did he believe all that separated us was the moat and glass? I lowered the camera and felt its weight around my neck. He continued to stare, the red eyes carrying a language that cannot be said. I glanced away, surveying the van that now seemed like a cage: the plush carpet, the padded dash, and sharing it, my two friends who munched away at chicken wings and legs. I glanced back at the staring creature and understood his gesture. It named me brother with desires as small as any beast's.

You may have noticed the piece is thick with specific detail. But did you see that the writer carefully selected these specifics and arranged them to lead you to the final insight that suggests he, like the creatures in Safari Land, is a captive of his own desires.

   After the lead that gets the piece under way, he describes the elephants, lions, zebras and apes as contented creatures that have given up their natural urges in this "strange world, where creatures . . . are tamed by having their desires met . . ." His response deepens and grows into personal insight when he encounters the gesturing bull gorilla with the massive fist filled with carrots. Of course, the beast isn't attempting to communicate what the writer feels; the writer only responds to its gesture in this way. He interprets it.

Did you also notice that even the details that may seem unnecessary at first glance serve a purpose? The new van, for instance, functions as a desire that makes the writer captive. His chicken-eating friends may be looked at as contented animals, his companions in captivity. Even the camera serves a purpose. It weighs him down or perhaps serves as a restraining noose. Or perhaps we go too far in our interpretation. The point is that this writer has selected specific details in an attempt to trigger in the reader a response similar to his own.

Before going on to the next writing task, we want to mention something about the arrangement of the Safari Land piece. It's constructed in a climactic sequence. The word "climactic" comes from the word climax — the point of greatest intensity that ends a series. To arrange a piece in climactic order, then, is to put the most significant part last. Aside from more sober works, a great deal of entertainment is arranged in this structure. A cane over his arm, a comic blithely strolls down a sidewalk. An uncovered manhole yawns before him. Unknowingly, he approaches its edge. Tension builds. But without breaking his gait he blindly steps over it. He takes another step then he stops, scratches his head and turns back, again stepping over the open manhole. He stops on the other side, this time to pick up a dime. After flipping the coin in the air and dropping it in his pocket, he swiftly turns and steps into the center of the trap. In the nick of time a workman's head pops up and serves as a stepping stone for our pedestrian. Then two steps farther on, he slips on a banana peel. Boom. The climax.

We hope this crude example serves our point. We're not asking you to write humor, but we do hope you are beginning to sense the underlying nature of a climactic arrangement. Reread the Safari Land piece; you'll see more clearly how it works.

The Safari Land piece is built inductively as well as climactically. The writer begins with a general statement about the overall subject — "Last week I toured Safari Land" — but holds back the main point until the end. Although most of your writing will be deductive — a structure that presents the main point in the lead sentence, with the remaining sentences serving as support — the inductive method has some strong advantages. It not only nudges the reader toward the main point and prepares him to accept it, but it also helps the writer generate some suspense. Moreover, the inductive arrangement seems to be a natural order in which to present personal insights. Think about how we come to new personal knowledge. Don't we begin by noticing particular experiences? Don't we combine them with other experiences and finally, once they click together, say Ah ha? This "ah ha" experience comes to us piece by piece; it comes inductively. To arrange our papers in a way that reflects that process makes sense.

Take a look at the next illustration. Notice how the student blends his inner responses with the specific details he has associated with them.

Since he's dealing with personal insight, he arranges the sentences inductively, the climactic point coming at the end. First read the selection through without studying the marginal comments. Then reread it along with the commentary for a more thorough understanding.

While walking through the supermarket last night, I became uneasy about my life. I had just come from home where I had seen the evening news. There had been a report of earthquake destruction in Central America. The report featured a film of a city that collapsed. It showed lost children roaming through the ruins and men and women in shock, sitting in the rubble of their homes. It showed heaps of bodies waiting to be cremated. A reporter's voice commented on possible starvation and epidemic. The whole thing hit me hard. I thought about the emptiness the survivors must feel and about how they must feel about the future. But life, my life, couldn't stop. My refrigerator and cupboards were empty; I had to work the next day, and there were places to go and people to meet, as the saying goes. So, an hour later, I was pushing a cart through Ralph's, but I still didn't feel good. Something was eating away at me. I hurried to stock up on groceries for the week—some oranges, apples, a head of lettuce, juice, milk, a chicken, and three pounds of beef. I began to notice other people shopping around me:

A general lead that introduces the main elements. It gives the reader some direction.

"The report featured" begins the concrete description of the report's specifics that relate to the writer's feelings.

"The whole thing hit me hard" begins a sequence of the writer's inner responses.

"My refrigerator and cupboards were empty" prepares the reader for the next phase and ties back to "But life, my life, couldn't stop."

"So, an hour later" serves as an overt transition into the next supermarket phase.

The writer continues to blend in feelings — "I still didn't feel good. Something was eating away at me" — while generating a realistic description of the market.

some together, chatting and smiling, and some

alone, lifting items from shelves and comparing

prices. I pushed the cart toward the checkout

stand, trying to understand the feeling that

seemed to be deepening in me. Just foolishness,

I thought. I must have become lost in my

thoughts, for my cart slammed into another

shopper's. I glanced at her. Her eyes sparkled

at my folly. Her tan skin seemed golden and

each eyebrow was perfectly shaped. But then

over her shoulder I saw a poster advertising a

charity. A photograph of a half-naked child

holding an empty bowl, the eyes pleading, seemed

to leap at me. At that moment the images from

the news rose up in my mind--the ruined homes,

lost children, starvation--and I felt anger and

frustration as I realized how helpless I was,

and how spoiled.

The phrase "trying to understand the feeling" works to remind the reader of the main issue and nudges toward the climax.

"I must have become lost in my thoughts" begins the display of the shopper and starving child that crystallize the writer's personal insight.

The writer closes with his insight and reminds the reader of details mentioned earlier, thus creating a sense of roundness.

As a closing illustration, we offer the beginning paragraph of *Murmurs of Earth* by astronomer-writer Carl Sagan. Notice how Sagan has arranged it. He begins with a general lead that establishes the scene and sets up the middle. He follows with specific details from the experience and ends with his response. Aside from the arrangement, also notice Sagan's shift in point of view from "I" to "you" and back again. The shift is intentional. It's an attempt to create an impression that the reader is seeing what Sagan saw. Sagan tries to put the reader in the scene. (We suggest you avoid shifts of this sort, however, until you have mastered point of view.)

In 1939, before my fifth birthday, my parents took me to the New York World's Fair. It exhibited wonders. Lightning was made to crackle, blue and fearsome, between two metal spheres.

A sign read "Hear light! See sound!" and it turned out that, sure enough, such things were possible. There were buildings devoted to strange cultures and faraway lands of whose very existence I had been totally ignorant. The centerpiece of that World's Fair was the Trylon and Perisphere, a stately, tapering tower and a building-sized sphere in which was something called "The World of Tomorrow." You walked on a high-railed ramp and below you, in miniature, was an exquisitely detailed model of the future — graceful aerial skyways filled with streamlined automobiles and happy citizens purposefully intent on some futuristic business, the nature of which was difficult to divine from the perspective of my limited experience and abbreviated stature. But one message was clearly communicated: there were other cultures and there would be future times.

WRITING TASK

In no more than 350 words write a description that includes your inner responses to an experience. Most of your piece is to be made up of specific details. Blend in just enough of your responses to let the reader know where you stand in relation to the experience.

Your lead is to set the scene and take the reader into the experience. The middle is to be thick with specific details and arranged inductively with the main point or final insight coming at the end. At the end or near the end will be the climactic point; use it to showcase the most vivid part of the piece.

Remember to keep the readers in mind. That means you need to guide their attention. Do it by selecting specific details designed to trigger a response that agrees with yours.

Unlike the last piece, which requires you to seek out an experience to observe, this one may come from something you have done. We should offer a word of caution about using recalled experience. Often the specifics have faded with time. Writing that comes from recalled experience is often vague and general. It's important, therefore, to use the prewritten draft to fill in memory lapses.

Sit quietly, let your mind drift back to the experience, and record all the concrete details that come to you. Record your feelings also. Don't shut anything out. As an example, read the opening entries of the following extended list that helped the writer return to her tenth year. She used it to pull up specific details associated with a visit to a convalescent home.

Visit to The Palms

- 10 years old. I was mystified. Didn't know what one was — a convalescent home, that is. But I left with a childhood fear of being old.
- Two shabby palm trees out front. The buildings were pink stucco, though I didn't know what stucco was then.
- Old people everywhere. In wheelchairs sitting around the foyer. They seemed strange to my ten-year-old mind. Some babbled to themselves. Some slept, their heads bobbing forward and back. One woman stared at the stained ceiling and tapped her foot as if she were keeping time to music. Maybe the music was in her head, maybe in her soul.
- Smells: Urine. Disinfectant — Lysol? Everything was stuffy, no air. Felt I was suffocating.
- Walking down the hall. More people mumbling. One man who looked out of place, dressed in shirt and slacks, a full head of gray hair, seemed to be comfortable, but kept yelling "Help! Help!" Attendants in white walked by him, paying no attention.
- Confused. Why do people come here? Who wants to live like this? I didn't think of them as "people."
- My grandmother. Withered, shrunken, crippled — she had had a stroke. Seeing her made me realize they were all people because I remembered her as a younger, a different person. I remember . . .

And so on.

Often a fine piece of writing grows from the chaos of a prewrite such as this. This writer used the raw material for her list to construct a rough draft. She then edited and revised the rough draft and put it into final form. Then, after the final shaping, she did a polished copy that was as free of errors in spelling and punctuation as she could make it.

At this point we want to advise you against choosing a long-term relationship to describe. Relationships are much too complex for such a brief assignment. You might, however, pick just one incident from a complex relationship. Perhaps a date, argument, or chance meeting — a single incident with a limited scope; possibly an event that embodies the meaning of the relationship. But we feel it's best to stick to simple experience.

To gain a perspective on the kinds of experiences we're talking about, reread the illustrations — a day at the beach, a trip to Safari

Land, watching the news then going to the market, and Sagan's visit to the New York World's Fair. These are simple situations and each happens over a relatively short period.

When you study these illustrations and others in the text, don't feel they are models you must slavishly follow. They're not. We offer them as examples that embody the concepts all good writers need to master. We offer them as illustrations of general writing principles, not as models you must emulate.

Also keep in mind that most of the illustrations are final products of the whole writing process. They have gone through several drafts. So don't feel discouraged if your first efforts fail to come up to some standard you see in them. We want to encourage you to attempt a piece that challenges your skill; however, we don't want you to become discouraged because you attempt a piece beyond your skill at this point. Judge for yourself what you are capable of doing.

PART TWO

WRITING TASKS

Part Two presents a variety of tasks designed to teach principles of good writing. They range from short pieces that emphasize patterns of organization to longer, more complicated essays, and from personal, subjective pieces to more objective ones. Some are accompanied by many examples and thorough discussions that we hope will guide you through the possible pitfalls of the tasks. Others have a minimum of explanation and illustration. Some of the tasks impose structures; some are more open to personal approaches.

How should you approach this part? That depends on the skill you already have. There's no reason for you to start at the beginning and go to the end. Instead, your teacher will guide you through a sequence of tasks to help develop your writing strengths.

4 SPECIFIC EXAMPLES

We suggest an excellent way to make your point clear to a reader is to develop it through the use of examples, for an example can convert facts and assertions into concrete pictures that stick in a reader's mind. Writers generally use two kinds of examples: specific and typical. Here we will discuss specific examples; typical examples will be the next topic.

Topic sentences such as "Tommy, my little cousin, behaves like a monkey," "The year-round residents of Laguna abuse summer tourists," or "Waiters who work at Newport's slick restaurants seem to be better at intimidating customers than giving service." require examples if readers are to fully understand the writers' points. But too often, beginning writers will merely repeat what they have said in their topic sentences.

To see our point, consider the following student paragraph. Although the writer limits the topic sentence and provides readers a clear direction, the discussion that follows does little more than repeat the lead idea and offer some complaints. This is no way to develop a paragraph.

> Tommy, my little cousin, behaves like a monkey. You never know what he will do next. Sometimes I have to baby-sit him, and it's all I can do to keep up with his antics. No wonder his parents go out every chance they get. I don't know where he gets his energy or how he dreams up new kinds of mischief, but I think for the good of all concerned he should be put in a zoo.

This paragraph is nothing but a general blur. It's dull. No sensible reader would want to finish it. The writer leaves readers wondering what Tommy actually does. Is he funny? Destructive? Malicious? More than likely, since the writer hasn't done a good job, readers will supply concrete examples from their own experience to fill in the blanks. They may do it poorly, completely missing the writer's point. Since the writer's purpose is to communicate a specific point, the obligation to the reader is to do it as clearly as possible.

The remedy for this kind of writing is obvious: provide some specific examples of Tommy's behavior. But how do writers generate examples? Simple. They draw up lists of related experiences. In other words, they prewrite before they begin. Before rewriting the Tommy piece, this student created a list taken from baby-sitting experiences with Tommy.

> Tommy never sits still—jumping from furniture, climbing trees, sliding down banisters. Sometimes I think I should bus tables. Baby-sitting my cousin is no way for a bright college freshman to earn spending money. Tommy is a monkey.
> - Pans on stairs. I was dozing. Raining outside. I thought he was asleep. Wham. Crash. The creep!
> - I remember the time he climbed out the window and hid from me behind the air conditioner. He could have broken his neck. His dad would have broken mine.
> - Making pie. Tommy loves to bake, God help me. Took me an hour to clean up. Paprika, Jell-O, flour. Ugh!
> - UFOs. He is nuts over UFOs. Zoooooooom!
> - Aunt Jane's house. The science lab. The mushroom cloud.
> - Driving lesson. One time he "backed" the car from the driveway. Rolled across the street, over the curb onto Mrs. Dale's front yard. Through the rosebushes. I wasn't baby-sitting then. Thank the Lord for small things.
> - All and all I must admit I like Tommy. He makes me a nervous wreck when I baby-sit him, but I like him.

After this writer completed his prewritten draft, he decided to reshape the topic sentence of his first effort to reflect accurately what he wanted to say. Next, he evaluated the material in his prewritten draft and excluded the experiences that didn't fit. He then took the remaining material and filled in the brief entries with more detail in order to construct a rough draft. Finally, he edited and revised the rough draft and wrote the final version. During this entire process, the writer's goal was to develop his topic sentence by creating specific examples that would help the reader understand his point. Now, here's the polished draft. As you read, notice how each specific example helps you see Tommy's zany and nerve-wracking behavior. Notice also that since the writer uses several specific examples, he introduces each with a clear transition.

Whenever I baby-sit my little cousin Tommy, his zany behavior makes me a nervous wreck. | Once when I was baby-sitting him, he climbed out of a second-story window onto the roof of the garage and hid behind the air-conditioning unit while I frantically searched the entire house. | About a month ago, he made an "experimental cake," using the kitchen floor for his mixing bowl. It took me a frantic hour to erase all the traces of paprika, Jell-O, and flour before his parents returned. While I was nervously scrubbing up the mess, he was jumping from chair to couch and back to chair in the living room, chattering something about UFOs. | Another time he tried some gymnastics on the railing at the top of the stairs. I screamed in fright as he leaped to the stairway landing, bounced up and down on his toes, scratched his armpits ape-fashion and screeched. | The episode that shook me up the most, though, took place on a cold, rainy night in December. Tommy had gone to bed--or so I thought--and the only sounds were the splashing rain and crackling fire. I dozed in an easy chair in front of the fireplace, slipping deeper and deeper into a Tommyless world of quiet and peace. Wham! An earthquake? A bomb? World War III? As my heart floated down from my throat, I discovered what I should have known

Topic sentence that prepares the reader for examples of Tommy's zany behavior and its nerve-wracking effect.

Example 1: Notice the overt transition "Once" that guides the reader into the example. Also notice "frantically" that links back to "nervous wreck" in the topic sentence.

Example 2: The phrase "About a month ago" signals the reader that a new example is coming. The idea of being nervous is picked up in the word "frantic" and in the writer's rush to clean up the mess before Tommy's parents return.

Example 3: The writer makes the transition by using "Another time." He continues to weave in the point with the phrase "I screamed in fright."

Example 4: This is the longest and most dramatic example. The writer uses an entire sentence to serve as a transition and set the scene for what follows. He mixes in a great deal of concrete detail and uses dramatic questions to help keep the reader interested.

```
all along.  It was only Tommy.  I found him
lying in a grinning heap near the stairs sur-
rounded by pots and pans.  He had decided it
would be best to make his next cake in his room.
```

These four specific examples are vivid. They are clear. After reading them you should understand the meaning of this writer's topic sentence, for he has carefully crafted them to create an impression. And these examples are interesting, too. Interest is one good feature of examples. They dramatize the vague and abstract. Examples hold the reader's attention.

The examples that reveal Tommy's behavior are short narratives. But writers often shape examples in other ways. Sometimes they use them to capture exact moments of experience, like snapshots that freeze a moment in time. These verbal snapshots, when appropriate for a subject, help a reader to see the point.

Jane van Lawick-Goodall uses short, visual examples to illustrate the social behavior of chimpanzees she has studied in Tanzania. This paragraph from one of her books illustrates the technique of presenting examples like photographs in an album. As you read, notice the stress Goodall puts on visualizing experiences. Although she uses few overt transitions, notice how she guides the reader into each of the first four examples by beginning them with "I saw" and "I watched." She varies the openings of the last two sentences after she has set the pattern in the reader's mind.

> While many details of their [the chimpanzees'] social behavior were hidden from me by the foliage, I did get occasional fascinating glimpses. I saw one female, newly arrived in a group, hurry up to a big male and hold her hand toward him. Almost regally he reached out, clasped her hand in his, drew it toward him, and kissed it with his lips. I saw two adult males embrace each other in greeting. I saw youngsters having wild games through the treetops, chasing around after each other or jumping again and again, one after the other, from a branch to a springy bough below. I watched small infants dangling happily by themselves for minutes on end, patting at their toes with one hand, rotating gently from side to side. Once two tiny infants pulled on opposite ends of a twig in a gentle tug-of-war. Often during the heat of midday or after a long spell of feeding, I saw two or more adults grooming each other, carefully looking through the hair of their companions.

For this particular paragraph the verbal snapshots are effective. These visual examples communicate more than a lengthy discussion would. You might also notice how Goodall varies the lengths of the examples. The shortest is only ten words; the longest, divided into two sentences, is forty-one. In order, they are the longest first; then the shortest; next two of middle length; then one that is quite short; then one of middle length as a close. We aren't suggesting you follow this pattern, but we are suggesting that variety in the length of examples adds to the pleasure of reading the paragraph. Whenever you use several examples in a paragraph, vary their lengths. Variety will help keep your reader interested.

Not all paragraphs developed by specific examples are as visual as Goodall's. Often writers will use examples that may be characterized as incidents or events. The following student writer uses three specific incidents as examples to illustrate a relationship between a particular film and murder.

> No one has yet shown a direct relationship between murder in Hollywood films and murder in real life, but after a film about street gangs called *The Warriors* opened in 1979, rival gangs clashed in or near some theaters. In Palm Springs, during an intermission in the showing of *The Warriors,* some members of a Fontana motorcycle gang made several sexual comments to a local girl. The Family, a rival gang, came to her rescue. Violence exploded. A member of the Blue Coats killed a nineteen-year-old member of the Family with a Saturday Night Special. In Oxnard, two gangs clashed on opening night of *The Warriors.* When people crowded into the lobby someone, yet to be identified, stabbed an eighteen-year-old to death. In Boston several gang members leaving a theater featuring *The Warriors* taunted a sixteen-year-old boy with a line from the script. A brawl broke out. Someone used a knife. Six hours later the boy was dead.

One effect of these specific examples is that they are convincing. They convince in a way that no abstract discussion could ever do. But when you use isolated examples, such as these related to gangs, you must keep in mind their limitations. They do not hold up well in logical argument. They are not "proof." Their value lies in their emotional impact. They serve well enough for ordinary communication.

WRITING TASK

Write a paragraph using a series of specific examples, which may be short narratives, verbal snapshots, or specific incidents. Keep in mind that they must be written in concrete language and must illustrate a limited topic sentence.

Once you have a subject, go through the various drafts — you know: prewriting, rough draft, editing and revising, final and polished draft — to get to the finished paragraph.

In case you can't find anything to write about, select something from the list of general subjects below. We offer the list with fear and trembling. Too often college writers will leap at a suggestion, then mechanically develop a subject in which they have no interest. Papers of this sort are boring to write and boring to read. So, although we offer the list, we urge you to accept it as a starting place. And remember, you must still shape any general subject you choose into a workable topic sentence.

fortunetelling	sports
superstition	fads
films	food
jobs	dreams
music	relatives

5 TYPICAL EXAMPLES

Typical examples differ from specific examples in that they are timeless and general rather than particular. Most specific examples can be assigned times and dates. For instance, Tommy's baby-sitter could probably say, "My zany cousin Tommy made an 'experimental cake' at 7:14 P.M. on March 6, 1979." Goodall could assign times and dates to her specific observations of chimpanzee social behavior, as could the police to the gang murders that followed the viewings of *The Warriors*. Typical examples, on the other hand, have no exact times and dates. Writers often compose typical examples from experiences gathered from many observations. Therefore, they seem timeless. And while they are usually written in concrete language, they tend to be general in nature.

In her work on chimpanzees, Jane van Lawick-Goodall offers a typical example of how the creatures prepare for bedtime. This extended example comes from many observations. While casting it in concrete language, Goodall offers the example as typical of their nightly behavior — that is, on any night chimpanzees will prepare for bed in this manner. Notice the way Goodall begins with background information. She leads into the topic sentence, which directs the reader toward her example of the chimpanzees' nesting practice.

At that time of year the chimps usually went to bed late, making their nests when it was too dark to see properly through binoculars, but sometimes they nested earlier and I could

Background information pointing toward the visual example that is typical of chimpanzee nesting practice.

49

watch them from the Peak. | I found that every
individual, except for infants who slept with
their mothers, made his own nest each night. |

Topic sentence that identifies the focus for the reader

Generally this took about three minutes: the
chimp chose a firm foundation such as an upright
fork or crotch, or two horizontal branches. Then
he reached out and bent over smaller branches
onto this foundation, keeping one in place with
his feet. Finally he tucked in the small leafy
twigs growing around the rim of his nest and
lay down. | Quite often a chimp sat up after a
few minutes and picked a handful of leafy twigs,
which he put under his head or some other part
of his body before settling down again for the
night.

Writer introduces the extended example that describes the typical nesting process. Notice how "Generally" sets the example in motion.

Notice how "Quite often" serves to introduce a variation in the typical process.

Also notice Goodall's use of concrete words throughout the piece.

Do you see how Goodall shaped this example as typical of chimpanzee nesting behavior? The example comes from many observations, not from one particular one. We suggest, though, that the success of Goodall's typical example lies not only in carefully generalizing from several observations but also in meticulously using concrete details to compose the piece. These concrete details help us see the typical behavior.

Now study another paragraph developed through a typical example. This paragraph, hatched in the mind of a student writer, focuses on the funeral rites practiced by an imaginary tribe called the Dubako.

The Dubako Indians of South America are
perhaps unique in their joyful approach to
funerals. | When a member of this tiny tribe
dies, the whole community turns out for an
entire day of riotous celebration. The fire
pit in which the deceased will be cremated is

Topic sentence that focuses the paragraph for the reader

Writer introduces one extended example of a typical Dubako funeral.

first used for the roasting of pigs, dozens of them over a period of several hours. The morning is spent in almost continuous eating, interrupted only for the telling of stories, often wholly imaginary, about the dead--not just about the present tribe member, but about all the dead of previous generations. By afternoon the body of the deceased, which has been carefully hidden during the storytelling, is now brought to a small clearing. It is nap time. The members of the tribe lie down around the body--the most honored position is right next to the corpse-- and sleep for several hours, hoping to be visited by the spirit of the deceased, who is left seated to guard the tribe from a sneak attack by an enemy. The nap period is brought to a close by the beating of drums which simultaneously announce the beginning of the dance. Male and female, old and young, dance individually and in groups, drinking a fermented beverage from a supply carefully saved for this occasion by the deceased himself. The night is for lovemaking. The Dubakos are ordinarily monogamous, but on this evening pay no attention to the conventions of daily living. If a woman conceives on such a night, the child will be considered a special blessing, a sign that the spirit of the deceased is still concerned about the welfare of the

Notice how the writer has worked in concrete details to make his work more vivid. The Dubakos aren't merely going to cook in the fire pit; they are going to roast pigs — dozens of them.

Also notice that the writer is not responding to the details but instead presents them objectively as Goodall did. However, a writer may work in responses if they seem appropriate.

Have you noticed how the writer has arranged his work? "The morning is spent . . ." "By afternoon . . ." "The night is . . ." and so on through a day's cycle

tribe. Those who do not partake of the lovemaking gather the children together in the clearing by the still-seated guest of honor and play
games, tell stories, and sing songs until early
morning. At dawn the corpse is cremated in the   *The last sentence closes the cycle.*
fire pit as in silence the tribe says goodbye
to the departed companion.

      The chimpanzee and Dubako illustrations have been extended examples. But whether you should write long or short examples depends on the demands of your material. Often you will write short typical examples. Unlike Goodall, who uses examples based on what she has seen, the writer of the following paragraph on slang terms develops the topic sentence through a series of typical examples taken from David Dalby's linguistic research.

      Linguistic researchers have discovered what   *Topic sentence*
they believe is a close tie between some American
slang terms and the Wolof language of West
Africa, spoken by many slaves. | An American   *Four representative examples which typify*
says "I dig," meaning "I understand" and "I   *the connections between Wolof language*
agree." It may be that this term is derived   *and American slang*
from the Wolof word dega, pronounced "digger,"
which means "understand." | "Jive" seems to be
related to Wolof jev, which means "to talk
about in a negative manner." | The Wolof word
hipi, meaning "to open your eyes" possibly gave
us the slang words "hip," "hep," and "hippy."
There is even speculation that the common
Americanism "OK" is only a corruption of Wolof
waw kay, which means "all right" or "certainly."

We'll close this section on typical examples with a paragraph from psychologist Erich Fromm. Notice that the examples Fromm uses differ from the other illustrations we've presented in this section. They are not grounded in observation or research. They are logical generalizations about human behavior. Fromm uses them not as factual information, but to impress his reader with the idea that people with different attitudes will view an experience differently.

> What is, for example, the attitude of different people toward a forest? A painter who has gone there to paint, the owner of the forest who wishes to evaluate his business prospects, an officer who is interested in the tactical problem of defending the area, a hiker who wants to enjoy himself — each of them will have an entirely different concept of the forest because a different aspect is significant to each one. The painter's experience will be one of form and color; the businessman's of size, number, and age of trees; the officer's of visibility and protection; the hiker's of trails and motion. While they can all agree to the abstract statement that they can stand at the edge of the forest, the different kinds of activity they are set to accomplish will determine their experience of "seeing a forest."

Though Fromm's paragraph is structurally complicated — instead of arranging his examples one after the other he mixes them throughout — still, he is following the method of developing his point with typical examples.

WRITING TASK

Write a paragraph using one extended typical example or several short typical examples. You may develop your paragraph through observations, representative facts, or logical generalizations. Remember, although these examples tend to be general, they should be written in concrete language. As always, we suggest that you select your own topic, but in case you become stumped, select one from the following list.

1. observations: typical behavior in:
    elevators
    medical offices
    nursery school
    classrooms (student/teacher behavior at the start/end of class)

2. representative facts:
        cruelty to animals
        safety in nuclear plants
        dying rivers/forests/deserts
        reclaimed rivers/forests/deserts

3. logical generalizations: attitudes of
        parents   politicians
        teachers   advertisers
        students   artists
        salespersons   police
        waitresses or waiters   civil servants
        mechanics   doctors

A warning. When developing a paragraph through typical examples, you may fall into the trap of being too general. For instance, if you choose to write a paragraph using logical generalizations and dealing with the subject of politicians, you will still need to narrow your focus. You can do it by writing about a small group of politicians such as members of your city council. Or you may do it by writing about the way politicians respond to a particular situation, as Fromm does with businessmen, painters, hikers, and military officers.

One more thought. Do we need to remind you about working in drafts?

6 CATALOGUING

Cataloguing a great many details is another effective pattern you might use to develop a paragraph. A detailed catalogue serves as a way to thrust a reader into the middle of an experience. Often a writer will announce a catalogue in a topic sentence that leads readers to expect descriptive details. Then the writer will follow with a sentence that sets the pattern in motion. The writer of the following example does just that. As you read this short paragraph, notice how the details that the writer catalogues follow from "I saw . . ."

Last summer I attended an out-of-doors concert that erupted into a riot. From where I sat on a distant grass-covered knoll, I saw a guitarist smash a microphone against a fan's head, a herd of drunks hurl beer bottles at the dodging musicians, a group of girls dressed in punk rock styles shaking their fists and shouting for blood, and I saw club-waving security guards wade into the crowd as innocent bystanders scurried for shelter. The whole time I thought, this is insane, this is insane, while overhead

Topic sentence sets the time and event writer plans to describe.

This sentence is the core of the pattern. It sets the visual quality of the piece and catalogues the fragments of detail: (1) guitarist smashing a fan, (2) drunks hurling bottles, (3) girls shaking their fists and shouting, (4) club-waving guards, (5) bystanders scurrying,

This writer closes with personal response while weaving it with auditory details.

a police helicopter buzzed and in the distance

sirens wailed.

How can readers fail to get involved in this pattern? Tugging at their emotions and pulling at their senses, the rapid presentation of concrete details demands readers' attention.

Not all catalogues are this emotionally gripping. Sometimes writers use them to tantalize their readers. Catalogues of this sort generate expectations and promise excitement. Paul Theroux uses this technique in a paragraph in *The Great Railway Bazaar,* a book that describes his trip by train across Asia. Theroux uses two catalogues in a single paragraph. The first — which begins "Anything is possible . . ." — creates the atmosphere of the train. The second — which begins "It was my intention . . ." — catalogues the various railroads Theroux will ride during his journey. As you read notice how Theroux uses a colon to set up each catalogue.

Then Asia was out the window, and I was *Topic sentence that sets the paragraph in motion*

carried through it on these eastbound expresses

marveling as much at the bazaar within the train

as the ones we whistled past. Anything is possible *First catalogue*

on a train: a great meal, a binge, a visit from

card players, an intrigue, a good night's sleep,

and strangers' monologues framed like Russian

short stories. It was my intention to board *Second catalogue*

every train that chugged into view from Victoria

Station in London to Tokyo Central: to take a

branch line to Simla, the spur through the

Khyber Pass, and the chord line that links Indian

Railways with those in Ceylon; the Mandalay

Express, the Malaysian Golden Arrow, the locals

in Vietnam, and the trains with bewitching names,

the Orient Express, the North Star, the Trans-

Siberian.

Theroux's piece reflects the pattern of the paragraph about the concert-turned-riot. He opens with a topic sentence that leads the reader to expect what follows. He then writes a sentence to lead into each catalogue. Unlike the first illustration, Theroux's paragraph doesn't end with a response. We suggest that whether or not to end with one depends on what follows in the next paragraph.

Besides generating excitement and building expectations in a reader, a writer may also use the cataloguing pattern to present a great deal of information in a condensed form. Barbara W. Tuchman uses this technique in *A Distant Mirror* to give her readers an impression of the fourteenth century's understanding of distant places. One of the problems a writer faces when arranging catalogues of this sort (or any sort, for that matter) is how to present the details in an orderly fashion. Tuchman solves the problem by first introducing the catalogue with a colon, then beginning each major element with a key word and following it with one or more descriptive details. The key words are *forests, horned pygmies, brahmins, men, cyclopeans, monoceros, Amazons, panthers, trees,* and *snakes.* As you read, study how Tuchman has followed this plan.

> Faraway lands, however — India, Persia, and beyond — were seen through a gauze of fabulous fairy tales revealing an occasional nugget of reality: forests so high they touch the clouds, horned pygmies who move in herds and grow old in seven years, brahmins who kill themselves on funeral pyres, men with dogs' heads and six toes, "cyclopeans" with only one eye and one foot who move as fast as the wind, the "monoceros" which can be caught only when it sleeps in the lap of a virgin, Amazons whose tears are of silver, panthers who practice the caesarean operation with their own claws, trees whose leaves supply wool, snakes 300 feet long, snakes with precious stones for eyes, snakes who so love music that for prudence they stop up one ear with their tail.

So far we have used illustrations by writers who have jammed their catalogues into single sentences. This is the most common practice. But often writers will catalogue a series of questions. Later in her book, Tuchman uses this pattern to make her readers aware of the kinds of mysterious questions the fourteenth-century mind puzzled over.

> For all the explanations, the earth and its phenomena were full of mysteries: What happens to fire when it goes out? Why are there different colors of skin among men? Why do the sun's rays darken a man's skin but bleach white linen? How do souls make their way to the next world? Where lies the soul? What

causes madness? Medieval people felt surrounded by puzzles, yet because God was there they were willing to acknowledge that causes are hidden, that man cannot know why all things are as they are; "they are as God pleases."

As we said, cataloguing is a quick way to involve your readers. It's a device — nothing more — to thrust them into an experience or capture their intellect. Its underlying effect is made not through logic but through bombardment.

WRITING TASK

Write a paragraph built on the cataloguing pattern. Be sure to write an opening sentence that prepares the reader for the catalogue and follow with a sentence that sets the catalogue in motion. Remember, a catalogue can deal with most any subject, but its main purpose is to quickly involve your reader; therefore, you must work to create a strong impression with the material you select. To get you started, here are a few suggestions. Keep in mind that you can shape them to your own purposes.

1. **Take a walk down main street.** Visit some part of the town where you live and record an extended list of physical details you feel convey the dominant feeling of the area. Build the list into a paragraph.

2. **Visit a store.** Walk through a department, hardware, liquor, shoe, drug, or dime store. (Hmmmmmm! Do dime stores still exist?) Or sit around a pool hall, beauty parlor, bar, cafeteria, library, or street corner. No matter where you visit, record your impressions, then develop them in a paragraph according to the cataloguing pattern.

3. **Sit on a rock.** Go to a park, grove of trees, lake, hilltop, bird sanctuary, or empty football field. Record your impressions and build them into a catalogue.

4. **Review your life.** Reread some journal entries that focus on your life. Build a paragraph by cataloguing the high or the low points — the peaks and the valleys. Or if questions about your life come to you, build a paragraph out of them.

5. **Capture an experience.** Record the dominant impressions of an experience you've had, then build the impressions into a catalogue.

Remember, you want the reader to get involved with your material, so try to make it vivid. The key thought behind this pattern is bombardment. Give your reader plenty of detail, but be sure to arrange it in an orderly fashion.

7 ANECDOTE

逸話,
軼事

An anecdote is a brief story which illustrates a point or a person's character. Simple enough. But unlike other patterns we've discussed, anecdotes seldom make direct statements. They suggest rather than declare; they need to be interpreted, never accepted at face value.

Time magazine used the following anecdote to introduce a piece about Pete Rose's pride in his baseball ability:

> The plane carrying the Cincinnati Reds bucked and yawed through a storm front, scattering drinks and scrambling stomachs. Peter Edward Rose, the irrepressibly proud captain of the Reds, used the moment to tease a teammate whose fear of flying far exceeded opposing pitchers' fears of his bat. "We're going down!" Rose shouted. Then the punchline. "We're going down, and I have a .300 lifetime average to take with me!"

Brief as it is, this anecdote shows something about Rose's humor, pride, and enthusiasm. In other words, it does what some anecdotes are supposed to do: it reveals character.

The example also illustrates some other aspects of anecdote writing. The opening line — "The plane carrying the Cincinnati Reds bucked and yawed through a storm front, scattering drinks and scrambling stomachs" — sets the stage for the story through description. Many anecdotes require stage setting, but don't get lost in description when writing an anecdote; its purpose is to add reality and help the reader visualize the incident. This anecdote also includes some dialogue. Often anecdotes do. And, finally, the Rose anecdote works indirectly. Only two words serve as straight comments on Rose's character: "irrepressibly proud." The whole anecdote, then, needs to be interpreted to reveal

59

parts of Rose's character. So keep in mind that anecdotes often involve description and dialogue and often work indirectly.

James Phelan uses an anecdote in *Howard Hughes: The Hidden Years* to reveal Hughes's capricious character and the fear his whims stimulated in his attendants.

> During Howard Hughes' years of seclusion in the Desert Inn in Las Vegas, he would demand the same meal every day for lengthy stretches. At one point, according to his long-time aide, Gordon Margulis, he was having two scoops of Baskin-Robbins' banana-nut ice cream with every meal, so his staff kept it constantly on hand.
>
> One day, when the supply needed to be replenished, it was learned that the flavor had been discontinued. Hughes' staff panicked. Someone telephoned the Baskin-Robbins office in California and asked them to make a special batch of banana-nut. They agreed to make up the smallest batch they could on special order — 350 gallons. "We still had a few scoops of the old banana-nut when the new banana-nut arrived," says Margulis, "so we felt all set for the rest of Hughes' lifetime."
>
> When the ice cream was served to Hughes the next day, however, he ate it and declared: "That's great ice cream, but it's time for a change. From now on, I want French Vanilla."

The Hughes anecdote is part of a much longer work. This is usually the case with anecdote. Phelan uses it as a quick means to reveal Hughes's character. Speed and impact give it punch. Punch, or surprise, as opposed to reasoned discourse, is characteristic of most anecdotes. The punch may merely generate a belly laugh, such as the banana-nut ice cream caper. Or it may tug at a deeper emotional awareness.

In *Desert Solitaire* Edward Abbey uses an anecdote to make a point about the plight of Navajos living in a world that has little respect for their heritage.

```
It will not be easy.  It will not be easy

for the Navajos to forget that once upon a time,

only a generation ago, they were horsemen,

nomads, keepers of flocks, painters in sand,

weavers of wool, artists in silver, dancers,
```

Abbey begins setting up the anecdote by calling to the reader's mind what the Navajos once were.

Notice how he uses a catalogue to work in a great deal of detail.

singers of the Yei-bie-chei. But they will have to forget, or at least learn to be ashamed of these old things and to bring them out only for the amusement of tourists.

A difficult transitional period. Tough on people. For instance, consider an unfortunate accident which took place only a week ago here in Arches country. Parallel to the highway north of Moab is a railway, a spur line to the potash mines. At one point close to this road this railway cuts through a hill. The cut is about three hundred feet deep, blasted through solid rock with sides that are as perpendicular as the walls of a building. One afternoon two young Indians--Navajos? Apaches? beardless Utes?--in a perverted Plymouth came hurtling down the highway, veered suddenly to the right, whizzed through a fence and plunged straight down like helldivers into the Big Cut. Investigating the wreckage we found only the broken bodies, the broken bottles, the stain and smell of Tokay, and a couple of cardboard suitcases exploded open and revealing their former owners' worldly goods--dirty socks, some underwear, a copy of True West magazine, a comb, three new cowboy shirts from J. C. Penney's, a carton of Marlboro cigarettes. But nowhere did we see any conchos

"For instance, consider an unfortunate accident" announces the anecdote.

Abbey gives some background information that leads up to the incident.

Now he moves directly into the story.

Abbey catalogues the contents of the wreckage to show the reader what today's young Navajos possess. A sharp contrast to the proud possessions of former Navajos. At this point the contrast becomes even more direct — the dreams of drugstore cowboys juxtaposed against the reality of the past.

of silver, any buffalo robes, any bows, arrows,

medicine pouch or drums.

                Some Indians.   *Abbey closes with an ironic comment —*
                                                        "Some Indians" — to show what an
                                                        insensitive white man's response might be.

The pride of the ancient Navajo has been bartered for the cheap goods of modern society. That may be one way to look at these paragraphs. Or perhaps the criticism goes much deeper. Modern America has sold the goods and the dreams the goods represent to the Indians, thus diminishing their lives. Beyond that, just as the Navajo are diminished, so too are we diminished by the same forces that have driven these Indian boys to the fantasies of Tokay and *True West.*

Do we go too far? But remember anecdote speaks indirectly. When you read one you must prowl through it to get the point. When you write one, you must shape it for a reader to get the point.

WRITING TASK

Write an anecdote that reveals character or makes a point about a social issue. Keep in mind that anecdotes suggest rather than declare the writer's concern. They also involve some descriptive stage setting so that the reader can visualize the experience. And, most importantly, they end with some punch that drives the point home.

If you have been doing Daily Writing as described in Part Three of this book we suggest you reread some of your entries. They may offer the thread you can weave into a fuller tapestry.

If you choose to write an anecdote that illustrates a social concern, be sure to stick to a particular case that suggests the larger issue, as Abbey does in his anecdote of the Navajo youths. For instance, if you're concerned over the health care of the infirm, you might select a particular case from a local convalescent home as the focus for your anecdote. If you're concerned about the behavior of authorities, parents, students, politicians, choose a particular case from your experience as the focus. Do you see what we mean? Remember, two pages devoted to a concrete anecdote is often more valuable than reams devoted to explanation and analysis.

8 SHORT COMPARISON AND CONTRAST

"My dad's a better baseball player than your dad!"

"Did anyone ever say you look just like Dustin Hoffman?"

"It's a good movie, but I like the book better."

"Get your hair cut — you look like a wild animal."

"Men are all alike."

These bits of imaginary conversation are all examples of comparisons or contrasts. We're sure you've heard such comments many times in your life. They're not very specific, so they won't work well in writing, but in casual conversation they hold up.

Comparison points out similarities; contrast points out differences. Both are common patterns for communicating information and ideas. They are used not only in conversation but in all forms of writing — essays, research projects, examinations, letters, reports, and so on.

Sometimes a comparison or contrast pattern will be a brief· part of a longer work and come at the end of it, such as this illustration from a paper on inflation.

> No matter how bad inflation has hit your pocketbook this year, you can at least be thankful you don't live in Japan, where the inflation rate is twice that of the United States.

Often, though, a comparison and contrast pattern will take up at least a paragraph and sometimes extend for several paragraphs.

Whenever you line up two things for discussion, you'll almost always be comparing and contrasting them. Keep in mind, though, that for this pattern to be effective, the subjects must be members of the same group. For instance, one writer might effectively compare and contrast a bee with a snake because both are living creatures. Another writer might effectively compare and contrast a bee with a helicopter because both are things that fly. But we doubt that any writer could effectively compare and contrast a helicopter with a snake no matter what the purpose. So when you employ this pattern, we suggest you make sure your subjects are clearly related.

Read the following paragraph which a student wrote as part of a museum report and which combines both comparison and contrast. There are a few techniques we'd like you to watch for as you read. First, notice how the writer presents both subjects — elephants and mastodons — in the topic sentence. Also notice how the writer uses the topic sentence to lead readers into a comparison and contrast structure. Third, notice the brief phrases the writer uses to remind readers of the comparing and contrasting process: "Like the modern elephant" and "Unlike the elephant." Brief phrases of this sort help guide readers' attention so that they can smoothly shift their thought from one point to another. And, finally, notice the sentence that pivots the paragraph and moves it from pointing out similarities to pointing out differences between the two beasts.

After you've read the paragraph, we suggest you reread it along with the comments in the margin so that you can more firmly grasp the pattern.

When I first saw the reproduction of the prehistoric mastodon, I thought of elephants I had seen in circuses and zoos. Like the modern elephant, the mastodon is large with legs that remind me of sturdy tree trunks. The ancient beast had large, floppy ears and a long trunk which he could use as a tool for gathering food. But after a closer look, I saw some major differences between the modern elephant and the prehistoric mastodon. The mastodon's tusks grew longer and curved upward at a sharper angle.

Topic sentence sets up the two elements to be compared and contrasted — mastodon and elephant.

Brief presentation of the similarities between the two creatures

"But after a closer look . . ." serves as a pivotal sentence to guide the reader into the contrast section.

Brief presentation of the differences between the two creatures

Unlike the elephant with its thick, almost hair-

less hide, the mastodon was matted with long,

thick hair. | And, although the mastodon was

large, it was not as tremendous in size as its

modern descendent.

The final sentence reminds the reader again of the two elements presented.

As a final comment on this illustration, we'd like to point out the writer's use of concrete details to develop the comparison and contrast pattern — sturdy legs, floppy ears, curving tusks, hairless hide, and long, thick hair. No matter what patterns you employ, try to include concrete detail.

Comparing and contrasting two subjects does not always take place in the same paragraph. Sometimes a writer will devote a paragraph to one or the other. Read the following illustration in which the writer compares fat to thin people. The writer begins by linking the comparison to her father, but quickly shifts to overweight people in general. Her paragraph is an appeal to see beyond surface differences to the deeper similarities among all people. (If we were talking about examples here, we would point out that this writer selects typical details that all human beings share.)

My father is fat, but he, like all fat

people, is similar in significant ways to

thinner human beings. | Fat people have eyes

that see and ears that hear and tongues that

speak. Too often, like most people, they see

rejection, hear ridicule, and speak self-

deprecatingly. Fat people work, play, serve

their country, and, like everyone else, they

bleed when wounded. With age their skin

wrinkles and their hair grays. In the end they

must face the terrible void that everyone must

Topic sentence that leads the reader to expect a comparison

The series of concrete details that link fat people with all other humans

Notice how "like most people" helps keep the reader focused on the writer's intent.

The phrase "like everyone else" also helps keep the reader focused.

face--death. No matter what their size, they

are human, as human as all humans. | Why, then,

are they berated for being overweight?

After linking fat people to the common fate of death, the writer ends with a question which implies a purpose for the comparison.

We hope you see that comparison paragraphs offer little organizational difficulty. Once the subjects have been selected, you simply go through the ways in which the two are similar. We suggest, though, that you play close attention to the order in which you discuss the similarities. Save the most dramatic for last.

There are two basic ways of developing paragraphs by contrasts: the block pattern and the point-by-point pattern. Let's look at the block pattern first.

The block pattern is quite simple. First you sketch the outstanding points of one subject; then you sketch the outstanding points of the other. You always end with a comment that brings the two subjects into focus. This pattern is easy to organize if the subjects are brief and not too complex.

Read the following illustration that contrasts the "negative addict" with the "positive addict." As you read, notice how the writer swings from one section to the other with the phrase "On the other hand." He also sets up the closing comments with the phrase "In any case. . . ."

The word addict is usually used in a nega-

tive way, but when used in a positive fashion,

it has a different significance. | A negative

addict may be someone who smokes until his

breath grows weak and raspy and his lungs decay.

At a greater extreme, he may be a person hooked

on heroin, alcohol, or gambling--or on any

compulsion that so dominates his life that it

threatens both his existence and the existence

of his loved ones. | On the other hand, a posi-

tive addict may be addicted to jogging,

swimming, or meditating--activities that sustain

Although the two subjects are not clearly identified in the opening sentence, the writer gives the reader a clear idea of what to expect.

First block presents details related to the negative addict.

The phrase "On the other hand" announces the movement into the second block that presents details of the positive addict.

his health and help him live vigorously. He

may be addicted to diary keeping, spending up

to two hours a day writing down his experiences

and thoughts. Some claim that concentrated

reading may be a positive addiction that helps

the reader sustain intellectual involvement

with his own growth and his society. | In any   *The phrase "In any case" announces that*
                                                 the two subjects will be brought together in
case, unlike the negative addict who seems bent *order to close the paragraph.*

on destroying himself and those around him, the

positive addict perpetuates his life and becomes

a better person through his compulsion.

Whenever a subject is complicated and writers need to contrast several differences, they will usually use the point-by-point pattern. The reason is simple. Point-by-point development holds a reader's attention when the material gets complex. But writers face one difficulty when using this pattern. They must avoid the monotony of repeating such phrases as "in contrast to" or "on the other hand." In the block pattern these kinds of phrases sparely scattered throughout a piece serve as guides; in the point method, if a writer frequently uses them, they become tiresome.

Writers don't want to tire their readers. They will, therefore, weed from their work all unnecessary transitional phrases. They will then arrange their sentences so that their readers can clearly see the shift from one subject to the other. Often they will mix their sentence structures by using semicolons to both link and set off contrasting points.

Study Gilbert Highet's contrast of early Greek teachers called sophists with their rival teacher Socrates. Notice how Highet counterpoints one difference with another. Also notice how he arranges his sentence structure so that the beginning of each independent clause clearly identifies the subject he's presenting.

To some of his contemporaries Socrates looked   *Topic sentence that opens with some*
                                                 background information before suggesting
like a sophist. But he distrusted and opposed   *the contrast between Socrates and the*
                                                 sophists

the sophists wherever possible. They toured the whole Greek world; Socrates stayed in Athens, talking to his fellow-citizens. They made carefully prepared continuous speeches; he only asked questions. They took rich fees for their teaching; he refused regular payment, living and dying poor.

These first few differences are organized by the semicolon.

They were elegantly dressed, turned out like film-stars on a personal appearance tour, with secretaries and personal servants and elaborate advertising. Socrates wore the workingman's clothes, bare feet and a smock--in fact, he had been a stonemason and carver by trade, and came from a working-class family.

As the differences become more complex, the writer divides the details into sentences. This detailing also adds structural variety to the paragraph.

They spoke in specially prepared lecture halls; he talked to people at street-corners and in the gymnasium, where every afternoon the young men exercised, and the old men talked, while they all sunbathed.

The writer returns to the semicolon structure.

He fitted in so well there that he sometimes compared himself to the athletic coach, who does not run or wrestle, but teaches others how to run and wrestle better; Socrates said he trained people to think.

The writer leaves the contrast to develop Socrates more fully, thus accentuating his method as superior to the sophists'.

Lastly, the sophists said they knew everything and were ready to explain it. Socrates said he knew nothing and was trying to find out.

He closes by bringing the sophists back into the process and suggesting that Socrates is superior.

Structurally, Highet's paragraph is quite simple, yet he effectively works in a great deal of detail about the sophists and Socrates. Of course, his sympathies are clear: he applauds Socrates while making the sophists look like egocentric materialists. Unless you are required to write an objective report, we recommend you also make your attitudes clear to the reader.

WRITING TASK

Write a short comparison or contrast paragraph. You may choose to develop your paragraph around the similarities of your subjects or around their differences according to the block or point-by-point pattern. For this task we recommend you stick to one pattern and not try to mix the two.

When you begin your comparison or contrast paragraph, be sure to start with a prewritten draft with your subjects as the focus. Then, after you've determined what the topic sentence will be, select from your prewrite those details that fit your purpose and arrange them in a list that reflects it. For instance, Highet might have built his contrast of the sophists with Socrates from a list such as this:

Sophists	*Socrates*
traveled the entire Greek world	stayed in Athens, teaching fellow citizens
gave lectures and speeches	asked questions — no formal speeches
accepted high fees	accepted no fees, died poor
like film stars on tour, secretaries, servants, fine clothes	wore workingman's clothes; went around with bare feet; from a working family; once a stonecarver
talked in lecture halls	talked in public places where men of all kinds gathered — especially the gymnasium; thought of himself as a coach training people to think
claimed to know everything	claimed to know nothing

When you phrase a topic sentence for this task, be sure it clearly announces a comparison or contrast pattern. It is also good practice to identify the two subjects you will discuss, and, if not writing an objective report, your attitude toward them. For example, re-examine the topic sentences from three of the last illustrations.

> My father is fat, but he, like all fat people, is similar in significant ways to thinner human beings.

> The word *addict* is usually used in a negative way, but when used in a positive fashion, it has a different significance.

> To some of his contemporaries Socrates looked like a sophist. But he distrusted and opposed the sophists wherever possible.

Here are a few more to consider:

> Although *Star Wars* takes place "long ago in a galaxy far away," most American moviegoers will recognize it as just another Western in disguise.

> After visiting Warren Beatty several times last summer, I was intrigued by the difference between the private man and the public image.

> The difference between the old America and the new America is reflected in the two national sports: baseball and football.

> All cacti are succulents, but not all succulents are cacti.

> In practice both coaches stress fundamentals and conditioning, but on the sidelines during the game, Burns is a tiger while Stevens is a pussycat.

All of these topic sentences point clearly to comparison and/or contrast. They all specify the two subjects the writer will discuss, limit the territory the writer will cover, and often suggest an attitude. That's what we want you to do with your topic sentence.

Here are some possible subjects.

1. Compare or contrast two films you liked or disliked.
2. Compare or contrast two pets.
3. Compare or contrast two teaching styles or teachers.

4. Compare or contrast two outstanding athletes who play the same position.

5. Compare or contrast two dress styles.

Or, as with all writing tasks in this section, select your own subjects to compare or contrast.

9 EXTENDED COMPARISON AND CONTRAST

As we have said, comparison and contrast patterns often extend beyond a single paragraph. After all, within this pattern writers develop two or more subjects, an act which may require more space than most readable paragraphs contain. Moreover, writers sometimes mix comparison with contrast, as in the piece that both compares and contrasts mastodon with elephant. Unlike the mastodon/elephant illustration, the mixing may demand more than a single paragraph to adequately develop the subjects.

As an illustration of an extended comparison and contrast, study the following student piece. The writer develops the similarities and differences in his grandfathers. We suggest you notice how he presents the similarities in the first paragraph and then follows with the differences arranged in blocks. Unlike the author of the block pattern illustrations in the last section, this writer divides his blocks into two paragraphs and links them with the connecting phrase "on the other hand." There's a reason for doing it — the blocks are long; better to make the reader's way easier by separating them.

comparison

In several general ways my grandfathers were similar. | Both immigrated to America from Europe to escape military service. Peace-loving men, they were determined to leave petty national

Topic sentence that sets up the comparison

First part deals with the similarity of peace-loving immigrants.

quarrels behind. Both settled first in New York City, married American girls, and then moved to Nebraska to raise their families in the open spaces of the Midwest. They shared a belief in the simple life: hard work, thrift, honesty, and church on Sunday. They also shared the disappointment of seeing sons return to Europe to fight in a war which they felt was "none of our business." Fortunately, the sons survived and raised their families too, bringing warmth and joy to my grandfathers' old age.

This point groups several similarities. Notice how the writer introduces his points with "Both" or "They."

They shared the same simple values.

They also shared the sorrow of war touching their lives indirectly and the joy of their sons surviving to raise families.

contract

Sharing so much, they were so different in personality. Grandfather Spender was aloof and serious. He loved to read and to spend his evenings writing long entries in a diary. Our visits to his house were brief and quiet. Sometimes he would read a passage in German aloud while we children stared uncomprehendingly at his eyes filling with tears. I never knew him well, but I admired him and secretly sympathized with what I understood to be a homesickness for his native Germany.

Topic sentence that unifies the next two paragraphs by setting up the differences in personality. Obviously, these differences could not be structured in a point-by-point pattern.

contrast

On the other hand, visits to Grandpa Kaluski's house were always noisy. Most of the noise was provided by Grandpa Kaluski himself, who loved to play the accordian while we kids did our best to polka on the packed dirt of the

"On the other hand" clearly identifies this paragraph as an extension of the preceding one.

backyard. Always jovial, proud to be an American,

he never, within my hearing at least, mentioned

Poland or indicated any interest in Polish

things--that is, except the polka. We used to

take long walks together through the fields,

sharing secrets, singing songs, and making plans

for my future. When he died I felt a loneliness

I had never before experienced.

By the way, did you notice how smoothly the writer works in the difference in nationality? He doesn't hold it up as a major difference, but keeps to his focus — the differences in personality.

No matter what the length of an extended comparison and contrast piece, the structural principles don't significantly vary, as the grandfathers Spender and Kaluski piece illustrates.

Writers tend to handle comparisons in one fashion — by lumping the subjects together. This is the most natural and efficient way to do it. Notice how inefficient it would have been for the writer of the last illustration to present his grandfathers' similarities in blocks.

> My grandfather Spender immigrated to America to escape military service in Germany. He was a peace-loving man, determined to avoid petty national quarrels. He settled first in New York City, married an American girl, and then moved to Nebraska to raise his family in the open spaces of the West. He believed in the simple life: hard work, thrift, honesty, and church on Sunday. The biggest disappointment of his life was seeing his son return to Europe to fight in a war that was "none of our business." Fortunately, his son survived and raised a family, too, bringing warmth and joy to my grandfather's old age.
>
> My grandfather Kaluski came here to avoid military service, too. Just like Grandpa Spender he settled in New York City first, married an American girl, and moved to the wide open spaces of Nebraska to raise his family. He, too, believed in the value of a simple life. He also saw a son return to Europe to fight. His son also survived and gave him many grandchildren.

No matter how the writer tries to avoid it by changing the wording here and there, the piece sounds repetitious and trite. All the power is spent in the first block. Comparison tends to bring things closer to each other, so we suggest you always go with the natural tendency to lump similarities together.

Writers tend to structure short and relatively general contrasts in blocks and long and relatively specific contrasts by points. Contrast tends to separate things — to put one thing here, the other over there. In the second paragraph about the two grandfathers, the writer deals with the general subject of their personalities, but he discusses different activities for each one. Consequently, he arranges the information in the block pattern. On the other hand, if his focus had been more specific, he might have structured his paragraphs point by point.

> Grandfather Spender was slender, built like a whip-thin birch; Grandfather Kaluski was massive, built like a deep-rooted oak. Grandfather Spender would spend hours in solitude with his fingers curled around a pen, writing in his diary; Grandfather Kaluski would surround himself with us children and move his beefy fingers over accordion keys, bellowing for us to polka. . . .

And so on.

For further study we offer two more extended pieces, both developed by contrast. The first writer uses the block pattern, the second the point-by-point method. When reading the first one, we suggest you notice that the two blocks have similar content, but that the writer emphasizes the general nature of her subjects; consequently, there's no need to use the point-by-point method. Also notice how she displays her attitude. Unlike an objective report, a personal piece of this sort benefits from the personal tone.

I've only lived in two communities in California, hating both, but for different reasons. | Each has its own logic, I suppose, but this little girl from the Midwest would prefer a place less extreme in lifestyle than either Sand Point or the Peaks.

Topic sentence indicates discussion of differences and attitude of writers.

Second sentence explains reason for hate — lifestyles are too extreme.

Sand Point is a tourist-hating hangout for the locals. The attitude of the area is loose and casual. The motto of the Sandy kids who live there is "Have a good time." And they do. There are never-ending parties, lots of

Block of information about Sand Point

drugs, and surfing all day long. Their only

educational goal is a semester or two at the

local community college. Only the adults in

this area are employed. Most of them are

Democrats, unmarried, living together in low-

cost housing. Cops patrol the Point intensively,

and it's not unusual to find fugitives hiding

beneath Mustangs and Falcons or escaping through

a yard.

The only evidence of law enforcement you

see at the Peaks is an occasional security guard

informing someone that his Mercedes or Porsche

is parked in the wrong place. The whole environ-

ment revolves around stuffy money and finding

new ways to show it off. High-class young adults

here jog daily on the greenbelts wearing their

John Kloss sweats, and they are never caught

without Virginia Slims at invitation-only

parties. An Ivy League college is their future,

sorority and frat all the way. Kids from the

Peaks earn play money at Marie Callendar's

during dull summers. Their fathers are car

dealers and their mothers contribute time to

charities, eat lunch at quaint, expensive

restaurants and shop at Neiman-Marcus or I.

Magnin. These Republican families have every-

thing, including a mistress for Daddy.

Block of information about the Peaks contrasting it with Sand Point

```
     In the space of an hour last week I saw
```
Concluding sentences bring the two places together and reject both, thus reminding the reader of the introduction.

```
a Porsche in the Peaks and a beat-up Edsel in

Sand Point both sporting a "Save the

American Dream" bumper sticker.   If these are

examples of the American Dream, count me out.
```

In the following illustration the writer focuses on his past high school experience. In the first paragraph the writer briefly gives his topic and attitude. In the second paragraph, he presents the differences between his old, condemned campus and the new one built to replace it. In the third paragraph, he presents the differences in faculty attitudes that developed after moving to the new campus. If the writer had used the block pattern, his piece would have been much longer. But since he is interested in developing parallel elements, he uses the point-by-point method.

In the first paragraph, notice how the writer announces in the topic sentence his plan to structure his material around three points: safety, versatility, and pleasantness of the environment. He then fills in each point with contrasting details. Before writing the second paragraph, from a prewritten draft, he shaped a list that looked like this:

Old Campus	*New Campus*
SAFETY	
made of brick	reinforced concrete
built in 1903	just built
earthquake hazard	earthquake safe
wooden stairs	concrete stairs
loose banisters	metal railings
exit into crowded halls	exit into outside
VERSATILITY	
auditorium condemned	TV studio
one gymnasium	little theater
	two gymnasiums
cramped rooms	outdoor amphitheater
PLEASANTNESS	
bell tower	uniform appearance

brick walls	chain-link fence
tree-lined entryway	near street
windows that opened	no windows

Once the bare details of the list were established, the writer still faced a major task — to present the material in an interesting way. He avoids monotony by varying his details within each main point.

Unlike the second paragraph, the third follows a simple development that briefly lays out three differences in faculty behavior since moving to the new campus. As you read the piece, notice how the writer weaves the details together and swings from one point to the other.

A couple of years ago in high school I learned progress isn't so hot. | Redwood High School got a new campus that was safer and more versatile than the old campus, but for all its faults, the old place is a more pleasant campus to attend.

Besides giving some background, sentence 1 sets the writer's general concern and attitude — "progress isn't so hot."

Sentence 2 serves as the topic sentence — sets down the three main differences to be developed.

The old brick buildings, built in 1903, were an earthquake hazard, officials claimed, so they were replaced with new buildings of reinforced concrete designed to withstand all but the most severe shocks. | The new buildings have concrete stairs with metal railings instead of creaky wooden stairs with dangerously loose banisters. All the new rooms now empty into a concrete quad, instead of into crowded hallways where panic could be a serious problem in case of a tremor. | The new campus is more versatile with its TV studio, little theater, two large gymnasiums and outdoor amphitheater for assemblies and pep rallies. The old school

The writer begins the discussion with safety. Notice how the contrasting details all reflect safety concern.

The writer presents versatility as point 2. As with safety, the contrasting details reflect the point.

had a boxy, cold auditorium, which had been
condemned long before the rest of the buildings,
one tiny gym, and plain, cramped classrooms,
which were constantly being remodeled to keep
up with educational trends. These new features
are fine, but I miss the bell tower, the brick
walls, the tree-lined entryway, and windows that
really opened. In the new buildings there are
no windows at all, and the buildings, set near
the street behind a chain-link fence, are
finished with a uniform, flat-topped, smooth-
surfaced beige monotony to them that makes the
whole place seem more like a maximum-security
prison than a school. I guess I'm pretty young
to be talking about the old days, but after
moving to the new buildings I felt less human.

More importantly, there were changes in
the faculty's human attitudes. Before moving
into the modern buildings, the teachers used
to dress casually, often the women in slacks,
blouses, and sweaters and the men in jeans,
polo shirts, and tennis shoes. After making
the move, as if attending a formal occasion
the women began to show up in snappy dresses
and high heels; the men in suits and white shirts
with ties knotted around their necks. Before
the move classes were informal. Teachers would
often set aside their notes to share personal

He goes to point 3 — the pleasant environment of the old campus. Notice the shift. While the new campus seems safer and more versatile, the writer clearly appreciated the old campus more.

He closes the paragraph in a way that reflects his human concern over progress — the last sentence circles back to the first.

To start paragraph 3 he picks up "human" to aid the transition from one paragraph to the other while laying down his topic — the change in faculty attitude.

Point 1 deals with attitude toward dress.

Point 2 deals with faculty attitude toward class organization.

experiences related to whatever subject they
were covering. After the move local educators
began to see our new school as a showcase, so
we had hundreds of visitors tramping through
our classrooms. All these outsiders seemed to
have made our teachers nervous; consequently,
they became more formal in their lessons.

Finally, in the old days the best teachers used
to hang around after school. They would lounge
on the grass under the sycamores and talk with
students about social issues or their subjects.
Once in the new buildings, when the last bell
rang they, like almost all the students, bolted
for the doors as if escaping into freedom.

Point 3 deals with after-school faculty-student encounters.

The closing sentence ties back to the closing sentence of the last paragraph — the school has become a prison.

Now that you've had several examples to consider, it's time to write.

WRITING TASK

Write an extended comparison and contrast piece. Since this work is to be more than a single paragraph, we suggest you select subjects that will allow you to show both similarities and differences.

Here are some suggested subjects. You don't need to use them, but they may help you to get started. If they don't work for you, feel free to develop your own. Compare and contrast:

1. your life with the life of someone you envy.
2. your current life with the life you led several years ago.
3. an effective with an ineffective teacher, boss, or parent.
4. an ideal neighborhood you conceive with the one you live in.
5. your public with your private self.
6. two paintings of a similar subject by two different artists.

7. your values with your parents' values.
8. two films of the same genre — two thrillers, two musicals, two comedies, or whatever.
9. your high school experience with your college experience.
10. an area where you once lived with the area where you now live.

Remember, first develop an extended list of similarities and differences. Then use the list to aid you in structuring your paper. Next, write a clear and limited topic sentence and develop your work according to fundamental comparison and contrast techniques.

10 ANALOGY

Earlier we said that to write an effective comparison (as well as an effective contrast) pattern, you need to use two subjects from a common group. Analogy is a special kind of comparison that works only when you compare subjects from different groups. In other words, unlike ordinary comparisons that present the similarities of two things very much alike, an analogy presents similarities between things basically different. An analogy, therefore, is figurative, not literal.

Often analogy is used for descriptive purposes, functioning as part of a larger pattern. For example, read the following paragraph from surgeon Richard Selzer's collection of essays *Mortal Lessons*. Selzer begins with a quick comparison between a scalpel and the bow of a cello. He then compares the way a scalpel cuts to the movement of a slender fish.

> One holds the knife as one holds the bow of a cello or tulip — by the stem. Not palmed nor gripped nor grasped, but lightly, with the tips of the fingers. The knife is not for pressing. It is for drawing across the field of skin. Like a slender fish, it waits, at the ready, then, go! It darts, followed by a fine wake of red. The flesh parts, falling away to yellow globules of fat. Even though I've used it so many times, I still marvel at its power — cold, gleaming, silent. More, I am still struck with a kind of dread that it is I in whose hand the blade travels, that my hand is its vehicle, that yet again this terrible steel-bellied thing and I have conspired for a most unnatural purpose, the laying open of the body of a human being.

The main purpose of analogy is to explain. Sometimes it serves descriptive purposes; then it is closer to metaphor. Selzer's paragraph skirts description. To a slight degree it serves explanation by comparing the known to the unknown — the scalpel's handle to a cello bow or tulip stem and the moving blade to a slender fish. His analogy helps the reader to feel and see the scalpel at work.

Usually analogies are more elaborate and functional, less descriptive and lyrical. Often a writer will bring one into a work in order to illustrate an abstract idea. Julian Jaynes uses analogy in this fashion when trying to explain just how limited human consciousness is. He compares the conscious mind to a flashlight searching in a dark room for an unlighted object.

> Consciousness is a much smaller part of our mental life than we are conscious of. How simple that is to say; how difficult to appreciate! It is like asking a flashlight in a dark room to search around for something that does not have any light shining upon it. The flashlight, since there is light in whatever direction it turns, would have to conclude that there is light everywhere. And so consciousness can seem to pervade all mentality when actually it does not.

By comparing the abstract to specific, concrete, seeable things, a writer can make an abstract concept a little clearer. The same is true of complicated experiences.

A writer might, for instance, decide to communicate the complicated thrill of a love affair. How? Well, the writer might do it by comparing it to a roller coaster ride — by using analogy. Although a love affair and a roller coaster ride are totally different experiences, they do share some general characteristics. Both have moments of heightened anticipation and exhilaration. Both capture a person's full attention. Both provide occasional surprises. And both, perhaps, end too soon. An analogy that is used to explain a complicated experience of this sort would be much longer than the above examples. A writer would develop it in a special pattern by introducing the subjects in the topic sentence.

The following illustration represents such a pattern. In it the writer compares getting a college education with a trip through a car wash. She sets up her subjects in the topic sentence. She then gives a brief description of the aspects of the car-washing experience that she wants to develop in her comparison. Next, she weaves together the experience of being a student with that of a car being scrubbed. Note that she doesn't try to describe every detail of the car-washing experience, but instead selects only what she needs in order to make the connections between the two experiences — no more. We want to stress the importance of selecting appropriate details when writing anything, but especially when writing an analogy. If you include too much description, you may side-track your reader.

Like a trip through a car wash, a college education is an unveiling experience. | The car arrives, its brilliance dimmed by layers of dust accumulated on the road. Sprayed and brushed repeatedly is it moves down the line, the car begins to regain its true color. | So too, a student enters the educational process, his potential hidden by inexperience and mis-conceptions about the world. He may resist at first, but gradually the repeated immersions in coursework and the buffeting of his professors will begin to have an effect. He will discover previously unsuspected talents and interests; he will begin to view the world differently; he will become more tolerant of others as he learns of the complexity of human affairs. | If he is lucky he will find two or three teachers who seem to speak directly to him, who have the skill and patience to put the final, polishing touches on his education, just as a small group of wash boys clean up the last specks of dirt on an automobile. If all goes well, what emerges from the process is a person better equipped to serve as an example to those who still labor under their private accumulations of ignorance and prejudice.

Topic sentence presents two subjects and clearly leads the reader to expect an analogy.

Two sentences about the car wash set up the comparison.

Writer compares educational process to previous statements about the car wash.

States second similarity between education and car wash

As you can see from the illustration, analogy differs from ordinary comparison in that the writer focuses more on one subject than the other. She uses the car wash merely to get the reader thinking about a college education in a certain way.

We want to pass on a word of caution here. It's a mistake to carry an analogy too far. If the writer had extended the car wash analogy by comparing the preliminary vacuuming of the car to a college orientation course and a wax job to upper division art courses (or any other courses, for that matter) the paragraph would have become ridiculous. Remember, the value of analogy lies in its power to suggest. It helps a writer lead the reader to experience something in a different way.

Now, let's examine another pattern built on analogy. Unlike the last illustration, this one relies on suggestion more than direct comparison. This paragraph, from Donald Hall's essay "Four Kinds of Reading," compares certain kinds of reading to a narcotizing experience. The paragraph comes after others that discuss reading for information, literary experience, and intellectual awareness. As you read, notice the way Hall suggests the relationship between reading and narcotics by using such words as *narcotic, opium, daydream, drug, addict,* and *trip.*

> But most reading which is praised for itself is neither literary nor intellectual. It is narcotic. Novels, stories and biographies — historical sagas, monthly regurgitations of book clubs — are the opium of the suburbs. The drug is not harmful except to the addict himself, and is no more injurious to him than Johnny Carson or a bridge club, but it is nothing to be proud of. This reading is the automated daydream, the mild trip of the housewife and the tired businessman, interested not in experience and feeling but in turning off the possibilities of experience and feeling. Great literature, if we read it well, opens us up to the world, and makes us more sensitive to it, as if we acquired eyes that could see through things and ears that could hear smaller sounds. But by narcotic reading, one can reduce great literature to the level of *The Valley of the Dolls.* One can read *Anna Karenina* passively and inattentively, and float down the river of lethargy as if one were reading a confession magazine: "I Spurned My Husband for a Count."

Sometimes analogies, especially ones that attempt to suggest more than they state, just don't work. When you use an analogy, be wary. Often an analogy can be flat, confused, and indirectly comic — usually because the writer hasn't thought through the comparison. It is easy to become blinded by a brassy style and lose sight of the concrete images words call to the reader's mind. For example, read Norman Mailer's attempt to compare Marilyn Monroe to a fine violin. Although Mailer doesn't intend it to be, the comparison, which begins midway through the piece, is comic.

> So we think of Marilyn who was every man's love affair with America, Marilyn Monroe who was blonde and beautiful and had a sweet little rinky-dink of a voice and all the cleanliness of all the clean American backyards. She was our angel, the sweet angel of sex, and the sugar of sex came up from her like a resonance of sound in the clearest grain of a violin. Across five continents the men who knew the most about love would covet her, and the classical pimples of the adolescent working his first gas pump would also pump for her, since Marilyn was deliverance, a very Stradivarius of sex, so gorgeous, forgiving, humorous, compliant and tender that even the most mediocre musician would relax his lack of art in the dissolving magic of her violin.

Mailer has tossed too many vegetables into his stew. His analogy is just one more potato he dumps in to fill the pot. When you write an analogy, we suggest you serve up smaller portions and include some meat.

But where can we send you to look for analogies? The answer is simple — into your imagination. When you begin to look at one experience and see another, you are on the track of analogy. You will be starting to make figurative comparisons.

Usually, a short descriptive comparison, such as a simile or metaphor, unexpectedly falls like a ripe jewel onto the page. How can a writer plan such descriptive phrases as "With fingers the size of sausages he plucked the wallet from her purse" or "I touched her paper skin and thought of a snake"? Somehow, as though by inspiration, the mind generates them during the writing process.

Unlike a single descriptive simile or metaphor, an analogy can be thought out. Suppose you wish to talk about personal growth. You realize that physical growth can be clearly seen and charted, but that inner growth is evanescent. It exists, but cannot be held. It cannot even be fixed in the mind because, like smoke, its shape keeps changing. After a time, your rambling thought begins to shape itself into a topic sentence — "personal growth is much like the movement of smoke." You've seen one thing in another. You have an analogy.

As a closing illustration of analogy, study the following paragraph. In it James Thurber compares editor Harold Ross of *The New Yorker* magazine to a skilled mechanic.

Having a manuscript under Ross's scrutiny was like putting your car in the hands of a skilled mechanic, not an automotive engineer with a bachelor of science degree, but a guy who knows what makes a motor go, and sputter, and wheeze, and sometimes come to a dead stop; a man with an ear for the faintest body squeak as well as the loudest engine rattle. When you first gazed, appalled, upon an uncorrected proof of one of your stories or articles, each margin had a thicket of queries and complaints--one writer got a hundred and forty-four on one profile. It was as though you beheld the works of your car spread all over the garage floor, and the job of getting the thing together again and making it work seemed impossible. Then you realized that Ross was trying to make your Model T or old Stutz Bearcat into a Cadillac or Rolls-Royce. He was at work with the tools of his unflagging perfectionism, and, after an exchange of growls or snarls, you set to work to join him in his enterprise.

Thurber immediately introduces the comparison of Ross to a skilled mechanic.

He develops analogy by describing the skilled mechanic's sensitivity to automobiles, for Ross is skilled in a similar way in his work.

He shifts to Ross's handiwork.

Thurber returns to the analogy, this time comparing a writer's corrected manuscript to a dismantled car.

Did you notice that Thurber used many words and phrases associated with automobiles? *Sputter, wheeze, come to a dead stop, body squeak,* and *engine rattle* are just a few. These words and phrases help keep the comparison before the reader. They serve as the thread that binds the analogy. Whenever you use analogy, we suggest you do the same.

WRITING TASK

One problem in writing an analogy is that one will usually leap to mind while a writer is deep in the process of expressing thought. Because of the spontaneous nature of analogy, we don't want to stifle your creative expression with too much direction.

If, however, you need a nudge for training purposes, consider comparing one of the following with an idea, person, experience, or process.

a flowing river	a merry-go-round
the changing seasons	the phases of the moon
the passage of the sun	the changing tide
a spider web	running long distances
walking through a desert	mountain climbing
a tornado	a dark tunnel
a bird of prey	a slot machine
a crap game	ripening fruit
an unweeded garden	a cluttered room
a poker hand	a game of solitaire

Remember, the term to which you compare an idea or experience is not the subject of your piece. For instance, when Selzer writes "One holds the knife as one holds the bow of a cello or tulip — by the stem," he is not writing about a cello or tulip stem, he is writing about the process of surgery that starts with the proper handling of a scalpel. Be sure not to lose sight of your true subject.

11 CLASSIFICATION

Human beings love to classify. We speak of lyric poetry and dramatic poetry; farces, comedies, and tragedies; economy cars, sports cars, and luxury cars; and, all too often, the good guys and the bad guys.

A music teacher may classify students according to their voices: soprano, mezzo-soprano, alto, tenor, baritone, and bass. A political science teacher may classify the same students according to their political leanings: radicals, liberals, conservatives, reactionaries, and maybe even confused. The registrar, for statistical purposes, may classify them according to sex, age, major, grade point average, city or county of origin, or future educational plans. A female student may be content just to classify males: dreamy, attractive, passable, and no thanks.

The point is that any given subject can be classified in a number of ways depending on the writer's point of view and purpose in writing. For example, one student, in a paper on off-beat hobbyists, spends a paragraph classifying comic book collectors. She begins with a standard opening for classification pieces by clearly letting the reader know where the next paragraph is going and by presenting the categories she slips her collectors into.

Other fascinating off-beat hobbyists are comic book collectors. | These collectors, whether 16 or 60, at first glance seem to be a bushy-haired, disheveled, absentminded and disorganized lot. But after close examination you'll find

Opening sentence includes a transition from the preceding paragraph and announces the subject of comic book collectors.

These sentences supply background and a general description of collectors while establishing four categories.

89

their habits put them into one of four major
groups: the Antiquarians, Mercenaries, Idolators,
or Compulsive Completers. You'll be able to
find all these types rummaging through pile
after pile of unsorted, secondhand comics in
magazine marts scattered from New York to Los
Angeles.

The Antiquarian cares only for age value;
subject matter is of no concern. He's looking
for a 1933 <u>Funnies</u> <u>on</u> <u>Parade</u> from the days when
men were men and comics were comics. To the
Mercenary, value is all-important. Certain
numbers and titles ring a bell in his cash-
register brain and start him furtively checking
through a half dozen price sheets. A pristine
first edition of <u>Action</u> <u>Comics</u> (value: $4000)
would suit him just fine. The Idolator couldn't
care less about age or value. He's looking for
favorites: a <u>Sheena</u>, a <u>Flash</u> <u>Gordon</u>, or another
<u>Incredible</u> <u>Hulk</u>. Hiding in a corner, reading
those he can't afford to buy, he'll be the last
one out of the mart at night and the first one
back in the morning. The most frustrated
collector is the Compulsive Completer. He'll
examine and reject thousands of comics in his
search for a badly needed <u>Felix</u> <u>the</u> <u>Cat</u> to
complete a year's set or the one <u>Howdy</u> <u>Doody</u>

*In this section the writer presents the four
kinds of collectors along with supporting
details. Notice how she introduces each type
by using the label she's given it in the first
sentence of each section.*

missing from his collection. | But no matter

what the reason for collecting, these hobbyists

share a common trait: they love the thrill of

the hunt.

She closes the piece by identifying a common trait — all love the thrill of the hunt.

The writer of the above example wasn't just handed her classes; she discovered them. She then created labels to identify them for the reader. Discovering and labeling is often the process a writer follows in a classification piece. But sometimes a writer will use classes that already exist. Working with existing classes may be tougher than finding new ones. When doing it, the writer is obligated to offer some new insight into the groups, not merely to pass on well-chewed information.

For instance, in the following example from *Blood and Money,* Thomas Thompson spends a paragraph describing the different classes of surgeons. To make his material fresh, he describes each group according to its general personal characteristics, thus giving the reader a new way of looking at the people who might be plunging scalpels into their flesh.

> Among those who train students to become doctors, it is said that surgeons find their niche in accordance with their personal characteristics. The orthopedic surgeon is medicine's carpenter — up to his elbows in plaster of Paris — and tradition holds that he is a gruff, slapdash sort of man whose labor is in a very physical area of healing. Away from the hospital, the orthopedists are often hunters, boaters, outdoorsmen.
>
> The neurosurgeon, classically, does not get too involved with his patients. Or, for that matter, with anybody. They are cool men, blunted, rarely gregarious.
>
> Heart surgeons are thundering egotists, star performers in a dazzling operating theater packed with assistants, nurses, paramedics, and a battery of futuristic equipment which could seemingly lift the room into outer space. These are men who relish drama, who live life on the edge of the precipice.
>
> And the plastic surgeon? He is, by nature, a man of art, and temperament, and sensitivity. "We are the artists who deal in beauty lost, or beauty that never was," said one plastic man at a national convention. "Our stitches are hidden, and so are our emotions."

Unlike the author of the first classification example, Thompson doesn't use the opening sentences to list the classes he'll be describing.

There is no need to; most readers are familiar with orthopedic surgeons, neurosurgeons, and heart and plastic surgeons.

You've probably also noticed that the arrangement of a classification piece is quite simple. A writer will present the categories in the order that seems most appropriate. We do want to make one hard rule about classification arrangement: always give the name of the class in the first sentence that starts the group description. The name will help you keep the reader on the right track by announcing that a shift from one group to another will be taking place.

You face one danger here. Often a classification piece will get boring if you merely tick off one category after another. How do you avoid reader boredom? Create some variety. For instance, Thompson begins his first three group descriptions with "The orthopedic surgeon," "The neurosurgeon," and "Heart surgeons." After these three standard openings the reader might react with a ho hum. But Thompson anticipates this reader response, so he varies the last opening by beginning with a question: "And the plastic surgeon?" It's not a spectacular tactic, but it serves to nudge a drowsing reader. It's unexpected.

Now study the following example that classifies high school basketball fans. Since the writer creates his own categories, he mentions them in the opening in order to let the reader know what to expect. As you read, notice how clearly he arranges the classes: he presents one group with its description, then the next, and the next. Simple.

> A high school coach I used to know insisted there were three kinds of basketball fans: Friends, Romans and Countrymen. He was well aware that for Mark Antony, who used these words to address his fellow Romans after Julius Caesar had been assassinated, the terms were just three ways of addressing the same people. But for Pete Munson they represented distinct groups. Friends were the majority of fans. They loved to watch the game, didn't know much about it, never criticized the coaching, supported the team in victory or defeat, and ate a lot of popcorn. Nice guys. No problem. It was the Romans he had to watch out for. Aggressive, raucous, even vicious, they knew that the game was being staged by a dumb coach, incompetent or possibly corrupt officials, and greedy but inept players. What's more they told everyone about it — loud and clear:
>
> "Let Smith play, Munson!"
>
> "Hey, Honer, how much you get paid?"
>
> "Point hog! You had an open man!"
>
> After an hour of such abuse, my friend would seek the solace of a glass of beer and a small group of Countrymen. Countrymen were other coaches. They knew Munson was working miracles

with poor material; they understood his strategy; they sympathized with his decision to bench the uncooperative Smith. And
for the rest of the evening, at least, they helped him forget the
Roman words he feared most: "We come to bury Munson, not
to praise him."

Obviously, this classification piece is based on personal experience. It
represents the view of one man — Coach Munson — and may not fit
anyone else's experience. That's fine: the writer is attempting to give the
reader Munson's point of view regarding fans, not suggesting that every
high school coach would describe fans the way Munson does.

Beyond learning the general pattern of classification pieces, we also
want you to see that their main thrust is to describe what each class is
like. The examples we've used do just that. By this time you should not
only be aware of a basic classification pattern, you should also know
something about various types of comic book collectors, surgeons, and
basketball fans.

You may also have noticed that classification is closely related to comparison and contrast. In a comparison or contrast piece, though, the
writer's intention is to show how two items are similar or different. In
classification, the writer groups many similar individual items or cases
into one class that share certain characteristics. By implication they are
different from other individual items in the same subject area that are
placed in other classes. The focus of discussion, though, is on the nature
of each class rather than on a point by point contrast.

You can think of classification as another word for grouping or sorting. You have a large number of instances, too many to discuss individually, and you group, sort, or classify them into a small number of classes
according to some principle of similarity which is meaningful for your
paper.

It's very much like sorting the mail. When you drop a letter into the
slot at the post office, you take the first classification step yourself by
dropping your letter in the out-of-town slot instead of the local one. A
mail clerk going through the out-of-town mail conducts further classification as he sorts the letters into bags labeled New England, Middle
Atlantic, South Atlantic, Midwest, South, Southwest, Northwest and Pacific Coast. When a bag of letters arrives at a New England depot, it is
further sorted by zip code and later still by street address. Only then
does the name of the individual addressee become important.

When you want to arrange some information in a classification pattern, you must sort its components into meaningful groups. *Meaningful*
is the key word. Consider our post office analogy. For the first clerk to
decide to classify the letters alphabetically would not have been to sort
them meaningfully. Such a sorting would produce stacks of bags labeled

A, B, C, and so on through Z. This system would not serve the post office's purpose of passing mail from senders to receivers. A meaningful classification would be for the clerk to sort the mail by destination, not by alphabet.

In a different situation, the destination of a letter may not be the best way to classify it. Consider the needs of someone in business who receives bundles of mail daily — requests for charitable donations, advertisements, business reports, invitations, demands for business actions, and notes from old friends. Whether formally or informally, the executive will classify the day's mail according to the importance of each letter, perhaps arranging it in categories such as immediate response, eventual response, information only, and junk. Given the executive's situation, these would be meaningful classes.

Once you have your meaningful classes spotted, you need to be sure they're equally general. It just wouldn't make much sense to classify bundles of mail headed for the East under the labels New England, Middle Atlantic, Southeast, and Boston. These classes are not equally general. The first three are regions. Boston is a city — in fact, part of New England. Would Thomas Thompson have made much sense if he had classified surgeons under orthopedic surgeons, neurosurgeons, heart surgeons, plastic surgeons, and surgeons in training? Of course not.

Your classes should also be inclusive — they should cover the territory reasonably well. If the postal clerks had forgotten to label a bag Midwest, their system would not cover the territory of the United States. If you classify religions in America by referring only to Catholics, Baptists, Methodists, and Christian Scientists, you have not covered the territory. Of course the word *reasonably* has to operate here. Perhaps your paper can't include every specific instance, and if you think you've covered the territory and someone says, "Hey, how about the Poseidon freaks?" you may be justified in dismissing that person as a crackpot. If you want to avoid leaving yourself open to such criticism, you may have to resort to changing your subject to major religions in America and then define the term *major* as you see it. Realistically, such problems won't crop up too often, and if you avoid major omissions, most readers will accept the fact that you are characterizing prominent classes, which most cases fall into rather logically. Your classes should be exclusive, too, with no overlapping of classes. If the postal clerks have drawn their boundaries well, there will be no doubt that a particular letter belongs in the Mid-Atlantic and not the Southeast bag. If you are classifying television programs and you decide to group them as children's, Westerns, situation comedies, and educational, your classes are not exclusive. A children's program could be a Western or educational. The problem here is in the method of arriving at the classes. Children's is a class arrived at according to age; Westerns and situation comedies are classes arrived at according to content; educational is a class arrived at according to purpose. You can't mix methods of classification without confusing your reader.

In summary, then, hold these four points in mind while thinking through a classification piece. Develop meaningful classes, shape them at the same general level, make sure they cover the territory (keep them inclusive), and make sure they don't overlap (keep them exclusive).

Before going to the writing task, let's examine one more example. As with comparison and contrast, classification pieces often stretch into several paragraphs. But even in extended classification pieces, the same general principles of classification operate. An extended classification will usually include more background information and examples than shorter ones.

Now, keeping all this in mind, read the following example that classifies the humanlike creations of science fiction writers.

Scientists and space engineers are currently engaged in a universe-wide search for the presence of "life as we know it" on other worlds. No one can predict with certainty what such life forms, if they are discovered, will look like, but science fiction writers have done a good deal of speculation. Through their works they have created imaginary worlds for us, populated with intelligent and mobile plants, giant androphagous (man-eating) insects, and other forms of life lower or higher on the evolutionary scale than earthly humans. | Such nightmare worlds are fun to read about, but the serious work of science fiction, the exploration of human problems and possibilities, is best done in stories inhabited with humanlike

Since this is an extended piece, the writer leads the reader into it with background information.

The last sentence clearly indicates that a classification will follow by announcing the groups to be discussed.

beings: humanoids, robots, and androids.

A humanoid has some recognizable human

characteristics: intelligence, mobility, and

the ability to communicate complex messages.

It may have more body parts--two hearts, twelve

eyes, several heads; it may be physically more

animal-like--scaly skin, a furry body, a

reptilian face; or it may not breathe oxygen

or use water as its principal body fluid. These

details don't matter. What is important is that

a humanoid lives its life amidst humanlike

situations of conflicts and emotions. L. Sprague

de Camp's imaginary planet Osiris, for example,

is inhabited by highly emotional dinosaur-men

who have developed a capitalist economy.

This paragraph is devoted to humanoids. Notice the details: two hearts, twelve eyes, several heads, and so on. As with most writing, detail makes it vivid.

The writer closes the paragraph by referring to a work that deals with humanoids.

Robots are man-created entities, usually

of metal, with a long history and an evolutionary

process of their own. Although they get their

name from a play, R.U.R. (Rossum's Universal

Robots), written by the Czechoslovakian play-

wright Karel Capek, their metal beings go back

at least to early Greek mythology. The architect

and inventor Daedalus built a man of metal,

Talus, whose duty was to guard the island of

Crete for King Minos. Serving man by doing

housework, working in the fields, fighting wars,

and even playing football has traditionally

been a robot's reason for being, but once

The next paragraph is devoted to robots.

The writer gives some historical information about robots. Their physical characteristics aren't as interesting as those of humanoids.

created, robots have often evolved in unantici-
pated ways. "Revolt of the Potato Picker" by
Herb Lehrman describes a robot assigned to the
potato fields who develops a desire to be a
professional dancer. Other robots exhibit such

Follows with some examples from science fiction that deal with robots

human traits as loyalty, perseverance, and
greediness as well as the ability to love and
hate. Clifford D. Simak in "How-2" describes
a robot who learns to make other robots and
exhibits all the emotions of a proud parent.

Capek's robots were actually chemically
produced synthetic beings, not metal men, and

Presents the last group — androids

such fleshy creations are now called androids.
Not only do androids develop human emotions,
thus complicating matters just as robots do,

Have you noticed that the writer has arranged her groups according to how close they appear to and how much they act like humans?

but they present the added difficulty of
identification--it's not easy to tell who is
android and who is human. Sometimes the "person"
attempting to make such identifications finds
he is himself an android, a shocking discovery,
because androids ordinarily cannot reproduce,
nor do they have immortal souls. The love-hate

The androids are the closest to being human. The writer, therefore, focuses on the problems this group faces.

relationship between androids and humans commonly
leads to one of three possible developments:
the androids serve as man substitutes, allowing
one man to fill several roles in either his
work life or his love life; the androids resent
human superiority and try to take over human

affairs undetected; or androids and humans get

involved in tragic love affairs which cannot

be adequately consummated.

Using humanoids, robots, and androids as

characters allow the science fiction writer to

adapt his chosen literary medium for social

commentary and for relevant and philosophical

investigation of the complexities of human

affairs.

The writer ends the piece with a final paragraph that pulls the details together.

See how the classification pattern works? Fine. Now go on to write one.

WRITING TASK

Write a piece developed by classification. Since virtually any subject can be organized into classes, whatever interests you will probably work. A key to getting off to a good start will be your selection of classes. Avoid the obvious and the superficial. Don't classify sales people into the successful and unsuccessful or cars into luxury and economy classes. Such classifications and others like them don't merit your attention or your reader's. They're too obvious.

Here are some general subject areas you might consider classifying. Keep in mind that they need to be focused — that is your job.

teachers
jobs
department stores
students
coaches
policemen
books
TV programs
drivers
playgrounds

vacations
restaurants
boutiques
pets
athletes
lies
movies
disguises
smokers
sports fans

dates	affairs
love	lovers
doctors	nurses

If these don't work for you, you may want to use one of the following questions to lead you into classification:

1. What are the ways to obtain knowledge?
2. What are the ways to manipulate others?
3. What are the ways to bring joy to others?
4. What are the ways to make big money?
5. What are the ways to stop smoking?
6. What are the ways to get a person to say yes?
7. What are the ways to live without working?
8. What are the ways to cook a good anything?

Remember, if you develop your own labels for the classes you describe, announce them in the opening sentences. Also develop meaningful classes that cover the territory and don't overlap. We suggest that once you have your subject and have identified the classes, you draw up a list of details to use as an aid in writing your piece. And, of course, we assume you are working in drafts.

12 DEFINITION

When speaking, many of us toss away words like a gambler throwing quarters at a Las Vegas slot machine. But when writing, most of us try to use words precisely. We live with the knowledge (maybe even the fear) that on a sheet of paper our words can be examined — studied in context and explored in a dictionary; whereas in speech we relax with the knowledge that words melt like cotton candy on a warm tongue.

Trying to use words precisely can be a gut-wrenching business. Some words are so much a part of a specialized vocabulary that only certain occupational or recreational groups know them. Some are used so infrequently that few readers know what they mean. Some are so slippery that people understand them differently. But when you write, you have to struggle to be precise — painfully precise — in overcoming the specialized, the infrequent, the slippery word. Sometimes that means defining, briefly or extensively, any key word you use to make sure the reader understands what you mean.

A short definition will usually do for an obscure or specialized word. A synonym, a short phrase, a brief comparison — that's all you need.

Synonym	When my uncle returned from abroad, he gave each of us a grego, which is a jacket.
Short phrase	Some historians suggest that the American government during the last century conducted an unofficial pogrom, an organized massacre of helpless people,

	against Indians confined to reservations.
Comparison	Thallium, a metallic element resembling lead, is rare.

When you give a brief definition, always try to work it into the flow of your piece. Don't stop the movement, announce the word's meaning, then pick up the march. Also avoid misusing *when* and *where* in definitions. Don't write something like this:

Gregarious is when people flock or herd together.

Or this:

Gregarious is where people flock or herd together.

Gregarious is neither a time nor place — it's a mode of social behavior.

Brief definitions of this sort are easy enough. The real difficulty comes with extended definitions of abstract or general words, words such as *freedom, love, prejudice, equality, delinquent,* or *patriotism.* Words such as these have become so slippery you must define them. Usually the definition will be extended — a paragraph or more — so that your reader will have a clear idea of what any word of this sort means to you. To write an extended definition you can

1. use synonyms
2. give examples
3. discuss the word's origin
4. develop comparisons
5. tell what the word is not
6. create an anecdote to show the word in action

We don't suggest you try to use all these techniques in any single definition. We listed them to give you an impression of the possibilities.

Now let's take a look at an extended definition of patriotism. The writer starts with a topic sentence that suggests a broad meaning of patriotism. He then spends four sentences exploring what patriotism isn't. He follows with examples — brief ones — of patriotic behavior. He then spends a sentence on the origins of the word before moving into a comparison with parental love. He finishes the paragraph by reminding the reader of his opening thought, thus indicating he has covered the territory.

True patriotism is wishing your country well. It does not require chest thumping, flag waving, fiery speeches or parades. We use the word incorrectly when we confine it to ostentatious acts. It is not boasting, but service; not hatred, but love; not loud, but quiet. Quiet, loving service is what a patriot has to offer. The voter who puts public welfare above private greed is practicing patriotism. The person who expresses his opinion on local, state, and national problems; who dares to criticize elected representatives; whose personal behavior serves as a prod to the conscience of others is practicing patriotism. Those who do these things do so because they care about their country. We get the word <u>patriot</u> from the Latin for "fellow countryman," a term suggesting a loving relationship which is at the heart of patriotic behavior. One's love for his fellow countrymen and therefore his country is not unlike a parent's love for a child. The parent wants the child to realize his potential, to grow, to become better. He invests time and effort to this end. He supports the child through rough times, but he also demands certain standards of behavior. It would be a poor parent who said "My child, right or wrong," if that phrase is intended to convey an unthinking

This opening sentence clearly suggests that a definition will follow.

These four sentences tell what patriotism isn't. Since patriotism is such an abstract concept, the writer tries to give his definition life with image-producing phrases: chest thumping, flag waving, fiery speeches, and so on.

Because definitions tend to be inclusive, examples tend to be impressionistic and general such as these. The last sentence in this series comes back to the central point: wishing your country well.

Here the writer dips into etymology — word history — to set up the comparison that follows.

This comparison further illustrates what patriotism means to the writer.

support of whatever the child wants to do. By

the same token the phrase "My country, right or

wrong" should not be accepted blindly as a

patriotic position. | Wishing your country well

is harder and more complicated than blind loyalty.

The last sentence recalls the introduction and closes the paragraph.

Do you agree with this definition? Perhaps not. But agreement isn't what this writer is after. Instead he seeks understanding. There is no doubt that you have a strong impression of what he means by patriotism.

Extended definitions can be purely personal or they can be largely objective. A personal definition, like the one above, explains how a writer is using the term — "Never mind what other people think patriotism means; it means this to me." Such a strategy is useful if your purpose is to get a reader to see a word in a different light or if you are discussing personal experience with the term. Everyone knows, for instance, what *prejudice* means: "prejudging without adequate information." But to a six-year-old prejudice may mean waiting at a candy counter until all the adults are served. It may mean not counting as a real person, tolerated rather than truly listened to. It may mean being discriminated against on the basis of size.

An objective definition, on the other hand, seeks general agreement. It's the kind of definition that applies in all cases at all times. This requires detailing. The word *democracy* means "rule by the people." At this level, most people can agree with the definition without further discussion. But two opposing political forces may need to reach a more detailed agreement if they are to talk productively together. For example, who are the people? Everyone? Voters? Only those over twenty-one? A ruling class that claims to speak in the name of all? It would be meaningless to discuss the value of "democratic elections" without a comprehensive definition of democracy.

Objective definitions, therefore, should play it straight. The details should be spelled out. This isn't always easy. Millions of words have been written defining *liberal* and *conservative,* yet the water is still muddy. But we don't want to discourage you. Lots of terms you'll need to define aren't that difficult. You should, though, be aware of the complexity involved in objective definition.

Now let's examine an objective definition to give you an idea of how to go about writing one. One dictionary definition of *plagiarism* is "to steal someone else's ideas or words and pass them off as one's own." Okay so far, but a more extended objective definition gives the reader a better understanding of plagiarism and how it happens.

Plagiarism is taking the words or ideas of another and pretending they are yours. It is a serious literary crime, a form of dishonesty which, if discovered, carries heavy penalties. There are two kinds of plagiarism, the intentional and the unintentional. Intentional plagiarism is an act of either defiance or desperation. The defiant student sees no reason to learn about photosynthesis (for example) himself, and so he "rewrites" an article or textbook entry and brazenly submits it to the instructor as his own work. The desperate student probably agrees that the subject is worth knowing about, but he's neglected his studies too long. In panic he also turns in someone else's work, throwing in a few misspellings for authenticity. More often plagiarism is unintentional, a product of ignorance. The student is required to write on a subject he is not expert on. The instructor knows this and expects the student to turn to other written sources for information. Unfortunately, those other sources phrase things so well that the student cannot see any alternative ways of organizing the material. Instead of making the information his and then expressing what he has learned, he produces a patchwork piece of alternating amateur and professional sentences and paragraphs. He's not proud of it,

The topic sentence is a capsule definition.

Next the writer amplifies on the capsule definition.

Then divides term into two kinds

Divides first kind into two subparts

Explains one subpart

Explains the other subpart

Explains the other kind of plagiarism

but what can he do? | Well, fortunately, there are many things he can do. And in the process of following the tips presented below, he will not only learn his subject well, he will avoid the embarrassment of being charged with plagiarism.

The final sentences lead to the rest of the paper, discussing ways to avoid plagiarism.

An extended definition such as this is often used as just a part, usually near the beginning, of a longer paper. In a paper discussing the skill of bullfighting, for example, it may be useful to have a definition of the term *adorno*. Briefly, it means a kind of flowery theatricality by which the bullfighter shows domination over the bull. But an extended definition giving examples of *adorno* in practice would be helpful for the reader of such a paper.

You may also have noticed that these writers have used other patterns in their definitions. The writer who defined patriotism used examples and comparison. The writer who defined plagiarism used classification. Keep in mind that patterns seldom appear in pure form. They get mixed together. And nowhere do they get more mixed than in defining terms. So when you write an extended definition stay on your toes; use good horse sense. If you don't know what horse sense is, read the following extended definition by writer Earl Rudolph.

Horse sense is a judgment which reflects sound thinking. | It is not a blind jump into a decision which may lead to ruin. Horse sense is not a hasty conclusion which prompts action causing deep regret later. | In other words, horse sense is common sense. Anyone possessing this common sense would know better than to wear bathing trunks outdoors in December. He certainly would regret this action while recuperating from pneumonia. A sensible casting

The topic sentence puts the term into a general class. The two sentences that follow tell what it is not.

Next Rudolph gives a synonym.

Then three examples

```
machine operator will turn off his machine

before he attempts to retrieve a die which has

fallen into the mechanism.  A thoughtful home-

owner carries liability insurance to avoid
```
being sued by someone injured on his property.

These people all use horse sense or common   *Then a summary statement about the*
                                                examples
sense in making important decisions almost every

day of their lives. We see then that horse   *Rudolph returns to first statement.*

sense or common sense often requires sound

thinking.

There's always a limit as to how far a definition can go. We're sure you could sit down and list many more examples of horse sense than Rudolph does. But remember, in definition your goal is to give the reader a clear understanding of the term. That calls for personal judgment. When you've nailed down the term, stop.

WRITING TASK

Write an extended definition of an abstract or general word or phrase. Your definition may be personal or objective. In either case, develop your definition with several of the techniques discussed earlier: use synonyms, give examples, discuss the word's origin, develop comparisons, tell what the word is not, create an anecdote to show the word in action.

Here's a list of abstract and general terms of the sort that often need defining. You may use one of these — or better yet, select your own.

Abstract	*General*
bigotry	student
freedom	housewife
charity	teacher
courage	committee
responsibility	clubs
respectability	business

hypocrisy   English class
wisdom   athlete
happiness   entertainer
cowardice   leader

Or, if you wish, define any current slang term or phrase such as *macho, making it, foxy,* or *skating.*

13 CAUSE AND EFFECT

An eight-year-old bursts through the screen door, tears running down his cheeks, hand clasped over his nose with a few droplets of blood squeezing between the finger cracks. Dad puts down the dishtowel and turns from the sink with an "I'm an understanding poppa" look on his face.

"Sandra hit me," the boy cries. "She hit me right in the nose."

Dad begins to wipe away the droplets and tears. The screen door flies open again. The sister storms into the kitchen and shouts, "He threw the baseball at me."

"She tried to horn in on our game. She can't hit."

"I can hit better than you. Look at your nose."

And on and on and on.

At one level this drama illustrates normal child behavior. At another it illustrates cause-and-effect relationships.

We begin the drama with a clear effect — the bloody nose. We then fall back to a cause — a right cross. At first it all seems simple. We probe deeper: right cross to nose caused by brother tossing baseball at sister.

Hmmmmmm!

The plot thickens: tossed baseball caused by sister trying to join the game.

Here we stop, for we want only to give you an idea of what cause-and-effect patterns involve, not probe the roots of sibling rivalry.

When writers explain why something happened or what could possibly happen or the results of something happening, they are dealing in cause and effect.

Why did Sandra punch her brother? Does violence broadcast on TV stimulate violence on the street? Has the women's liberation movement changed college programs? Why do so many Americans revere John

Wayne? These are all questions that would lead you into using a cause-and-effect pattern.

A cause-and-effect piece may cover just causes or just effects or both. When the effect is clear, you won't need to spend much time discussing it, but you will need to explore its causes. For instance, statistics indicate that teen-age suicide is increasing. If you were to write about the problem, you wouldn't need to spend much space substantiating the fact. You would spend a great deal of space discussing why — the causes.

Sometimes a cause will be clear. Most readers would generally agree that children spend more time watching television than they spend in school. No need to prove it. Plenty of surveys already have. But if you were writing about children spending more time before a TV screen than in school, you would need to discuss what it might mean — that is, the possible effects.

Consider the following example. The writer assumes that her readers will not dispute the existence of a women's liberation movement. So instead of documenting the fact, she gets right to its effects on her college campus. She uses a basic pattern. First she lays down the liberation movement as a basic cause of the changes. Next she details the obvious effects.

The fallout from the women's liberation movement has settled on our campus and produced changes in both student body and curriculum.	*The topic sentence indicates the effect in broad terms.*
In the last few years over a thousand women, newly liberated or trying hard, have enrolled in classes to launch academic careers, prepare for new vocations, or seek self-fulfillment. The historical male majority on campus has given way to this inundation, and the balance is tipping more every year. Our typical student is now a twenty-six-year-old female.	*The writer introduces effect 1.*
No longer the husband hunters of yesterday, these women are dedicated and serious students. Their	*This sentence provides transition between effect 1 and effect 2.*
presence has led to the development of new courses and the revision of some old ones. Many	*Effect 2 begins.*

courses now give equal time to the contributions
innovating women have made to the fields of
science, literature, and philosophy. Teachers
have developed new courses in female sexuality
and women writers. Our campus has a women's
center and a new Women's Studies department.

Four subparts of effect 2.

Women even have their own athletic teams--not
powder-puff imitations of male teams, but the
real stuff, complete with leagues, spectators,
and championships.

*An effective closing sentence that shows
women making inroads in the most male-
dominated area of campus life*

Often causes and effects are classified as immediate and ultimate — those that are most apparent and those that underlie them. This writer presented the immediately apparent effects of women's liberation: changes in student population, curriculum, and the athletic program. She could have probed more deeply: changes in male roles as related to female roles, in student government, in relationships between older and younger women. But her intent was not to give the ultimate effects but only to present some immediate ones. The depth to which any writer goes always depends on the subject and how thorough the writer wishes to be. Getting to the ultimate causes or effects requires a greater effort than getting to the immediate ones. It takes more space than a short piece offers, because a writer will usually have to lay a foundation for the analysis.

In *The Seasons of a Man's Life,* a study that deals with the psychological development of men, Daniel J. Levenson lays a solid base before presenting some ultimate results that stem from internal conflict some men experience during the middle years. Halfway through the book Levenson explains the concept of Young/Old polarity — the problems men must confront as they move from youth to old age — and the Dream — the aspirations that motivate men in their youth. He then shows how the Young/Old polarity and the Dream might create conflict between middle-aged men and young adults.

At around 40 a man is deeply involved in
the Young/Old polarity. This developmental
process has a powerful effect upon his relationships with his offspring and with young adults

*Levenson spends two sentences to introduce
his topic and focus — the effect of
relationships with young adults.*

generally. | When his own aging weighs heavily upon him, their exuberant vitality is more likely to arouse his envy and resentment than his delight and forbearance. He may be pre-occupied with grievances against his own parents for damage, real or imagined, that they have inflicted upon him at different ages. These preoccupations make him less appreciative of the (often similar) grievances his offspring direct toward him. |

He begins to detail the effects.

If he feels he has lost or betrayed his own early Dream, he may find it hard to give his wholehearted support and blessing to the Dreams of young adults. When his offspring show signs of failure or confusion in pursuing their adult goals, he is afraid that their lives will turn out as badly as his own. Yet, when they do well, he may resent their success. Anxiety and guilt may undermine his efforts to be helpful and lead him instead to be nagging and vindictive.

The second paragraph begins with the topic of the Dream and focuses on its role in the conflict.

Levenson begins to detail the effects.

Levenson has gone much deeper than immediate gripes a middle-aged man might have with young adults; he explores the ultimate reasons buried deep in the male psyche.

We don't want to give you the impression that cause-and-effect patterns always deal with objective material, as the last two examples have. They don't. Cause and effect play an important part in self-analysis. The writer of the following example uses totally subjective material. He charts the effects the women's liberation movement has had on his life. As you read, notice that the writer builds his piece through examples taken from personal experience.

I'm not sure I like the effects that the women's liberation movement has caused in my life. Equal pay for equal work is fair enough, but the more subtle changes in women's attitudes toward men really bug me. I don't like being asked for a date, for one thing. Some weeks ago a girl in my philosophy class stopped me to ask if I would attend a Rolling Stones concert with her. My God! I didn't know what to do! Ordinarily, I'd go to a Stones concert with Dracula. But I was too dumb to accept on the spot, so I blushed and stammered out some stupid excuse. The whole scene made me uncomfortable. Then the service station I go to hired a female gas pumper. It embarrassed me to have her check my oil and to tell me I needed air in my front tires. I quit going there. I know there's no reason to feel she shouldn't be doing the job, but it made me feel inadequate somehow. The other day I opened the door to the library for a girl who was just behind me. She went through all right, but she gave me an awful dirty look as if to say, "I can do it myself, jerk!" I was just trying to be polite, but I guess I insulted her sense of independence. Every day I see examples of women becoming more aggressive and independent as a result of the liberation movement, and while it's easy to

The opening sentence clearly states the topic and personal focus. Sentence 2 shows the writer is interested in exploring attitudes, not issues.

Example 1: a brief narrative to illustrate effect 1

Example 2: another specific example that mixes details — "change my oil" and "air in the front tire" — with responses — "It embarrassed me" and "made me feel inadequate"

Example 3: the writer continues to use vivid detail in specific examples.

He closes by restating his agreement with the issues but keeping his personal reservations.

agree with the idea behind it, it's hard for

this male-person to accept these changes.

When setting up a cause-and-effect piece, we suggest that in the beginning sentence you include *cause* or *effect* or other words that let the reader know what pattern to expect. In the topic sentence of the last paragraph, the writer used both "cause" and "effect": "I'm not sure I like the effects the women's liberation movement has caused in my life." Although many words can guide a reader into the pattern, some writers start with a question that begins with *what* or *why*.

In the next example a writer explores the reasons people jog in southern California. She begins by asking why. Since people jog for a variety of reasons, she carefully qualifies each one she offers, thus avoiding the claim that any single cause drives all joggers to the streets. Qualifying causes in this fashion is an important technique to learn, for sometimes you will be faced with a clear effect but have only probable causes. When this is the case, qualify them.

Why is jogging becoming a popular activity in southern California? Perhaps because we live in a youth oriented culture, and those moving into middle life jog in a desperate effort to keep what nature is tearing from them. Others may jog to be part of "the scene," just as some people go to discos to be part of that scene. Or perhaps the cause is much deeper. Some jogging enthusiasts claim that extended periods of running can lead the jogger into meditative trances with all the benefits of quiet sitting. They see themselves as innovators in the tradition of "moving meditation," such as that practiced by Sufi whirling dervishes. Still others claim they jog merely to stay fit by burning off extra servings of cream pie, chocolate cake, ice cream, and jelly rolls.

The opening question clearly leads the reader to expect causes.

Qualifying words and phrases such as "perhaps," "others may," "some," and "others claim" clearly indicate the writer isn't claiming people jog for all these reasons.

We want to close with another example from a writer's personal experience. Too often when learning this pattern, writers feel they need to deal with earthshaking subjects — the causes of the energy crisis, the effects of nuclear proliferation, the causes and effects of terrorism. But to say anything meaningful about earthshaking subjects requires expertise. You probably don't have it yet. To write about earthshaking subjects, therefore, would mean you had to pass on common information from *Time, Newsweek,* or the "NBC Nightly News."

When my team, the Astros, won the summer softball championship a few years ago, I took a lot of sour grapes guff from my friends on other teams. They said we were just lucky or they accused our coach of stacking the team with the best talent. I guess there's a certain amount of luck in winning so much--we were undefeated in twenty-four games--but luck can't explain it all, and as for talent, we had some pretty ordinary players, really, including me.

The writer begins with some background information. He also rejects some immediate causes — luck and team stacking.

I think our secret was our short, intense, and infrequent practice sessions. We only practiced for an hour just before each game, never on other days. It doesn't seem like much, but it put us in the right mood to play well. By game time other teams were tired from daily practice but we were starved for action. We practiced hard. Bunting, sliding, throwing, and fielding. Although we were known for our hitting, we never had regular batting practice. Our coach said it was too boring for everyone but the guy batting. When we took the infield

This is the focusing sentence that presents the cause — short, intense, and infrequent practice sessions.

The writer presents the details of the session.

just before game time we concentrated hard on

running the patterns smoothly. A good infield

warmup is a thing of beauty in itself and puts

you in a good mood to play. | A lot of coaches

wouldn't agree with this approach, but I think

it was the cause for our success. After all,

we won every single game!

He closes by reminding the reader of his focus — the cause of the Astros' success.

Not earthshaking, but the writer uses a basic cause-and-effect pattern. When the time comes to write about earthshaking events, he'll be ready.

WRITING TASK

Write a piece patterned on a cause or effect structure. Depending on the subject, you may choose to explore immediate or ultimate causes or effects. If your subject is complex enough you may want to explore both the causes and the effects. As a way of getting started, you may use any of the following leads. But, as is always the case, you may create your own subject.

1. Write a piece about the causes/effects of an experience from your life that moved you emotionally.
2. Write a piece that presents the causes/effects of one of your strong interests.
3. Write a piece that presents the effects of an outside event, movement, or institution on your life.
4. Write a piece that presents the causes behind a family, institutional, or social custom.
5. Write a piece that presents the possible effects of a particular choice you must make.

Remember to limit your topic — the five areas we suggest above are general and therefore need to be focused. Be sure to announce to your reader in the opening sentences that you are writing a cause or effect piece. And, finally, be sure you know whether you are dealing with ultimate or immediate causes or effects.

14 DESCRIPTION

You've already had some experience with descriptive writing in Getting Started. We've emphasized the value of embedding bits of description in all but the most scientifically objective pieces. Descriptive details will bring life to classifications, comparisons, contrasts, examples — indeed, descriptive details will make all patterns you use more vivid. Moreover, when a descriptive paragraph is mixed with other patterns, it can tug powerfully on the reader's attention. Writers who use description effectively evoke scenes, people, situations, and actions by involving their readers' senses and experiences. So at this point we want to talk about description as a separate pattern.

That's difficult, for unlike development by examples, comparison and contrast, classification or analogy, descriptions aren't always cast in traditional structures.

In a descriptive paragraph there may be no topic sentence or overt transition to guide the reader. Writing effective description, therefore, often depends on cunning. Of course, to be cunning the writer must be tuned to what the paper needs and what the reader can follow.

Timing, then, is important — timing and the writer's sense that a pedestrian piece of prose can be elevated to a more vivid reading experience through a paragraph of description. In the piece that follows, a student who is also a police officer includes a paragraph of dramatic description in a paper that deals with the psychological requirements of being a detective. She begins by relating the abstract and clichéd views of what it takes. Then she develops a descriptive paragraph by using typical details from a detective's work life. As you read the illustration, note how the descriptive paragraph seems to flow from the opening one.

> To be a police investigator a person must meet some tough
> requirements. He must stay alert, keep calm under pressure,

and perform his job fairly. These are general requirements — the kind of requirements every citizen would expect every cop to meet, somewhat like the Boy Scout motto, "Be Prepared." But there's a much tougher requirement. Anyone who wants to be a detective must consider it to be the spine of his work. It has to do with the courage to meet the tedious, unglamorous day-to-day activities every detective faces.

In a year a detective is required to spend hundreds of hours in routine work behind a government-gray desk under the glare of fluorescent lights. He'll dial thousands of telephone numbers until a callus grows on his index finger. He'll get thousands of busy signals and few answers for his trouble. He'll spend hours filling out reports and sitting in courtrooms waiting to testify. Often he'll see the criminals he has described in his reports sent home by the court he sits in. In a year he'll spend endless hours driving crowded streets during a steamy summer and frigid winter. He'll eat pounds of hamburger, salami, and bologna for lunches and wash it all down with enough coffee to kill ten normal kidneys. The odds are he'll never be shot at, but he'll probably get spit on and cursed. No doubt some violent drunk or strung-out junkie will retch on his shoes. A dramatic life — no. Moreover, keep in mind how hard it is to stay alert, calm, and fair in the face of this kind of psychological torture.

The writer continues her essay by exploring the psychological effects of this kind of tedious routine. She develops most of the paper through objective research that supports her points. But without a descriptive paragraph that paints the detective's routine the information would not have much impact.

The illustration raises an obvious question. Is the description a true one? Yes and no.

It isn't true if you read it as objective information. Not every detective eats pounds of hamburger, salami, and bologna during a year of lunches. Not every detective gets spit on.

But if you read it for the writer's emotional intent, the paragraph is true. The writer wants to generate a feeling in the reader. She's not claiming to be objective. She's clearly biased. She has a point of view and uses a dramatic description to involve her reader in it. She is writing subjectively, not objectively. So, from an inner perspective — from the writer's emotional viewpoint — the illustration reflects a general truth. Moreover, within the context of the entire essay, it is effective.

Most writing draws from our creative juices, but description seems to draw the most. To use description effectively, you must be supple enough in your writing to turn the details to your writing needs. Nowhere is this more difficult than in attempting to describe the abstract — that level of experience almost impossible to communicate. One way to do it is through analogy. Another, perhaps one that wears better on the reader, is by finding descriptive details strong enough to make the reader see and feel the abstraction.

Michael Herr does it in *Dispatches,* a collection of personal essays about the Vietnam war. Through the use of concrete description he makes the reader feel how sensitive one becomes to sound while in a jungle filled with enemies. Before going on, think for a moment about how you would describe the abstract experience of straining to hear sounds in a world gone silent. Then study Herr's paragraph to see how he does it.

> There were times during the night when all the jungle sounds would stop at once. There was no dwindling down or fading away, it was all gone in a single instant as though some signal had been transmitted out to the life; bats, birds, snakes, monkeys, insects, picking up on a frequency that a thousand years in the jungle might condition you to receive, but leaving you as it was to wonder what you weren't hearing now, straining for sound, one piece of information. I had heard it before in other jungles, the Amazon and the Philippines, but those jungles were "secure," there wasn't much chance that hundreds of Viet Cong were coming and going, moving and waiting, living out there just to do you harm. The thought of that one could turn any sudden silence into a space that you'd fill with everything you thought was quiet in you, it could even put you on the approach to clairvoyance. You thought you heard impossible things: damp roots breathing, fruit sweating, fervid bug action, the heartbeat of tiny animals.

Like the police officer's piece, this illustration is subjective. Herr uses as much experience as he needs to make the reader feel the threatening silence. He draws from the past — "I had heard it before in other jungles" — and relates the past to the present he describes. He even flies into imagination to illustrate how the strain of listening leads one to hear the impossible, "damp roots breathing, fruit sweating, fervid bug action, and the heartbeat of tiny animals." Herr touches another abstraction: fear — the fear of being caught unaware by an enemy that moves through the silence.

Descriptive paragraphs aren't always this dramatic and subjective. Often they serve a functional purpose. They allow writers not only to set a scene but also to work in necessary background information. This use of description is particularly characteristic of news articles, but it can also work in various kinds of reports.

In a discussion of the Public Broadcasting System's change from telephone line to satellite transmission, Ciji Ware opens with a paragraph that not only describes the scene, but gives the date, place, and subject of the article.

> *more description*
> It was the morning of March 1, icy and raw with patches of snow crusting the low hills near the Washington, D.C., suburb of Springfield, Virginia. The birds had long since flown south, past the imposing 200-foot receiving tower which scoops up microwave signals coming from the downtown public television broadcast center in Washington. At the foot of the giant Tinker-Toy tower is the brand new PBS main origination terminal — two giant dishlike structures embracing a low-lying building like wrong-way earmuffs against the winter cold.

Whatever is being described, the writer must use concrete language and specific detail. Without them writers cannot lead their readers to see and feel what they have in mind. For example, study part of an article describing a hypothetical family situation titled "TV of Tomorrow" which was published in *Newsweek*. Although the setting is the future, the writer still uses concrete language and specific detail.

> The year is 1985, the setting a typical Video Communications Complex (formerly known as a "home"). As the "CBS Evening News with Roger Rather" fades from the 84-inch screen, Dad switches to the local pay-cable channel and sits back to enjoy *Jaws 4*. No one disputes his choice, for everyone is off on a different electronic trip.
> In the den, Mom has flicked on the video-cassette recorder and is engrossed in the soap-opera episode she missed last week. That will be followed by a homemade-for-TV movie of the family's recent trip to Disney Cosmos. Upstairs, meanwhile, Sis has slipped a plastic disk onto a turntable device wired to her own TV set. Now she is grooving along with a transvestite reggae group, this month's R-rated selection of the Vidiary Guild. Down the hall, Junior has tired of playing Super Pong and has dialed in a baseball game. Suddenly, the announcer interrupts to ask the audience: "What do you think the next pitch should be?" By punching some buttons on a small console, Junior informs the system's computer that he would opt for a slider — and, sure enough, it's a slider that ends the inning.

Fanciful? Certainly. But whether fanciful or not, the writer had to use description to help make the piece believable.

Sometimes descriptive paragraphs are absolutely necessary for a paper to be effective. This is often the case with reports that involve close observation. For a psychology class one student was asked to visit a preschool and select a child for a day's observation. Then she was to describe the child at school and draw some conclusions about how well the school's program was meeting the child's needs. The whole project took ten paragraphs. Having explained the program in the first paragraph, the writer devotes the second to a description of the child and his behavior.

At first glance John seems to be a typical four-year-old: scruffy sun-bleached hair, a few freckles, worn cords, short-sleeved shirt, and tattered tennis shoes on his feet. But behind his boyish appearance, he seems to be a loner. During the first fifteen-minute class session, he was the only child who did not raise his hand to answer a question or share an experience. He was attentive at first, but soon lost interest. Once he reached out a finger to poke a boy in front, then stopped, perhaps thinking better of it. Finally, his thumb went into his mouth. As soon as the class broke up, he headed for the monkey bars, where he climbed to the highest rung and sat, his eyes staring toward the distant hill. No one tried to approach him; the other children, most of whom chased around the play yard, seemed to respect his wish for privacy. Later, when the class regrouped for story time, John didn't show as much interest as he had during the sharing session. He seemed more interested in tracing the cracks in the wall than in listening to *Frog and Toad Are Friends.*

One last word about description. Often when beginning writers have little to say, their eyes will reach into the mind's landscapes and return with chunks of description. They'll then glue them onto their papers. This practice just won't do. Whenever you include a full paragraph of description in an essay, be sure it has a clear purpose. Description is not batting to be stuffed into assignments.

WRITING TASK

Write a description that evokes a scene, a person, a situation, or an action. Keep in mind that an effective description works to create a predetermined response in a reader. For instance, if you were to write about a teacher you see as absentminded, you would select details that reflect absentmindedness. Remember, too, that description often

works indirectly. Don't tell readers, show them. If you decide to describe an action, avoid slipping into narration — telling a complete story.

15 DEDUCTIVE ESSAY

If you're able to develop a topic sentence with examples, catalogues, comparisons, contrasts, and so on, you'll probably have little trouble writing a deductive essay of several paragraphs. But before we get into an explanation of the task, we want to offer a few general comments about the essay as we see it.

For one thing the word *essay* conveys the idea of personal involvement. A journalistic report which sticks to who, what, and when information about an event isn't an essay. A lab report describing the results of an experiment with scientific detachment isn't an essay, either. Yet an essay could be written on an event — a bank robbery, for example — or even on the effects of mixing Na and H_2O. To qualify as an essay, such papers need only to show in some way a personal involvement on the part of the writer.

In the earlier tasks in this book we have repeatedly suggested you seek topics and material in your own experience and thoughts. Even when you have used facts and ideas which were not in your personal storehouse, you have, we hope, passed them through the mixing box of your own values, personality, and experience before laying them on your written page. So the essay is only an extension of this method of working.

Secondly, the word *essay* also has a nonliterary definition: "to make an attempt," to give something a try. And that is what you do in writing— attempt to express in words, sentences, and paragraphs the richness and complexity of an experience or idea so clearly that others can understand it too. It's good to keep this dimension of the word *essay* in mind because it reminds you that just any expression of an idea won't do. A writer has to keep trying, keep playing with ways to express his thoughts. Each draft is an attempt. Even the finished paper is just the latest attempt whose worth, in the end, will have to be judged by a reader.

Finally, the word *essay* conveys the idea of a relatively short piece of writing on a limited subject area. Most books are not essays because they cover many parts of a subject. When writers use the word *essay,* they are thinking of short papers on single subjects.

So by our definition, an essay is a short written composition revealing the writer's personal involvement with a limited subject.

Of course, there are many labels given to different types of essays. We aren't going into all these because the dividing lines are so subjective. But we do want to mention a primary variable. It has to do with the way writers reveal their involvement in the essay. Sometimes writers use first person extensively and declare their opinions in every paragraph. At the other extreme the first person never appears, and writers signal their involvement through tone and diction. In an essay objecting to the way science tends to reduce everything to details, Lewis Thomas uses the direct involvement of the first person. He is describing how he felt watching the otters and beavers at the Tucson Zoo.

I was transfixed. As I now recall it, there was only one sensation in my head: pure elation mixed with amazement at such perfection. Swept off my feet, I floated from one side to the other, swiveling my brain, staring astounded at the beavers, then at the otters. I could hear shouts across my corpus callosum, from one hemisphere to the other. I remember thinking, with what was left in charge of consciousness, that I wanted no part of the science of beavers and otters; I wanted never to know how they performed their marvels; I wished for no news about the physiology of their breathing, the coordination of their muscles, their vision, their endocrine systems, their digestive tracts. I hoped never to have to think of them as collections of cells. All I asked for was the full hairy complexity, then in front of my eyes, of whole, intact beavers and otters in motion.

Joan Didion, discussing a state-sponsored experiment to encourage the use of public transportation and carpools on Los Angeles freeways, begins with a description of a monitoring center. She doesn't use first person or directly state her opinion in this paragraph, but she does reveal her involvement in the subject through her choice of words. As you read this section of her essay, notice the attitude revealed by the italicized words.

The *closed door* upstairs at 120 South Spring Street in downtown Los Angeles is marked *OPERATIONS CENTER.* In the *windowless* room beyond the *closed door* a *reverential hush* prevails.

From six A.M. until seven P.M. in this *windowless* room *men sit at consoles watching a huge board flash colored lights.* "There's the heart attack," someone will *murmur,* or "we're getting the gawk effect." 120 South Spring is the Los Angeles office of Caltrans, or the California Department of Transportation, and the Operations Center is where Caltrans engineers monitor *what they call* "the 42-Mile Loop." The 42-Mile Loop is simply the rough triangle formed by the intersections of the Santa Monica, the San Diego and the Harbor Freeways, and 42 miles represents less than ten percent of freeway mileage in Los Angeles County alone, but these particular 42 miles *are regarded around 120 South Spring with a special veneration.* The Loop is a "demonstration system," *a phrase much favored by everyone at Caltrans,* and is part of a "pilot project," another two words *carrying totemic weight on South Spring.*

Didion is clearly not viewing all this with admiration and awe but with a kind of doubtful cynicism. She forces us to view the engineers as a sort of priesthood worshiping gods of their own creation and cut off from the realities of life beyond the windowless room. Her involvement clearly shows.

Now we want to be more specific. This task will ask you to write a short deductive essay. The structure of a deductive essay is quite simple. It begins with an introductory paragraph that presents a central point. The introduction is followed by a discussion several paragraphs long, each of which includes a topic sentence and develops a subpart of the central point. The deductive essay ends with a conclusion that often restates the central point and ties together the loose ends. The paragraphs, usually a minimum of five, are linked by clear transitions. Diagrammed, a five-paragraph deductive essay might look something like this table.

Paragraph 1 *Introductory paragraph*	Information leading to the central point
	Central point
Paragraph 2	Transition and first subpoint presented in a topic sentence
	Development of the first subpoint

Paragraph 3	Transition and second subpoint presented in topic sentence
	Development of the second subpoint
Paragraph 4	Transition and third subpoint presented in topic sentence
	Development of the third subpoint
Paragraph 5 *Concluding paragraph*	Restatement of the central point and closing remarks

Please don't get the idea that a deductive essay needs to be as mechanical as the diagram might indicate. It doesn't. But we want you to understand that simple deductive essays have the same basic structure. How well writers use the structure depends on their skills.

With the diagram in mind, study the following deductive essay written by a student. The writer uses first-person point of view, clearly shows her attitude toward her subject, and organizes the material in a deductive structure. We suggest you read the essay through once; then read it a second time along with the marginal notes.

```
The Thirties: A Personal History
```

Members of my generation have grown up during a time when the majority of Americans have lived in relative comfort. Nevertheless, we have all seen photographs of the Great American Depression of the 1930s: images of anonymous men in dark suits and tweed caps selling apples on street corners; hollow-cheeked women cuddling infants in front of clapboard shacks; crowds milling before factory gates; hoboes gathered around campfires and eating from tin cans;

This introductory paragraph leads to the essay's main point, which is presented in the closing sentences and is developed primarily through a catalogue which sets up a contrast with the writer's point.

The writer's use of concrete detail makes the introduction interesting.

Model T Fords loaded with chairs, tables, mattresses, and boxes of clothes crawling along desert highways toward the Pacific. These dreadful memories, preserved in history books, seem totally grim. | But besides the dreadful memories, there are positive aspects of the Depression that haven't been preserved in history books. These memories are carried by people who suffered yet lived through the thirties.|

The central point comes at the end of the introduction — some people who lived through the Depression have some positive memories about the experience.

One positive aspect of the thirties my grandparents remember was the determination to overcome adversity it stirred in them. | Like many Kansas farmers in the early thirties, they were suffering from the country's sudden economic collapse, but they still had land and raised some crops. Then nature turned against them. Unrelenting winds swept across the plains, destroying crops and swirling away the topsoil. A drought came with the wind and destroyed any chance they might have had to grow a crop. Finally, the bank demanded payment on the farm's mortgage. They couldn't scrape together the money, so they lost the farm. But if economic collapse and a senseless act of nature destroyed them financially, these events toughened their will to overcome adversity. They moved to a small Kansas town. Days, my grandfather worked as a clerk in his uncle's store; nights, he

The opening sentence of paragraph 2 includes a transition and states the first subpoint of the central point: one positive aspect of the Depression for some people was the stirring of the determination to overcome adversity.

Also notice how "aspect" and "remember" tie back to words in the closing sentences of the introduction.

Paragraph developed through an extended example

studied law. My grandmother, who had taught before marrying, worked at the local school. By 1938 my grandfather had passed the state examination allowing him to practice law. By the end of World War II my grandmother was school superintendent.

I know there were many less fortunate than my grandparents, many who were fighting poverty all those years, but some people who lived through the thirties remember poverty as being different then. It seems another positive aspect of the Depression was that people could be poor without losing personal dignity. My mother has a childhood memory of a gray-haired man who knocked at the kitchen door one day and asked to do some work in return for a meal. Her father refused to allow him to work, but invited him to join the family for a lunch of soup and biscuits. After the meal he whittled little wooden birds for all the kids. My mother says that the whole family gave him the respect they would give any successful artist now. My retired neighbor knew out-of-luck businessmen and bankrupt investors who sold flowers on street corners and caddied at golf courses without losing a sense of personal dignity. Can you imagine such things today? Perhaps because there were so many people broke and hungry, it wasn't con-

Transition sentence that reminds the reader of the central point

Topic sentence

Paragraph developed through brief examples

Rounds off the paragraph with a question and reminds reader of the subpoint

sidered a failure not to have a regular job.
People respected each other anyway.

Another positive aspect some people
experienced during the thirties was the sense
of community it created in them. Many people
carry stories about grocers who supplied out-
of-luck neighbors with food on credit and
charged no interest. Others talk about going
to wedding showers without enough money to buy
a nice gift and the guests all digging into
their pockets and pooling their change to buy
a community gift for the bride. My aunt
remembers over a hundred people turning out to
help repair a neighbor's house that had partly
burned down. But perhaps the most startling
example of the sense of community I've heard
comes from my friend's family experience. Her
grandparents were forced to move from the
countryside to Boston, where they rented a one-
bedroom apartment. At the time, my friend's
grandmother was seven months pregnant and started
having labor pains. A doctor, selected at random
from the phone book, came over immediately, completed a quick examination, then called for hot
water. He delivered a healthy, six-pound girl.
A week later the new parents got a bill for
$7.32, the cost of home delivery. Since the
move and rent had taken all their money, they

Transition integrated in topic sentence 3

*Paragraph developed through a
combination of brief general examples and
an extended narrative example*

couldn't pay. But when other people living in
the building--all of whom had been complete
strangers to them until the baby was born--heard
of the couple's plight, they chipped in pennies,
nickels, dimes, and quarters. They sent the
fee to the doctor. Less than three days later,
the doctor drove up with a backseat of groceries.
He said his nurse had sent the bill by mistake,
so he used the payment to buy groceries for them.
At one time I might have seen this aspect of
the Depression as an act of charity; now I see
it as an act of community.

   Indeed the historian's portrayal of the
Depression as a grim time for Americans is
accurate, but we must remember that a personal
history that doesn't get into books parallels
the social upheaval we've read about.│ It's the
history carried in the minds of people who
endured through that time. Often those memories
have some positive aspects.

Conclusion reasserts that the historical view of the Depression is accurate but that another kind of history lives in the memories of people who lived through it. The central point is restated.

Now that you've studied the diagram and one writer's short deductive essay, we want to give you some clear guidelines for writing a five-paragraph deductive essay.

Central Point

There's a story of a math teacher who used to begin a course in geometry by tossing a piece of chalk from the back of the room. Hitting the board, the chalk would make a white spot. The teacher would then shout, "Take a point in space."

In writing a five-paragraph essay the beginning spot may be called the thesis statement or the main idea or the controlling idea or the central point. Since the name makes no difference, we'll call it the central point. Before beginning an essay, you should have a central point clearly etched in your mind. Better yet, have it written on a sheet of paper.

The central point serves the same function for the essay that a topic sentence serves for a single paragraph. It is not just an announcement of a subject area, but a limited statement about a subject area. For instance, "trees" can serve as a subject but not as a central point. "Sequoias are becoming extinct" can serve as a central point because it has a limited subject — "sequoias" — and a limited predicate — "are becoming extinct." If you can phrase a limited central point and stick to it, you're off and running. The reality of the writing situation, though, is often not that simple.

Often the beginning writer will start with a general subject such as "crime." The first reaction will be to gaze at the horizon and say, "The central point is that-a-way," then mount Old Paint and head for the library. After hours of frantically searching through books and magazines, the writer will have compiled reams of notes — which will be distilled into a central point such as "Organized crime is a major problem in America."

An overly general central point of this sort makes most sensitive readers moan — makes their collective stomach hurt. They might scream, "So what's new?" But imaginary responses aside, this particular central point needs limiting. It's just too broad. Moreover, it's way outside the writer's experience. Sure, the writer might have read Mario Puzo's *The Godfather,* but would having read a novel about the Mafia make anyone an authority on organized crime? We doubt it. In fact, even an authority would have trouble handling a central point like "Organized crime is a major problem in America" in five paragraphs.

Rather than run to the library, a better way to handle a general subject like crime is to turn to personal experience. Using personal experience, the writer might come up with a central point like this: "Petty theft and vandalism in my apartment complex make most of us living there fearful."

The writer of the model essay above started with a general subject — the Depression. She limited it by focusing on some positive aspects of that time, which she had learned about through personal experience — that is, through the stories told to her by relatives and friends. Whenever you come up with a central point that doesn't bring to mind specific material, it's probably too broad. Keep working to limit it until you have plenty to write about. Then write it down on a sheet of paper; it will serve as the intellectual core for your essay. Remember, a workable central point should be limited — phrased in a complete sentence with a limited subject and predicate — and it should come from your experience.

Prewriting, Subpoints, and Plan

Once you've found a "point in space" — a central point — you're ready to collect material and organize it. Sounds simple, but often this is where essay writing gets complicated.

No matter how thoroughly you work at sharpening a central point, you may not discover what's really on your mind until about halfway through the prewriting. You might begin with a central point like "Sequoias are becoming extinct" and find yourself commenting more and more about what a loss it would be for future generations if the majesty and beauty of these trees were to disappear. You might even have some conservation ideas which would help reverse the situation. If you include these comments you will no longer be dealing with the strictly informative material your original central point calls for. That's okay. You can change the original central point to fit whatever emerges in your prewritten draft. A new central point that would better fit the emerging essay about Sequoias might read something like this: "The vanishing Sequoia must be saved." We're suggesting here that as you work with an essay you may need to sharpen and refine your central point as you go. That's just a natural part of the writing process. Don't expect that the first phrasing of a central point will be perfect.

With those thoughts in mind, here's how you might proceed. After you've written the central point, take an hour or so to write down everything you can think of related to it. Don't worry about spelling or grammar (you can clear up such errors in the final draft), but instead work at generating detail and ideas. After you've finished, let the piece set awhile. When you return to reread it, do so without a break. While rereading the prewritten draft begin to organize the material according to subpoints. We also suggest you write a phrase or two to remind yourself which bits of supporting information will come under which subpoints. The subpoints will become the topic sentences for the discussion paragraphs.

Once this sorting is completed, you'll have a written "sketch" of your final paper. Sketches are very personal planning methods. They may be reworked into formal outlines if that fits your nature. For instance, a preliminary outline of "The Thirties: A Personal History" might look like this:

Introduction   *Central point:* Although historians paint a grim picture of the Depression, it did have some positive aspects which are carried in the memories of people who lived through the thirties.

Paragraph 2   *Subpoint 1:* The determination to overcome adversity was one positive aspect the thirties stirred in some people.

My grandparents' will to survive toughened during the Depression.

Paragraph 3   *Subpoint 2:* Being poor without losing dignity was another positive aspect of the thirties.

Example 1: My mother's story of the gray-haired man.

Example 2: My neighbor's stories of out-of-luck businessmen and investors.

Paragraph 4   *Subpoint 3:* A strong sense of community was another positive aspect some felt during the thirties.

Example 1: Some grocers carried neighbors on credit without charging interest.

Example 2: Some people would chip in to buy community gifts for showers.

Example 3: The story of my friend's grandparents who had to move to Boston.

Paragraph 5   *Conclusion:* The thirties were grim years, but people still found positive values in them.

Or perhaps your plan might take on the characteristics of a true sketch. One writer we know likes to draw boxes that represent paragraphs of the final essay. She then fills in the spaces with brief reminders of what will go into the various sections. When she's ready to write the final draft, she uses her prewritten material to flesh out the sketch. A sketch of "The Thirties: A Personal History" might look like this:

Paragraph 1 *Introduction*	Set up contrast by using negative images
Central point	For individuals the Depression had some positive aspects.

Paragraph 2 *Discussion paragraphs* *Subpoint 1*	One aspect: stirred the will to overcome adversity

	Grandparents' life on the farm Loss of farm Overcoming economic collapse

Paragraph 3 *Subpoint 2*	Second aspect: some people were poor but still treated with dignity.
Brief example	Mother's memory of gray-haired man — toys
Brief example	Neighbor's story of busted businessmen
Clincher	What would happen now?

Paragraph 4 *Subpoint 3*	Third aspect: many had strong sense of community.
Brief example	Grocers give credit.
Brief example	People without money chipping in for community gifts
Extended example	Family anecdote: having a baby at home in a strange town

Paragraph 5 *Conclusion*	The Depression was a grim time, but some remember positive aspects.

The form your planning takes is up to you. Some writers construct very specific outlines, delineating subpoints and sub-subpoints until every item to be included is listed. Others list main subpoints only and informally jot down some ideas under each one. Some outline in complete sentences. No matter how you go about it, have a plan — that's the message.

Because your plan should grow from your material and purpose, we don't want to lay down rigid rules, but you should keep in mind one general principle: start strong and finish strong. You have to have some good stuff early to keep a reader interested. And the most emphatic position in an essay is near the end. (The same is true to a lesser extent for sentences and paragraphs.) In practical terms, unless you have a good reason to do otherwise, keep the material with the most impact for the end, and present the next-strongest early. Weaker or less interesting material, assuming it is important to include, should come somewhere in the middle. This strategy will prevent your essay from tailing off at the end.

Introduction

Now, with a clear, though possibly tentative, central point and a plan for presenting subpoints and supporting material, you are ready to begin writing an introduction. For most of your papers one paragraph of introduction will probably be sufficient, though several paragraphs are often appropriate for long papers.

Effective introductions do more than offer writers chances to clear their throats — offer more than series of aimless, dull comments — but instead focus papers by clearly presenting the central points in ways that will draw in readers. Here are some traditional introductory methods:

1. descriptions of personal experience that allow the reader to identify with the writer
2. statements of striking facts or statistics that surprise the reader
3. a provocative quotation or interesting question
4. a definition, but not one merely taken from a dictionary
5. a glance at an opposing argument or attack on a commonly held opinion
6. an anecdote or narrative closely related to the topic

Any one of these is a fine way to begin a deductive essay if it fits your subject (see *Introductions* in the Index for Writers for illustrations of the various introduction forms). We want to make one strong suggestion, though. Always end the introduction with the central point. The introduction to "The Thirties: A Personal History" ends with the central point. The writer opens with a general contrast, develops the contrast by using a catalogue of images, then closes with two sentences that clarify the central point.

> Members of my generation have grown up during a time when the majority of Americans have lived in relative comfort. Nevertheless, we have all seen photographs of the Great American Depression of the 1930s: images of anonymous men in dark suits and tweed caps selling apples on street corners; hollow-cheeked women cuddling infants in front of clapboard shacks; crowds milling before factory gates; hobos gathered around

campfires and eating from tin cans; Model T Fords loaded with chairs, tables, mattresses and boxes of clothes crawling along desert highways toward the Pacific. These dreadful memories, preserved in history books, seem totally grim. But besides the dreadful memories, there are positive aspects to the Depression that haven't been preserved in history books. These memories are carried by people who suffered, yet lived through the thirties.

An introduction of this sort acts somewhat like a funnel — it begins big and narrows at the bottom. The funnel method is a good way to begin deductive essays. A diagram of it looks like this:

general subject introduced
becoming more specific
narrowed
to
the central point

You begin in the first sentence with a broad statement of the subject; then in several sentences using specifics you narrow to the central point. Do you remember the workable central point developed from the general subject crime? "Petty theft and vandalism in my apartment complex make most of us living there fearful."

One funnel introduction that leads up to that idea looks like this:

Crime seems to be a way of life for some Americans. Over the past few months I've read of political payoffs, gang violence, and dope smuggling. Just last week, daily papers and news magazines featured stories and photos of looters rampaging through the blacked-out streets of a storm-torn town. They seemed delighted to be carting away goods from demolished stores and homes while shouting, "It's Christmastime! It's Christmastime!" But reading about theft and vandalism in other parts of the country doesn't have the same effect on me as experiencing it in the apartment complex where I live. Petty crime committed in distant places seems unreal. When it happens next door, the fear it creates cuts deep.

As with most preliminary central points, the wording of this one gets changed in the process of writing the introduction. Nevertheless, all the elements of the original are still present, and the writer has managed to arrange the material according to the funnel method.

He begins by presenting the general subject of crime. Then in the second sentence he becomes a little more concrete by naming some crimes. In the next two sentences, he writes even more specifically by alluding to a well-publicized example of criminal acts. In the fifth sentence he narrows the focus to crime in his apartment complex. And finally, he completely reveals the central point.

We suggest the funnel method is a good way to start a short deductive essay. By using it you will put the central point of your essay clearly before your readers just before they begin to read the discussion part of your paper.

Discussion

Once you've completed the introduction to your deductive essay, move on to the discussion. If you can write paragraphs with topic sentences, you should have no trouble putting together a discussion of a central point. If you haven't already done so in the planning stage, the first step you should take in writing the discussion is to turn the subpoints into topic sentences. You will then develop these topic sentences in separate paragraphs by expanding the ideas and details you listed in your plan. Feel free to develop the subpoints by using examples, catalogues, comparisons, contrasts, causes and effects, classifications, or any combination of methods. In other words, develop the discussion in any way that fits the material. The writer of "The Thirties: A Personal History" developed the essay's central point mainly through specific and extended examples, but we want to stress that different central points require different strategies.

The main difference between writing individual paragraphs and writing a complete discussion has to do with the need to link all the paragraphs in a discussion with transitions. In a short paper, transitional markers are usually combined with topic sentences and are often achieved by a single word or short phrase, usually a key word repeated from the central point. But sometimes in the third or fourth paragraph an author will restate the central point to remind the reader of the essay's purpose. We suggest you reread "The Thirties: A Personal History" to see how one writer uses transitions to link the essay's paragraphs. But to give you an idea, notice the repetition of key words carried from the central point to the topic sentences:

Central point as stated in the final two sentences of the introduction:

But besides the dreadful memories, there are positive aspects to the Depression that haven't been preserved in history books. These memories are carried by people who suffered yet lived through the thirties.

Topic sentence 1:

One *positive aspect* of *the thirties* my grandparents *remember* was the determination to overcome adversity it stirred in them.

Topic sentence 2:

It seems another *positive aspect* of *the Depression* was that people could be poor without losing personal dignity.

Topic sentence 3:

Another *positive aspect* some people experienced during *the thirties* was the sense of community it created in them.

These are not the only transitional techniques working between paragraphs, but by repeating key words from the central point the writer keeps the essay's purpose before the reader.

Conclusion

Finally, a successful essay should conclude, not just stop. Conclusions, like introductions, are important; they stand out as the first and last contact you'll have with the reader. While an introduction serves to hook the reader and to present the paper's focus, a conclusion completes the focus and may echo the central and supporting points, along with their applications.

In other than descriptive and process writing, an essay will usually have a conclusion in a paragraph separate from the discussion. There are several standard ways to develop concluding paragraphs. For instance, an effective conclusion may

1. offer an answer to a question, a solution to a problem, the result of behavior raised in the introduction and explored in the discussion; or point out that there is no clear answer, solution, or result, thus showing the issue's complexity;
2. present a quotation, especially one that amplifies the central point or varies another quotation already presented in the introduction;
3. relate a relevant anecdote that the reader will be likely to remember and that echoes the central point;
4. rephrase the central and supporting points, followed by a closing sentence or two to turn the reader's mind back to the paper.

A word of caution. The conclusion must grow from the paper; it should not open a new subject by raising questions not explored in the discussion. Also keep in mind that the tone should be consistent with the rest of the essay. (See *Conclusions* in the Index for Writers for some specific examples.)

Titles

Once you've got the introduction, discussion, and conclusion written, all that's left is the title. There's only one general principle behind titles: keep them simple.

But whatever you do, don't title an essay "Assignment 13." The title should suggest the essay's content, not the sequence of the course. And don't underline or put quotation marks around your own title. If you use part of a quotation or the title of another work as part of your title, however, use quotation marks or underlining, whichever is appropriate for that part.

One Last Thought

We have very limited intentions for this task. We've tried to give you only the most basic elements of the deductive essay. We're a little fearful that you'll approach the writing of a short deductive essay rigidly. That would be a mistake because within the general framework we've presented, approaches to the deductive essay are as varied as the people who write them. As a writer you have to find the voice and method of development that fit the idea, emotion, knowledge, and experience you wish to communicate. Your choices will vary with your subject matter and your attitude toward it. The more you write, the more choices you will see as possibilities. It's the real challenge writing offers. Enjoy it.

WRITING TASK ══

Select a subject you feel personally involved in either because you hold strong opinions about it or because it has touched your life directly. Once you have your subject, write a five-paragraph essay exploring it. You can go about this task in one of two ways. You may take each step to your instructor for review, or you may work through the steps on your own. In either case, we advise you to follow this procedure:

1. Select a broad subject and shape it into a central point. Be sure your central point is clearly stated in a sentence. Keep your central point as simple and clear as possible, but also keep in mind that it may change as you develop the essay.

2. Develop a prewritten draft using the central point as the center for your thought. Once you feel you have enough information, reread your draft and start to develop a plan.

3. Organize a plan on a separate sheet of paper. Include the central point and subpoints that will make up the discussion paragraphs. Fill

in brief phrases to remind yourself what material you will use in the development of the subpoints.

4. Once you have a plan, write an introductory paragraph that presents the central point in the closing sentences. Remember, the introduction should serve a purpose by giving the reader important information related to the central point. Also remember that the central point you started with may need to be reshaped to fit into the introduction.

5. Once the introduction is completed, shape the subpoints into topic sentences and develop the discussion section of your essay. You should have at least three discussion paragraphs, each built around a subpoint cast in a topic sentence. Also be sure to use clear transitions linking your paragraphs together.

6. After you've completed the discussion section, write a conclusion that restates the central point and adequately closes the essay.

7. Write a title — a simple one. Don't put quotation marks around it.

8. As a final step, reread your entire essay to be sure that all the paragraphs are linked by transitions.

16 INDUCTIVE ESSAY

The inductive essay moves from specific detail to a generalized central point presented in the final paragraph. It therefore differs structurally from a deductive essay, which starts with an introduction that presents a central point, moves through a discussion of several paragraphs that present subparts of the central point, and ends with a conclusion that often restates the central point. This deductive pattern is especially effective when you are trying to get information to blurry-eyed college teachers buried to their nostrils in blue-book exams. The pattern's repetitiveness can bore less harried readers, however.

Sometimes the writing situation will be such that you won't want to reveal your central point in the opening paragraph. You may want to save it for the end so that it will have more impact. Or you may want to develop two sides of an argument before revealing your own position. In either case the inductive essay will serve the purpose.

The inductive essay is often used to present personal insights. By presenting personal experience and responding to it you inductively lead a reader to a central point — an ah ha! experience. Of course, unlike brief inductive paragraphs, in which the insight comes at the end of several sentences, in a full inductive essay it comes at the end of several paragraphs.

By this time you must be painfully aware of the process of mixing concrete details and inner responses in personal writing. You are also probably aware of the importance of using overt transitions that help to guide a reader's attention. But you probably aren't as aware of the need to integrate background information into your work, yet more than likely you have been doing so.

Background information functions as the mortar that holds personal writing together. Through it you supply a reader with information necessary to follow the train of your thought. In other words, background information establishes the situation for a reader. This is especially important in personal writing and specifically in constructing personal inductive essays.

Now let's move on to an example of an inductive essay that presents a personal insight. As you read it, notice

1. that the essay begins with a general comment announcing the writer's concern without stating it in a formal central point
2. that the next three paragraphs detail separate but thematically related experiences that lead up to the writer's insight
3. that the final paragraph clearly declares the writer's attitude
4. that the writer uses background information to guide the reader's attention

Also keep in mind that since inductive essays are much more flexible than deductive essays, the writer of an inductive essay doesn't build each paragraph around a topic sentence but instead gently leads the reader from paragraph to paragraph.

What follows is a student's inductive essay. We suggest you read it through, then reread it along with the marginal comments.

Growth

I have been becoming more aware lately of just how much meaning is summed up in the commonplace word <u>growth</u>.

Notice how the lead gives the reader the general focus without becoming too specific.

After spending August working as a counselor at a YMCA camp in the Sierras, I headed home to Orange County. Since the thought of a trip through Los Angeles always depresses me, calling up visions of housing tracts pasted together and of jammed freeways that lead to the city's concrete heart where gray towers spear into the afternoon pall, I decided to take the longer but more scenic route north of LA and over the

Lead for the first paragraph gives some background.

"Since the thought of" gives a response to past experience and backs it up with specific details.

Cajon Pass. I was in for a surprise. When I crossed the last ridge just before sunset and began the descent to the coastal plain, I saw that the fields of crops and citrus I remembered having been there had vanished. In their places were housing projects, shopping centers, gas stations, trailer parks, and schoolyards. The whole scene reminded me of a huge bowl heaped with junk and covered over with a layer of haze thick as gauze. I felt I was entering a nightmare. Certainly all this growth couldn't have happened in a single month, but then I remembered I had not traveled this particular route for almost ten years. I wanted to escape the numbing scene, so I stepped on the gas pedal and pointed my VW toward the city of Irvine and my home.

Irvine is a new city being slowly carved from a massive cattle ranch, according to the designs of a master plan. I can remember my parents saying they had moved to Irvine because it would never have the growth that came to Los Angeles. The next morning I was up early. It's my habit to jog just after sunup. I set out on my usual run: an easy jog to a nearby field, then a harder run across a mile of open space to the high school where I usually do four leisurely laps around the track, and then

"I was in for a surprise" prepares the reader for the specific details that follow in the next few sentences.

"The whole scene reminded" begins a response shaped in an image that suggests all the clutter and pollution the writer has associated with LA.

"Certainly all this growth" gives the background of the writer's thought. Using the key word "growth" is important here. The reader will associate it with building.

"I wanted to escape" begins another response.

Notice how the two paragraphs are linked by "Irvine."

The lead of this paragraph supplies the reader with more background.

"The next morning" sets up the next sequence that begins with background information related to the writer's usual run. If the writer didn't present this information here, he would have to work it in later.

Even though much of this is background, the writer works in specifics.

I head for home along a road that takes me to the crest of a hill and down a path that leads to my back gate. At the field I saw things had changed. All along its perimeter builders had terraced the hillsides and poured concrete slabs for housing foundations. Ahead, adjacent to the school, they had framed eight apartment buildings. I did four spiritless laps with my view of the field and hills glutted by the new construction; then I started up the road to the hill's crest. I grew sad as I ran. Just one month earlier, wildflowers, rabbits, squirrels, sparrows, meadowlarks, and ground owls thrived in the field along the road. Now, the builders had scraped them clean of vegetation. I saw no life. I did see heavy bulldozers and earthmovers, like the gorged offspring of ancient mastodons, standing in the fields. At the hill's top, I paused to catch my breath. Below, in the northern half of the city, I saw where builders had cleared other fields for construction and had sawed down whole eucalyptus stands that once protected orange groves from harsh winds. I couldn't get over the thought that all this leveling had happened in a single month. I felt as if I were in the presence of a demonic force whose power I couldn't grasp. It had changed the old growth of flowers, trees,

"At the field" sets up the specifics that follow.

Notice how the writer uses guiding words like "along" and "ahead."

This section includes background information mixed with a great deal of detail. He contrasts the hills and fields as they were with how they are. Notice how "now" is used to guide the reader from past to present.

Here the writer shapes a response into an image by comparing the machines to prehistoric creatures.

He continues to document the "growth" he sees.

He moves from the concrete details to his inner responses.

and wildlife into the new growth of houses, apartments, and shopping centers.

Here he brings out the idea that the old growth of living things has been replaced by a new growth.

That afternoon, while driving to campus, I passed more construction in the part of Irvine set aside as the industrial center. Here, the growth seemed to move upward rather than outward. I drove through the awesome shadows of multi-storied buildings with the afternoon sun flashing through the steel skeletons rising in what had once been strawberry fields. I had seen it all before--this part of the city had been under development for years--but after my experiences driving back from the Sierras and jogging through my neighborhood, the growth took on a new meaning. The thoughts from Joni Mitchell's "Big Yellow Taxi" came to me. I had heard the song often, but this time its thought seemed to capture what I was thinking. I recalled the words "paved paradise and put up a parking lot."

"That afternoon" serves to show time has passed and introduces the new sequence of experiences related to observing growth.

"I had seen" presents more background information and pulls together the experiences the writer has been recording.

He brings in a quotation. Notice that he gives all the important information related to it — the name of the song and the vocalist. He also places it near the end of the essay because it serves to bring his thoughts together.

Maybe southern California or Orange County or the city of Irvine fail as examples of paradise, but it seems to me that each field and hillside no matter where it is holds a little bit of paradise. All this new growth was bringing to me a sense of loss--not just for my neighborhood, but for all neighborhoods that are giving up their bits of paradise to more

Notice how the writer refers to the song by bringing out the idea of paradise.

The entire paragraph provides a showcase for the writer's insight. He closes by raising a question about the dangers of unchecked growth. But notice how he has tied it to other communities, thus linking his insight to the experience of others.

housing tracts, shopping centers, and industrial

complexes. And, finally, the question comes to

me: just as the unchecked growth of vines will

destroy smaller plants by blocking out the sun,

won't the unchecked growth of buildings smother

people who must live in their shadow?

The final question embodies the central point.

WRITING TASK

Write an inductive essay according to the information we've given in this section. Begin by selecting an insight from your experience with which others might identify. Then select a quotation from an article, book, poem, song, or lecture that reflects your personal observation.

Next, prewrite the essay by developing an extended list of experiences you associate with your insight. Using the list, develop a rough draft. Remember to write a general lead that launches your entire essay and a conclusion that provides a showcase for your insight and central point. Since this is a full essay, you will need to arrange your paper in paragraphs. The author of the illustration arranged his main paragraphs around a drive from the Sierras, a morning jog, and a drive to campus. If you search, you will probably find some simple dividing points for your essay.

As for the quotation, we suggest you place it near the end. It will then serve as a logical lead to the final insight, and it will also follow the details and responses you've accumulated to that point; therefore, it will have more psychological impact on the reader. In order to integrate the quotation into your essay, be sure to mention its source — both the person and place it comes from. (For more information on using quotations see *Quotations* in the Index for Writers.)

One final thought aside from structural considerations. Keep in mind that your writing will be serving four main functions: (1) to describe your experience, (2) to record your inner responses, (3) to guide the reader, and (4) to supply background information.

17 ASSOCIATIONAL ESSAY

By this time you would probably have little trouble arranging a paper covering the advantages and disadvantages of a particular job, the effects of the energy shortage on your campus, the process of preparing for an overseas journey, or the reasons for supporting one political candidate over another. This is the stuff of the intellect. This kind of material lends itself to organization in reports.

But what of personal growth? What of insight that comes from life's disruptions and joys? How do writers go about exploring feelings over ending a relationship, losing a friend, becoming an adult, seeking truth? How do writers deal with feelings about succeeding, failing, aging, and dying. How do writers share insights that come from experiences such as these? They put them in reports, right?

Not likely. Separating, growing, seeking, failing, succeeding, aging, dying — this is the stuff of emotion. More often than not, these subjects can't be handled in formal patterns, but need to be handled through less direct means. That's the function of the associational essay. This pattern offers the means to explore elusive areas of experience — that is, a way to search through life's nooks and crannies to see what experience has stored there.

This exploration usually involves the intuitive rather than the intellectual part of the mind, for the explorer abandons logical constraints in order to make more creative connections between separate memories drawn from personal experience. These memories often span a writer's life history by associating bits and pieces from the past and present that connect to a subject. Associational essays, then, tend to reflect the flow of psychological time instead of the procession of chronological time.

They often begin with an event or a thought important to the writer's current life, then skip to childhood memories that connect with the present, hop forward to the not-so-distant past to make other connections before returning to the present. They may leap ahead, just as everyone's thought does, to construct a possible future. Sometimes they even include dreams and fantasies, hopes and fears, and, at times, philosophical musings.

At this point you probably sense that the writing of an associational essay requires a more creative touch than the writing of standard patterns. It does. The fact that it does presents a problem. As with most creative forms, the associational essay follows no clear pattern; therefore, we can't give you hard and fast rules. What we can do is give you some general guidelines.

Begin by recalling an experience that holds a great deal of emotion for you and that has brought some insight about yourself. Don't worry about whether or not the experience will seem earthshaking to your reader. Often the slightest experience, while appearing to be ordinary to others, may hold tremendous emotional energy for you. It's your job to show the emotion of the experience to the reader.

Once you've identified the experience and insight, draw together a list by associating memories you connect with the experience. In this prewriting phase, you shouldn't waste time evaluating the associations, you should only record them — no judgment, just writing.

After collecting the raw material, you need to shape the whole essay. Like all finished writing, the associational essay has a beginning, a middle, and an end. But unlike the deductive essay, here the beginning merely suggests where the essay is headed. It never sets down a controlling idea. In fact, if your subject can be reduced to a controlling idea, we recommend you drop it and start over.

The middle of the associational essay weaves together memories connected with the central experience, but the bulk of the details will come from the past. The paragraphs, though less organized than traditional patterns, should begin with lead sentences that give readers a sense of order. Never let readers stumble in disordered associations, but guide them each step of the way.

The end of the essay reveals the insight you've gained from the experience. This revelation, however, should be suggested, not flatly stated as the moral of your experience. Such suggestion is often hard to achieve. To make writing the conclusion easier, we suggest you use an image or thought that circles back into the essay and indirectly captures the point.

One last thought: since the strength of an associational essay comes through the power of suggestion, the method of development is suggestive description. But before you can use description to suggest, you must have a clear understanding of what you want the reader to feel — a sense of loss; the pain of separation; the joy of discovery; the fear or acceptance of success, failure, aging, death. Once you have a clear understanding of your intent, you can select descriptive details that suggest the feeling. Often you may go through several drafts before you know exactly what it is you're after — that's the nature of creative writing — but before you write the final draft, you should have an exact understanding of what you're doing.

By way of illustration, we offer the following associational essay. The writer relates an experience he had returning to the home and neighborhood where he was born and raised. His parents have moved to a new house, and his former home is to be destroyed. He uses the experience to indirectly communicate his feelings about change and to share an insight that comes to him through the encounter. As you read, notice that the writer never flatly states a moral or controlling idea, but suggests his feelings by describing early memories he associates with growing up in the old neighborhood. The use of suggestion creates subtle suspense and prepares the reader for the final insight. First read the entire essay. Then reread it along with the marginal comments.

Allie, Allie Oxen Free

In the middle of my freshman year in college I returned to my hometown to visit the old neighborhood. It was the last time I could go home. Home--the word has a deep meaning for me.

Opening sentence sets up the event that organizes the essay and suggests the direction.

Driven out by a severe drought, my parents came from the cornfields of Nebraska to the house where they lived for thirty-five years. I was born in the back bedroom because, as my mother said, "there just wasn't enough time to get to a hospital."

The writer supplies some background information that shows the family connection with the house and neighborhood.

My earliest memories center around playing in that house: pushing trucks over the hardwood floors, my pajama knees mopping up the morning dust; rummaging through my mother's pan drawers and banging them on the linoleum; and hiding behind the overstuffed couch whenever I

The writer catalogues a series of memory experiences he associates with the house and neighborhood. Notice how these descriptive details move from the time he was a baby to starting school.

was called for lunch. The backyard seemed to
stretch the length of a football field and was
the place I would chase my older brother and
sisters until falling down, breathless and
sweating. Before I started grammar school, I
knew all the neighborhood's marvelous places:
the avocado tree where my friends and I used
to climb to an ancient tree house that had been
built by children before us, the park where the
old-timers would sit on benches and laugh at
our wild games, the abandoned garage where we
used to spy at the neighborhood through knotholes.

All that came back to me as I drove to pick
up my parents for a final visit. You see, my
home and the surrounding two blocks were to be
destroyed. The City Council, those faceless
champions of change, had condemned the neighborhood and planned to replace it with a civic
center.

This paragraph gives more background and suggests the writer's attitude toward change.

As I turned onto the street where my parents
had bought a tract home, I saw my father, a
little stooped since retiring after years of
hard labor, standing before the recently seeded
lawn that was beginning to sprout slivers of
grass. In work boots, khaki trousers, and plaid
shirt, which had become faded and thin from
too much sun and too many washings, he didn't
seem to belong to the stucco house packed with

The writer's brief description of his father suggests his father is out of place in this new environment. Also notice the implied contrast; his father who once grew corn has been reduced to growing grass and forced into the more convenient life of modern conveniences.

all the modern conveniences I knew my parents
had avoided most of their lives. I pulled to
the curb and he climbed in.

"Where's Mom?" I asked.

*The dialogue and comments let the reader
know the writer is resisting the change.*

"Not coming," he said. "Let's go."

That was all he had to say to make me
understand that Mom didn't want to make a final
visit to the old place and to make me realize
I didn't either.

As we drove, he filled his pipe, lit it,
and began puffing--the smoke carrying the smell
of Sugar Barrel, a smell I will always associate
with him, and floating out the window. We chatted
about anything important. "How're classes?" he
asked and I answered routinely, knowing that
neither of us wanted to say much about losing
our home. Then we were on the old street, and
the memories seemed to rise in my blood.

I first saw the old store the Hungarian
couple used to run. The advertisements were

*The next three paragraphs enlarge
particular memories. Notice how each
begins with a clear lead sentence.*

peeling off the walls, the windows had been
boarded up, and the screen door dangled stiffly
from one hinge--empty, abandoned. But I
remembered how I once spent summer afternoons
sitting in front of it and playing Monopoly
with my friends or chess with old man Jefferson.
The car seats we used to lounge on were still

*The writer creates a sense of change by
contrasting past to present.*

there, but the stuffing had been torn out and

only the springs remained.

      Then we passed Mr. Sallings's house. Tall
and bony, Sallings was the neighborhood's
mysterious figure. The few times I saw him in
the sunlight he wore a gray suit and had gray
hair and skin. But more often I saw him moving
behind the curtains where he paced the darkened
parlor or rocked in a creaky chair. I was told
he had been "that way" since "losing his wife."
He wanted only to be left alone. One morning
I learned that he had "left" the night before.
I never heard of him again.

*Why does the writer include the mysterious
Mr. Sallings?*

      We drove past the vacant lot that had been
the scene of many of my childhood joys. Each
Independence Day the neighborhood fathers would
set up a fireworks display and thrill us kids
for hours. In the spring we held war games
there. Costumed in makeshift army uniforms and
wearing plastic helmets and carrying plastic
rifles, we dodged through the tall grass and
dove into foxholes, shouting "TATATATATA, Gotcha!
C'mon, you're dead!" During the summer, the lot
served as the center for our nightly game of
hide-and-seek. As my father and I drove past,
I imagined hearing Billy Kieler's voice, the
loudest and most melodic among us, echoing
throughout the neighborhood, "ALLIE ALLIE OXEN
FREE! ALLIE, ALLIE OXEN FREE!" Billy was the

*The writer uses the vacant lot to create a
collage of childhood games.*

How does the memory of Billy Kieler fit in?

first of my childhood friends to move away.
How much had his life changed, I wondered. Yes,
how much?

Then we were in front of our old wood-frame
home. My father climbed from the car. I looked
straight ahead. "Coming?" he asked. But before
I knew I had made a decision, I said no. I
turned in time to see him walk the five steps
up to the front porch, unlock the door, and
step inside. No, I just could not bring myself
to see the house empty, abandoned.

*Writer's earlier feeling about not wanting
to make this visit ends in the decision not to
enter the house. The words "empty" and
"abandoned" echo the statement about the
store.*

I sat staring at the front lawn and recalled
how I had spent hundreds of Saturday mornings
mowing the lawn, trimming the hedges, and hoeing
around the rose bushes. I had hated to spend
my Saturday mornings in such labor since I hadn't
inherited my dad's love of growing and caring
for things. Now the grass was brown and the
hedges and rosebushes were dying and I missed
the unvarying routine those secure Saturday
mornings brought.

*By weaving past with present the writer
suggests a desire for permanence.*

In a few moments he was returning, lugging
a heavy toolbox in each hand. I saw he breathed
a little heavy. I went to help him.

*This bit of dialogue sets up the final
insight.*

"Hard going?" I asked.

"It's the last time for me," he said as we
hefted the boxes into the car.

At first I didn't make the connection be-

tween his words and mine. I had referred to
the difficulty he had carrying the boxes. He
referred to much more. He referred to the illusion I wished to keep. I glanced up the street
to the vacant lot and wished I could hear those
comforting words that meant everything was okay,
that the game was over and I could return home:
ALLIE, ALLIE OXEN FREE!

Of course, life is not a game, unlike the childhood games mentioned above. Although it may be hard, the writer must, as his father has, accept the change. Do you know the meaning of Allie, Allie Oxen Free?

Did you notice how muted the essay seems, yet how it still communicated a great deal of emotion? The writer patiently develops the scene and memories through description that suggests a deeper meaning than he reveals. When he does comment, he doesn't shout; he comments in a quiet way.

WRITING TASK

Write an associational essay. We recommend you follow this procedure:

1. Select an event that means a great deal to you and brought you some personal insight.

2. Use the journal to trigger memories you associate with the experience. Collect the raw material in extended lists.

3. Decide what you wish to communicate to the reader. Use it as the essay's guiding principle.

4. Write the essay by beginning with the main experience. Follow with a development of the experience while weaving in the associations you've collected.

5. Round off the essay by stating or implying how you feel or what you've learned from the experience.

Remember, the primary method of development should be description. You will need to work in some background information and responses, but the main intent is to suggest the meaning of the experience, not to explain it.

18 GIVING DIRECTIONS

Giving directions is a practical kind of writing that everyone uses sometime. You may, for example, want to explain how to get to a particular place, how to perform an experiment, how to assemble a kit, or how to create a craft project.

Giving directions demands special attention to clarity — the assumption of such writing is that your reader will actually follow your directions. Basically, you'll be saying "Follow Me," so write clearly. If you don't, your reader will get lost.

Select a subject you know well. You'll have to present a sequence of steps and comment on them, so write about something you have done yourself.

Select a narrow subject so you can handle it thoroughly. "How to sew" wouldn't do, but "How to make a wall hanging from a piece of discarded sheet" would. On the other hand, avoid subjects which are easily reduced to recipes. We have something more interesting in mind.

Once you have selected a suitable subject, organization is easy, as most procedures naturally fall into a chronological order of steps. As you work through these steps, though, keep the following practical points in mind.

1. Early in the paper, specify the materials needed so your reader can have them ready before he begins the process:

> For this project you will need 30 feet of #10 wire and a pair of ordinary household pliers.

2. Make comments and add details on some steps to avoid being monotonous and to help your reader visualize the process:

Press down three or four times on the silver squirter marked "chocolate" so that dark, sticky syrup slips down the sides of the glass to the bottom.

3. Give some reasons for some steps:

Clip the design to the tracing paper to avoid those little shifts which destroy accuracy.

4. Define special terms as you go:

The needle must oscillate — swing to and fro freely. If it does not, loosen the screw at the bottom of the dial.

5. Finally, include comments about what not to do:

Don't tighten any bolts until all have been attached loosely or the framework will slip out of alignment.

The introduction and conclusion should be brief. At the beginning, specify the process you are writing about and perhaps comment on the reason for doing it, its level of difficulty, or the overall approach you will be presenting. At the end, a sentence or two to signal a close is all you need.

Before writing this paper, examine the following directions given by Delia Ephron:

How to Cut Off Your Jeans

It seems like the easiest thing to do. Then you do it and somehow one leg comes out shorter than the other. This time you're going to do it right.

Brief introduction gives reasons for following these directions.

The trick is this: cut one leg first, then match the second one to it. Never cut off both legs at the same time and never cut jeans while wearing them.

The writer presents overview of process and tells what not to do.

You will need one pair of used jeans,

Specifies materials needed

scissors, ruler and a felt-tip pen (like a
Pentel).

Put on the jeans and look in the mirror.   *Step 1*
With the pen, mark one leg an eyeballed two
inches above the knee if you want Bermuda shorts,
four inches above the knee for short shorts.
Take off the jeans, lay them flat on a table,   *Step 2. Comment*
and cut off the leg even with the mark. Don't
worry if your cutting is a little crooked. You
can correct it later.

Put the jeans back on and look in the   *Sequence of steps with comments*
mirror. Now you are going to find the length
that is you. Experiment by turning under the
bottom edge of the cut-off leg and adjusting
the material up and down until you find a length
you like. You'll know it when you see it, but
it's hard to predict ahead of time. It will
depend on such things as your taste and the shape
of your thigh. When you find the right length,
mark it on the cut leg with the pen. Then take
off the jeans.

Lay them flat on a table or the floor. Now   *A key step presented with cautions*
here's the important part: Place the ruler
perpendicular to the side seam and even with
the mark and draw a line across the jeans. The
ruler must be perpendicular to get a straight
line. Cut the leg carefully along the line
through both layers of fabric at the same time.

Now cut the second leg to match the first.　*End of sequence*
Fold the jeans in half along the fly so that
the cut-off leg is on top.　Make sure the waist-
band is even all around.　Using the ruler and
pen, mark the length of the cut leg on the uncut
one.　Cut off the second leg.　Align the legs
again to make sure they match.

The cut edges look unfinished now.　If you　*The writer closes by commenting on final results.*
run the jeans through a washing machine a few
times the material will unravel into a nice
fringe.

WRITING TASK

Write a paper giving directions for the successful completion of a specific and limited task. Introduce briefly; specify materials needed; give details, comments, and reasons for the steps; and guide your reader by explaining what not to do when appropriate. When the process is complete, bring the paper to a close in one or two sentences. Remember, since basically you're saying "Follow me," write as clearly as you can so the reader will not get lost.

19 INFORMING AND ADVISING

We're sure you've encountered written attempts to guide you through a step-by-step process to complete a task — preparing a dinner by recipe, putting together a model, developing a photograph, setting the wake-up switch on a new clock radio, connecting the components of a stereo, repairing a flat tire, cleaning a paintbrush, making a pair of shorts from jeans, and so on. This kind of writing usually involves particular procedures laid out in chronological sequence. The writer's purpose is to march you from point A to point Z without any mishaps. In other words, the writer is saying "Follow me, I'll get you there."

A how-does piece is close to a follow-me piece, but the writer of a how-does piece mainly intends to give the reader information: how does a bill pass through Congress; how does one successfully interview with a prospective employer; how does one eat a formal dinner; how does a detective get an impression of fingerprints; how does one evaluate a restaurant, college, hotel, novel, marriage prospect; and so on.

Unlike writers of follow-me pieces, writers that answer "How does . . ." will not expect readers to do what they're describing but intend instead to satisfy a curiosity or to give advice and guidelines that cannot be applied in any procedural way. For instance, a follow-me piece about changing a flat tire would have clear steps toward successfully doing the job, whereas a how-does piece about evaluating a college could be approached from many angles.

The how-does, then, is mainly informational and advisory, not necessarily procedural, although procedure could be a part of it. And because of its nature, when you write one you must be not only informative but also interesting. Writing a how-does will give you a chance to use several patterns to make it interesting — vivid description, specific and informational examples, comparisons, contrasts, definition, anecdotes to make a strong point, and even analogy to make the strange familiar.

We can suggest no single way to arrange a how-does piece; you need to stay on your toes and keep up with the needs of your subject. A how-does piece does, however, tend to fall into the same general pattern as the deductive essay — that is, it has an introduction, which is brief and usually interest catching or dramatic; several paragraphs in the discussion; and a conclusion. You won't need to worry about a central point because your contract with readers is clear: you're going to give them some advice and information.

For an impression of how a how-does paper might develop, read the following excerpt from Roberta Ridgely's *The Tijuana, Mexicali, Ensenada Shopping, Restaurant and Entertainment Guide, Olé.* Ridgely informs and advises her readers about eating at the open stalls of Tijuana and Ensenada and passes on some general dining and drinking guidelines for them to follow. As you read, notice how Ridgely weaves together description, which creates a picture of the experience, with information and advice. She also defines some Mexican terms, uses narrative examples, and tells general anecdotes. She includes numbered guidelines, characteristic of some how-does pieces but not always necessary. And note this, too: Ridgely has clearly identified her reader — the first-time tourist visiting Tijuana and Ensenada, Mexico.

Eat, Drink and Be Careful

In the days of taco carts on Revolucion, Tijuana's tourist avenue, I eschewed chewing their wares. I've never eaten from a Tijuana clam cart. Nor have I bought a street vendor's churro (pastry fried in deep fat), thought by some to be a best buy. (I wonder if it isn't just a bargain in cholesterol.)

This brief introduction sets the piece in motion.

Ridgely assumes her readers will know what "tacos" are but defines the less familiar "churro." Then she generally suggests caution when eating at open stalls.

In Ensenada, however, I once let the then-director of the Chamber of Commerce direct me to a particular clam cart in that seafood wonderland. As a sweet sea breeze swept the street corner, fresh clams were pried open before my eyes and seasoned with fresh lime juice, sherry,

Paragraph 2 gives an exception to the cautionary advice but suggests you should know what you are doing when you eat seafood.

and a zinger of chili. Served up in a plastic

cup, the concoction was ambrosial. I supported

that cart many seasons, perhaps spurred on by

gringos who not infrequently crowded around to

ask, "You're not going to eat that stuff RAW?"

    Since the agricultural products of Mexico

so often find their way unsuspected to our tables,

it seems foolish not to partake of her bounty.

About two years ago I threw caution to the winds

one sweltering day when a hot santana was blowing

and I was parched. As my car turned a corner

near Tijuana's downtown park, I saw a boy and his

mother selling plastic cups piled high with

spears of melon, papaya, cucumber, pineapple,

with or without a sprinkle of chili powder. I

gratefully sated my thirst, and suffered no ill

effects whatsoever. These fruits have since

become so popular they're sold on the main

tourist drag, where thousands of visitors succumb

as I did.

    Oh, the summer of '74! It will linger in

memory as the advent of the luscious mango peeled

and sculpted to look like an artichoke formed

of orange sherbert. Firmly impaled on a stick,

it can be eaten with or without chili sprinkle.

This is a delicacy of mainland Mexico but never

before had it penetrated Tijuana's Av. Revolucion

nor Ensenada's Blvd. Lopez Mateos. I bought

Ridgely develops this point through a narrative example, packing it with plenty of vivid description.

In paragraph 3 Ridgely shifts to agricultural products and zeroes in on the fruit stands. Again using vivid detail she develops a narrative example, the point of which is that generally fruit is okay to eat. Through the description Ridgely shows how the fruit may be served.

In paragraph 4 Ridgely narrows her focus to the mango. She describes the way it should be served, gives some information about where to get it and the price. She also advises her readers about identifying a good mango and demanding a fresh one.

the sticks all summer (the price finally settled
at 40¢ in Tijuana). It was either that or a
cold beer. If you're tempted, always peer closely
at the mango to verify that the fruit still
glistens moistly. Then you'll know it's freshly
peeled and wondrously juicy. If the mangos look
dry, demand "Fresco!" and the vendor probably
will sigh and peel one just for you. . . .

   If you wish to follow my personal rules
(unscientific but I think sensible) for staying
well in La Frontera, then you will:

In this section Ridgely gives some general guidelines for dining and drinking.

1. Frequent the better restaurants. . . .
    There you're sure to be served bottled
    water. Even if there is nothing terribly
    wrong with local water, bottled water says
    something for the quality of the restaurant,
    don't you agree?
2. Never drink from a faucet, unless you're
    staying at a hotel or resort that has put
    in its own water-purification plant. All
    the other reliable inns will keep a filled
    water pitcher in your room.
3. If you're not used to highly seasoned food,
    don't plunge into it. Anywhere in this
    world unfamiliar cuisine can put you off
    your feet for a few days. Go easy. Some
    estimable Mexican dishes are almost bland.
    Basque and Spanish food is even more so.

Many tourist-oriented restaurants deliberately
serve food which from a Mexican point of view
is underseasoned. You're expected to use
your own discretion.

4. Understand Mexican hot sauce and the art of
applying it.

Ridgely develops point 4 in detail, which suggests Mexican hot sauce may be a real danger to tourists.

    In the last century and during part of this
one, at the mineral-springs resorts which were
the foundation of California tourism, local
yokels often played a cruel joke on naive
Easterners, who were served sulphur water disguised as chicken soup.

In paragraphs 6 and 7 Ridgely develops a general anecdote to make her point — actually, she develops two in a comparative way. The result (implied) of drinking sulphur water and eating too much salsa picante would be the same — several hours in the hotel restroom.

    These days Californians often hear about
another mean joke: Patrons of Mexican restaurants
look on poker-faced, the story goes, as an
innocent, assuming the little dish on his table
to be some sort of cold soup (maybe that gazpacho
he's heard about), downs it with a gulp. What
he's swallowed, of course, is salsa picante--
hot sauce. It will take him some time to put
out his fire.

    Salsa picante, if not sitting on your
restaurant table, will be brought to you. It
comes in several confusing varieties, all loosely
called Salsa. To my mind the best (and the
easiest to learn to like) has tomatoes and other
fresh ingredients such as cilantro and onion
chopped in, adding a fresh wild taste to mitigate
some of the hot. This is known as Salsa Ranchera.

Ridgely follows with some concrete information about salsa and advises which is the best.

```
    There are other varieties.  If you find

yourself in something less than an A-rated

restaurant, beware of a variety that looks like

pure Tabasco.  Because they think it's sort of

self-embalming, the proprietors of these joints

often let it sit around for days till it gets

kind of scummy.

    Were I a newcomer to Mexico's snappy and

satisfying cuisine, I'd eat no hot sauce the

first day.  The second day I'd treat it as if

it were radioactive, experimenting with a micro-

scopic amount on the tip of a spoon and distribut-

ing it as widely as possible in one of my servings.

But eventually I would try it, for this is a

taste which grows on you and can add immeasurably

to the spice of Mexican cookery.
```

She ends with some solid advice cast in a loose procedural form.

How does one eat in a border town? Now you know enough to avoid the greasy food like tacos and churros served in open stalls, and have some information about selecting clams and fruit, along with general advice for dining and drinking. If you were a tourist headed for the Baja border, this information and advice would come in handy.

A final comment on the point of view in Ridgely's piece. She writes in the first person "I" because she comes to the information from personal experience. But if she had written from research, she would probably have used an objective viewpoint. Keep that in mind. When you participate in an experience, write from the "I"; when you are an observer or researcher, write from an objective stance.

WRITING TASK

Write a paper that informs and advises your reader about a subject that falls within your expertise. Keep in mind that this paper is not to give a procedure for readers to follow in a step-by-step fashion but

should cover the problems and situations readers might encounter within a territory new to them. Your paper will guide readers by anticipating any difficulties they might face and by offering guidelines to handle them.

Remember, pick a subject that will capture readers' interest. Use plenty of concrete details to keep readers pinned to the page. Keep in mind, too, that like all extended writing projects this one should include a variety of developmental patterns. And, finally, if appropriate, use a numbering system to arrange the guidelines.

20 OUTSIDE REPORT

In classes other than English, you may be asked to write reports on places you visit. The kind of place will depend on the class — perhaps tide pools for marine biology, museums or galleries for art history, child centers for developmental psychology, or even night spots for social anthropology. Generally, although outside reports deal with different kinds of experiences, your instructors will want you to communicate both your observations and your interpretations.

The obligation to observe and interpret seems clear enough, but sometimes beginning writers go astray when doing outside reports. Some seem to believe their only obligation is to fill up two or three pages that generally describe what they saw and did — a kind of let-me-tell-you-what-I-did-last-Saturday paper. They may include details of what they observed, but they leave the meaning of the observations to the imagination. This is shoddy practice and will usually be rewarded with a shoddy grade.

An effective outside report includes not only a writer's observations but also an interpretation of them — that is, not merely a record of what was seen but also the meaning of what was seen. But how? you may ask. Simple. By applying some of what you've learned in the class through lectures, discussions, and readings. An outside report is another means for you to demonstrate and apply the knowledge you've acquired during the semester.

For example, imagine for a moment that you're taking a sociology class. You've been studying nonverbal behavior as it can be observed in public settings. For a final project, you've been asked to write an outside report based on personal experience with nonverbal behavior. You decide to study waiters and waitresses in a local restaurant. Fine. Probably a good choice. You go to the restaurant and sit in an unobtrusive spot that gives you a clear view of most of the tables and the counter. You select two or three subjects to study. You record every significant gesture, body stance, facial expression. You leave with a notebook full of raw material, much more than you'll need for the full report. At home you sift through the material and organize it into rough form. Now you're ready to write. When you write the paper, you not only describe your observations but also interpret their meaning based on information you've gained from a study of nonverbal behavior. This final step of responding to the material from an informed viewpoint is what the instructor will be looking for when evaluating your paper.

Now study the following paragraph. It is a discussion paragraph taken from a report generated by the above assignment. As you read, notice how the writer mixes interpretation with his observations. Although the paragraph is mainly developed through concrete description, the bits of interpretation focus the details.

> I noticed that the waiter would nonverbally expose his interest in young female customers and his disinterest in middle-aged female ones. I watched him wait on two women in their early twenties. When he took their orders, he leaned forward and glanced with them at the menus as if he were acting as a friendly advisor. After collecting the menus, he paused for a moment to chat although neither one's facial expression showed much interest in what he was saying. While he talked and the women sipped from their water glasses, he dangled the menus at his side as if to suggest he was ready to receive their interest. Later, when he waited on three older women, perhaps in their late thirties, he stood erect, like a private during a military inspection, and hardly looked at them as he wrote on an order pad. He didn't lean forward or try to start a conversation, even though the women seemed friendly. When one called him back to request another item, he stood with the menus held before him as if they served as a protective barrier.

The topic sentence sets up the interpretation of this writer's observations — the waiter nonverbally exposes his interest and disinterest. The writer then details his observations in order to support his interpretation. He slips in fragments of interpretation, such as "acting as a friendly advisor," "ready to receive their interest," and "the menus held before him as if they served as a protective barrier" — which help focus the details. This is an effective paragraph, which not only reports what the writer saw but also demonstrates some understanding of nonverbal expression.

Sometimes you may be assigned to do an outside report that doesn't require a specific application of what you've learned during a class. Instead it may involve appreciation. No matter, because your obligations are the same — you must deliver a detailed rendering of your observations and your responses to them. The difference is that your responses will be more subjective — they will come out of personal awareness rather than out of a body of knowledge you've mastered.

The following paragraph is taken from an outside report on a photography exhibit. After giving a general description of the exhibit and the background of the photographer, the writer presents her responses to particular works. She begins this discussion paragraph with a topic sentence that identifies a quality of one photograph, then follows with a detailed description before presenting her response to it.

> Harold Chan's photograph "Night Wood" has a haunting quality. Fog rolls through the pines, but the fog looks more like steam. Leaning against a tree, a man dressed in black and wearing a white mask stares directly at the observer. With fog swirling around him, he seems ghostly, perhaps demonic. I thought of nightmare images. I felt pinned by his round black eyes. I felt almost as if I had been caught in a horrible dream and was unable to awaken. It seems Chan is depicting the strange forces that exist in the mind's forests where the sleeper may helplessly stumble.

This writer has carefully combined her observations with responses. Concrete description helps the reader see the experience, but the interpretation of the experience helps focus the piece.

There will be two distinct phases in writing an outside report. First, you'll set out to prewrite the report the way you would any task. You collect the raw material to use in the final draft by capturing concrete details and your responses to the experience. This note taking is an active part of the assignment. Don't try to write a report from memory. Such reports usually turn out inaccurate and dull.

After you've made your visit and collected notes, you begin the second phase — the actual writing. Begin by sifting through your material. Reread your notes. Reflect on what you've recorded. Is there anything to add? Do you see a general shape? Is there an outstanding point you might use to organize your report?

The general structure of an outside report is much like that of a deductive essay. Begin with an introduction that gives the instructor some background information and presents a central point. In this case the central point will capture the general point of your paper — the conclusion you've drawn from the experience. For instance, the report from which we took the first example has this central point:

> Waiters and waitresses expose their attitudes toward customers through nonverbal behavior.

The report from which the second example came has this central point:

> Harold Chan's black-and-white photographs have a haunting theme.

Once you've decided on a central point, you will be able to cut excess detail from your paper and focus your thought.

With the central point chosen and the introduction written, you need merely to organize the remaining material into a discussion. Remember, be sure to include not only detail but your interpretation of the detail. Keep in mind, too, that the discussion paragraphs can be built on any of the patterns you've mastered — development by example, comparison, contrast, analogy, classification, and so on.

The conclusion of an outside report is usually short, perhaps a brief reminder of the central point or a further observation that grows out of the experience and relates to the class you've been writing it for.

A final thought. When you write an outside report, don't spend any time telling your instructor why you went where you went. Don't include information that isn't related to the experience itself.

> Last Saturday my boyfriend and I were just sitting around the house because it was too cold for the beach and the snow had arrived in the mountains and we didn't have anything to do, so we went to do my report at the Marineland shark exhibit.

Save this kind of stuffing for another kind of turkey.

WRITING TASK ═══════════════════════════════════

We suggest you select a report that would be appropriate for one of your other classes. If you have not been assigned an outside report in another class, you might visit an art exhibit, museum, job site, nursery school, zoo, or even another college to use for a report.

Remember:

1. Make your visit and compile ample notes that include both details and responses.
2. Develop a central point to organize your material.

3. Write an introduction that gives your instructor any pertinent background information.
4. Write a discussion several paragraphs long giving the particulars of your report. Be sure to combine your observations with interpretation. Keep in mind that this is a chance to show your instructor that you can apply some information you've learned during the course.
5. End the report with a brief conclusion.

21 BOOK REVIEW

In newspapers and magazines reviews usually deal with recently published books. Reviewers, therefore, must assume that their audiences don't know the works. They see their role as mainly that of guides — persons who acquaint readers with a book's content and make judgments about its value. Since most reviews are short, ranging anywhere from 750 to 1500 words, a reviewer hasn't the space to comment on every aspect of a particular book but must select the outstanding features or the ones which will hold the greatest interest for the audience. There's a danger here, for if the focus is too narrow, the reviewer is not doing a good job of guiding the prospective reader. The reviewer must tread the middle ground between being too specific and too general.

When writing a book review, you will be treading the same path as the reviewer. You are bound to present some general information, yet you must develop enough specific information to make your report valuable. You will also need to work in your judgments about the quality of the book based on the specifics you select to develop. A big job, but not impossible. Although we can't give you any hard and fast rules for writing a book review, we can give you some general guidelines that should serve most of your book reviewing purposes.

Generally, you'll open with a paragraph that gives some specific information: title, author's name, type of work, author's general intent (which for a work of nonfiction can usually be expressed in a quotation), and your general attitude about the work.

After the introduction, you'll follow with an overview that should be designed to give the reader a general feeling for the book. If the work is fiction, identify the situation; write a brief description of the setting, atmosphere, and historical time; and summarize plot. If the work is nonfiction, you'll do much the same, but instead of a plot summary, you might present any important background, capture the general movement, and identify the high points of the work. If you are reporting on a collection of essays, you might give the collection's general focus and summarize representative pieces. Keep in mind that all this information should be integrated, not boxed into little compartments. We also suggest that before you begin an overview you ask yourself what your intended reader needs to know to decide whether or not to read the book. Remember, too, that no matter how you go about writing the overview, it should be no longer than a quarter of the length of your entire paper. Your goal is to give a reader a feeling for the work, not to rewrite it.

You'll follow the overview with several paragraphs that closely examine important elements in the work. If the work is fiction, you might explore how the writer deals with character, take a closer look at plot elements, or examine theme. You can sometimes handle a nonfiction work similarly: if a person is the focus, you might trace how the author handles his or her life; instead of plot, you might deal with the story line or life history. If the work deals with ideas, however, then you'll need to examine the central thought. When dealing with a collection of essays, we suggest you select representative pieces and examine them. You might classify, compare, and contrast them according to theme, style, or point of view. Throughout this section, you should quote from the work, but be sure the quotations fit what you are saying about the work.

After talking about some specific elements, you'll move on to evaluate the work and to conclude your paper. Most book reviews present balanced evaluations, the reviewers presenting both the strong and weak points, although in the end a review may tip toward recommending, recommending with qualification, or not recommending the book. Do the same when you evaluate a work. Select several specific examples you believe represent the book's strengths and weaknesses. Don't hedge. Be forthcoming with your judgments, but always support them with examples, usually in the form of quotations. After working your way through the evaluation, you'll be ready to make a recommendation. Is the book of value? Should it be read? If so, by whom — specialists, everyone, children? For what reasons? The recommendation, usually only a few lines, concludes the paper.

Sounds simple, right? If you carefully read the work you've selected for the review, it should be. After all, the overall pattern is clear:

Introduction, usually a single paragraph	Includes the title, author's name, type of work, general intent, your attitude
Overview, usually one or two paragraphs	Generally acquaints the reader with the work

Close examination, usually several paragraphs	A close look at significant elements of the work through analysis and quotations
Evaluation, usually several paragraphs	The weighing of the work's strong and weak points with the judgments supported by examples or quotations
Conclusion	The closing recommendation and evaluation

Although the overall pattern of the book review is fairly rigid, what writers do within it is flexible. Consequently, rather than give you a single illustration, we want to present several tips on how you might handle the tough spots.

The opening paragraph is a place where many beginning writers stumble. Remember, the introduction should include the title, author's name, type of work, general intent, and your attitude. Fine — no problems here. But too often the information is presented in Dick and Jane prose, something like this:

> This book is titled *The Executioner's Song.* It is written by Norman Mailer. It is a biography of killer Gary Gilmore that covers the time when he was once released from prison until his execution by a firing squad. Norman Mailer writes, "This book does its best to be a factual account of the activities of Gary Gilmore and the men and women associated with him in the period from April 9, 1976, when he was released from the United States Penitentiary at Marion, Illinois, until his execution a little more than nine months later in Utah State Prison." Norman Mailer's account is riveting, though at times he burdens the reader with unnecessary details.

All the important information is in here, but the passage is written in such a pedestrian manner that only the most dedicated reader would plow through it. Don't write an introduction in this manner. Instead try to integrate the information into flowing sentences. An obvious way to go about it is to cut the clutter and combine the sentences where you can. In the last paragraph, can you see a reason for stating the author, title, and type of work in single sentences? Does the type of book have to be stated, since the quotation makes its nature clear? A revised version, one that's much more effective, might look like this:

Norman Mailer's *The Executioner's Song* is "a factual account of the activities of Gary Gilmore and the men and women associated with him in the period from April 9, 1976, when he was released from the United States Penitentiary at Marion, Illinois, until his execution a little more than nine months later in Utah State Prison." Mailer's version of those nine months is riveting, even if he at times burdens the reader with unnecessary details.

The revised introduction not only gets the information to the reader; it flows. Work to get your introduction to flow; integrate the information; don't write Dick and Jane prose. The revised version also sets the principal verb tense for the entire report. Notice that it is written in present tense: *The Executioner's Song is* "a factual account . . . Mailer's version of those nine months *is* riveting, even if he at times *burdens* the reader . . ." The present tense is the principal tense you should use for book reviews. Also notice that Mailer's full name is only used once. After you've identified the author by his full name, refer to him or her only by the last. Don't use Mr. or Mrs. or Ms., either — use only the last name.

Now let's look at another example to see how someone else might handle an introduction to a book review. As you read this paragraph, notice how much information you get about the book in question — but not too much. The writer merely wants to prepare you for what's coming, not overload you with too many specifics.

> "What parents have to learn is how to become a match for their children, wise to their ways and capable of guiding them without letting them run wild or stifling them," claims Rudolf Dreikurs in *Children: The Challenge.* Dreikurs's self-help book offers parents ways to handle problems in child rearing that could improve if not revolutionize the relationships between parents and children.

Beginning writers sometimes stumble in the overview section because they feel overwhelmed with the task of creating a feeling for a work in such a short space. Aside from a paragraph of summary that captures the highlights of a book, you may also use a catalogue that captures the tone, atmosphere, or setting.

> Mailer creates life as lived in the rural West. In the section called "Western Voices" he evokes people struggling to make a living in gas stations, roadside cafés, movie theaters, small factories, farms, and country stores. It's a world filled with pick-up trucks, six-packs, country music, Monday night football, deer hunting, motorcycles, and honky-tonk violence. The city slicker

is suspect and the easy buck is hard to come by. The four-wheel drive Blazer, not the sleek Mercedes, is the status symbol. It is a world of macho, not of sophistication.

The catalogue thrusts the reader into the scene. Through the multiple listing of particulars, the writer can sweep into a work and give the reader a feeling for what it contains. Try it. In the overview a catalogue will help you to move in broad steps.

In the section that takes a closer look at the work, be sure to use quotations wherever you can to develop your thought. For instance, one writer of a book report on Dennis McNally's *Desolate Angel, a Biography: Jack Kerouac, the Beat Generation and America* wrote this paragraph to demonstrate one of the work's outstanding elements:

> McNally gives more than a detailed portrait of Kerouac and a historical rendering of the beats. He probes at the creative motivations behind their acts. He points out that Kerouac felt obligated to tell the truth "in all its delicate and hideous glory." He goes on to generalize that other artists of the period, such as musician Charles "Bird" Parker and painter Jackson Pollock, were motivated by similar principles. McNally writes, "Each artist had concluded that in the limbo of war and Cold War, only the most risky commitment to personal creativity and intuition could allow them to transcend the times." It seems that McNally isn't just speaking of artists of this time, but artists of all time.

When possible, let the author speak to your reader through quotations. But remember, you have an obligation to show the reader the significance of the quotation. Don't just quote and leave the reader to figure out its significance.

Here's another example from a review of John D. MacDonald's thriller *The Green Ripper*. In this paragraph the writer is trying to illustrate an important aspect of MacDonald's vision:

> Often MacDonald's view of the world seems grim. He creates a society headed for Apocalypse. "All the major currencies will collapse. Trade will cease. Without trade, without the mechanical-scientific apparatus running, the planet won't support its four billion people, or perhaps even half that. . . . There will be fear, hate, anger, death. The new barbarism. There will be plague and poison. And then the new Dark Ages." But keep in mind that a good thriller writer must create the potential for chaos. Would the actions of his hero in a stable world seem worth reading?

You should use quotations not only in the close examination of the work's important elements, but also in the evaluation. One writer reporting on Thomas Thompson's *Serpentine* wrote this evaluative paragraph. Notice how the writer has strung fragments of quotations together. Using several short quotations is often the only way you can support a broad judgment.

> A minor flaw in the book comes from Thompson's flagrant use of clichés in place of more thoughtful prose. He writes, "It was the dead of winter, 1967, and the prison walls were as cold as ice." He refers to Sobhraj's court room chicanery as a "bag of tricks." His girlfriend clung to him "like moss on an oak." Sobhraj tried to pass their tawdry affair off as an "epic romance more poignant than Romeo and Juliet." Trite expressions and clichés such as these mark every other page and blemish an otherwise powerful performance.

At other times you won't be able to support a judgment with quotations. Then you need to fall back on summarizing broad points to shore up the evaluation. In the paragraph that follows the one above, the reviewer of *Serpentine* pulls together some outstanding features of Thompson's central figure to support another evaluative point:

> Much of Thompson's powerful performance comes from his fascinating portrait of Sobhraj as a suave yet grisly nomad full of contradictions. A man without formal education who learned to survive in the rubble of Saigon, along the docks of Marseilles, on the boulevards of Paris, in the marketplaces of Delhi, and in several prisons, Sobhraj mastered ten languages, studied French and Indian law and read thousands of books ranging from thrillers to Eastern philosophy. He was a man moved by some ill-defined dream of material success that sent him blazing across much of Europe, though the Middle East, and into Asia, while he spouted romantic ideals and supported himself by befriending tourists, drugging them, and stealing their valuables. Born a bastard to an Indo-Chinese mother and Indian father in French-dominated Saigon under Japanese occupation, he was never able to establish permanent connections with either parent. But during the peak of his criminal career, he surrounded himself with hapless travelers he called his "family," then methodically poisoned or bludgeoned them to death and left the bodies smoldering at roadsides, dumped in the jungles, or floating in the surf. A complex portrait, one that should make any traveler to exotic places suspect the stranger's friendly smile and firm handshake.

As for the conclusion, we suggested that it should flow from the evaluation section. Beginning writers sometimes stumble here because they try to say too much. Since by this point the reader will already have a clear idea of your attitude toward the work, you'll usually need to do little more than write two or three lines to tie a recommendation together.

> Thompson's *Serpentine* is for every reader fascinated by the bizarre and criminal. It moves swiftly, and if you don't mind the bumpity-bump of the clichés, then you'll be enthralled roaming much of the world with Thompson as he tracks the life of Charles Sobhraj.

When you write a conclusion to a book review, keep in mind that besides making a recommendation and identifying the potential reader, you should also reflect your opening attitude and evaluation and rename the work and author.

WRITING TASK

In order to facilitate this task, your instructor will probably provide you with a list of books that will be appropriate. We suggest you take the list to the library or bookstore and browse through several of the books to find one that interests you. After you've made a choice, read the work carefully, noting its interesting aspects. Once you have a solid understanding of the book use the guidelines in the preceding discussion to write the review.

Remember, in writing the review try to give the reader a broad understanding of the work as well as your evaluation. Finally, arrange your report in this fashion:

1. An introduction that presents the title, author's name, type of work, general intent, and your attitude.
2. An overview that acquaints the reader with the whole work.
3. Several paragraphs that examine specific aspects of the work.
4. Several paragraphs of evaluation that focus on the work's strengths and weaknesses.
5. A closing paragraph that identifies the potential reader, renames the author and title, and reflects the opening attitude and evaluation.

22 PERSONAL ESSAY: CURRENT LIFE

If you've been doing Daily Writing, during the second week you collected raw material from your current life. You began by writing an overview that captured this period's dominant activities, impressions, and fantasies. On the following days of that week, you focused your writing by enlarging individual aspects of your current life. You described where you live, personal possessions, important activities, and special places. You also recorded your personal associations with these aspects of your life. Although roughly written, these entries probably come together as part of an account of who you are. We hope that they serve as a first step in achieving what Henry David Thoreau asks of every writer, "a simple and sincere account of his own life, and not merely what he has heard of other men's lives."

To go beyond the general knowledge you've acquired from family, friends, and society at large — to go beyond what you "have heard of other men's lives" — is to approach a deeper understanding of how you fit into the world, an understanding of who you are and what you want to be. Now, after the entries reflecting your current life have had time to incubate, we suggest you write a polished account of your current life — one that not only communicates the details of this period, but that also communicates your personal insights.

WRITING TASK

Write an inductive, associational, or deductive essay that gives an account of your current life. We recommend you begin by reviewing the Daily Writing entries to stimulate more thoughts. Record your thoughts. As you read and record new thoughts, make a general obser-

vation about your recent experience. Shape the generalization into a central idea and use it to select material for your essay. Then, once you've selected the material, use the central idea to organize the paper's development.

Remember, whereas the Daily Writing entries may be rambling, the finished essay should be organized and developed with focused paragraphs. Never set your reader adrift in unfocused material. Your central idea, although not necessarily stated, should be clear to any attentive reader.

23 PERSONAL ESSAY: DREAMS

Sigmund Freud, the founder of psychoanalysis, described dreams as forbidden wishes symbolically disguised to preserve the dreamer's sleep. But Freud drew his conclusions from limited information. He didn't know, as today's researchers know, that virtually all mammals dream. What forbidden wishes, one may wonder, could birds and infants have?

Since Freud's time, researchers have taken a new attitude toward dreams. They reject the notion that a set of standardized interpretations can be applied to them. They maintain that each person creates individual meaning from dream experience. For instance, if ten people were to dream of wandering through a strange city, the dream would have ten different meanings, one for each dreamer.

These contemporary researchers also maintain that dreams serve as bridges between our conscious and unconscious experience. Many researchers maintain that dreams sometimes indicate the dreamer's destiny by pointing out unrecognized aspects of the dreamer or by focusing on another person who embodies the dreamer's potential. Sometimes dreams provide what is missing in the dreamer's waking life — love, friendship, success, adventure, travel, or freedom. Dreams can sometimes serve as releases from tension, pain, fear, or other emotions that may interfere with waking life. Finally, today's researchers point out the practical nature of dreams. Just as dreams have sometimes helped artists and inventors solve problems in their work, they sometimes serve the same purpose in every dreamer's life.

If you've been keeping dreams as part of your daily writing practice, then perhaps you've made connections between your dreams and aspects of your waking life. If so, then you might like to develop dreams as a subject for an essay.

WRITING TASK

Begin by rereading your Daily Writing entries on dreams. Have any given you an insight into your life? Have any offered a solution to a problem you've faced? If so, shape a central point from your observation and use it to develop a deductive essay that deals with your dream experience as related to your waking experience.

24 RESPONDING TO QUOTATIONS

The writing tasks given on the next few pages ask you to respond in some fashion to the words of others. Each task begins with one or more quotations expressing an attitude, insight, or personal opinion. You should read the quotations carefully, relate them to your own experience or knowledge, then write an essay responding in some way to this stimulation.

These tasks are open ended. We are not asking necessarily that you agree or disagree with the quotations. Your paper shouldn't be limited to either an answer to or an amplification of the ideas expressed. Rather, you should let your mind speculate about the quotations and see where your thoughts lead.

Perhaps the quotation will arouse emotions, bring to mind nostalgic memories, or lead to philosophical thoughts. Take, for example, a short quotation from the writing of George Santayana: "To me it seems a dreadful indignity to have a soul controlled by geography." How could you respond in writing to this quotation? You would begin, of course, with prewriting — jotting down the thoughts that go through your mind as you read it.

- The old cliché — travel broadens the mind. Is it true? My aunt and uncle's trip to Europe just reinforced all their prejudices against foreign things.
- Haven't traveled much myself, so can't support or deny the cliché from personal experience.
- Why "soul"? More important than the mind, I guess. Harder to pin down than thought. He's not talking about knowledge in the sense of facts and stories to relate, but about something more fundamental, something closer to the self.

- A soul controlled by geography would be a person imprisoned in some fashion — tied down rather than soaring free — missing out on full potential — the fullness of experience.
- Americans are criticized for this — being provincial — not willing to see the value of other ways of life.

  Example — languages. We think everyone should speak English. I've read that this is a problem in our diplomatic relations — not only do our reps not speak the language, they ignore customs too. What do we miss when we travel and can't speak with the people? All we have for the experience is a lot of slides.
- The other word I wonder about is indignity. What does it mean here? Being insulted is an indignity, or having pie shoved in your face — not exactly what he means. Here it is more personal — something you do to yourself — a kind of failure to reach potential again.
- Even if we don't travel we can learn about other ways of doing things.

  Example — influx of Vietnamese gives us a chance to relate to another culture, probably in a better way than a whirlwind tour. Trouble is we sit back and wait for them to adopt our ways (and language). How do they manage to study in American colleges?
- The world is becoming Americanized, they say. Coca-Cola in Egypt and McDonald's everywhere. I read that the most successful McDonald's stand is in Japan. And rock music — is that an American export or just a world phenomenon of the times? Is it a way to get beyond the limits of geography?
- Jeans and T-shirts. I saw a picture of a little boy in Cambodia wearing a Butterfinger T-shirt. Where did he get it?

This line of thinking has taken us quite a way away from Santayana's original words, but the journey has suggested any number of possible papers:

- How your aunt and uncle's trip was wasted — what they failed to get out of it
- Where you would like to go and why
- The intangible benefits your own travels have given you
- Your experiences with the language barrier
- Your experiences with people from other countries now settled in your community
- Your failure to learn from newly arrived immigrants
- The good and bad aspects of Americanizing the whole world

It doesn't matter if any of these topics speak directly to what Santayana had in mind. The quotations should be seen as stimulators only. Use them as springboards to your own thinking.

The short quotations presented here tend to be general in phrasing; they are statements of attitudes, insights, or personal opinions. The specifics which support such statements are missing. But your paper should include them. If, for example, you choose to respond to the Santayana quotation by writing about the benefits you have gained from your travel experiences, don't just say they have helped you appreciate other customs; get specific — give the reader the anecdotes and the individual experiences which illustrate the point.

The quotations and questions on the following pages are designed to get you into the prewriting portion of the task. We hope they will be helpful, but ignore them if you don't need them. In no case should you assume that you must write in response to·any of these questions. Open up your responses. Give yourself permission to let your mind wander over the entire landscape of possibilities.

MAY SARTON

The reasons for depression are not so interesting as the way one handles it, simply to stay alive. This morning I woke at four and lay awake for an hour or so in a bad state. It is raining again. I got up finally and went about the daily chores, waiting for the sense of doom to lift — and what did it was watering the house plants. Suddenly joy came back because I was fulfilling a simple need, a living one. Dusting never has this effect (and that may be why I am such a poor housekeeper!), but feeding the cats when they are hungry, giving Punch clean water, makes me suddenly feel calm and happy.

Whatever peace I know rests in the natural world, in feeling myself a part of it, even in a small way.

Does this quotation arouse emotions in you? Do you envy the writer's apparent ability to find joy in such simple things? Do you reject the idea? Do you have your own ways of fighting depression? How big a role does the "natural world" play in your daily living? What simple things bring you peace and calm? Or do you really prefer excitement and a more hectic pace? Do you have friends or neighbors who might make interesting studies of either the simple life or the high-pressure one?

WRITING TASK

Write an essay of your own design that reflects your consideration of the quotation, comments, and questions that follow. Remember to use various patterns of development and details from personal experience and knowledge.

ROBINSON JEFFERS

I have never been ambitious, but it seemed unpleasant just the same to have accomplished nothing, but exactly nothing, along the only course that permanently interested me. There are times when one forgets for a moment that life's value is life; any further accomplishment is of very little importance comparatively.

FYODOR DOSTOEVSKI

Perhaps the only goal on earth toward which mankind is striving lies in the process of attaining, in other words in life itself, and not in the things to be attained.

MICHEL DE MONTAIGNE

The great and glorious masterpiece of man is to live to the point. All other things — to reign, to hoard, to build — are, at most, but inconsiderable props and appendages.

All three of the above quotations stress the importance of process (living) over product (accomplishments). How much do we judge others and ourselves on the basis of product? Competitive sports at all levels is one obvious example. Can you think of others? Can you think of times in your life when the experience itself turned out to be more important or worthwhile than the end result? Is the pursuit of a goal as important as the achievement? Or is lack of achievement really failure? How should success in life be measured?

WRITING TASK

Write an essay of your own design that reflects your consideration of the quotations and questions. Remember to use various patterns of development and details from personal experience and knowledge.

MARK KRAM

All of this brings us down to marbles, not the argot for brains but the real thing: perfectly round; so smooth; brilliantly colored; as precious to generations of children as any diamond. Has anyone seen a marble lately? Has anyone seen a marble in the hand of a kid? Most likely the answer is no, for the only things kids carry these days are transistor radios, slices of pizza and tickets to rock concerts. The marble belongs to a time that now seems otherworldly, when trees lined big city blocks as far as the eye could see, when barley soup was supper three times a week, when children had secret places.

Have things changed much since you were a kid? What did you do for fun when you were eight, or ten, or twelve? What did you do finally on "Mommy-there's-nothing-to-do" days? Schoolboys and girls used to survive the year by moving mysteriously through a cycle of ill-defined seasons — marble season, jacks season, mumblety-peg season, bottle-cap season — all without the aid of any adult direction or organization. Now, even the very young, boys and girls alike, get involved in soccer season, football season, basketball season, baseball season, camping organizations, and "lessons" of all kinds. Old-timers will tell you something valuable has been lost because of all this organization, carried out under constant adult supervision. What do you think? Should kids be left alone more? Should they be allowed to invent their own activities? Are their lives too scheduled? What's the difference as you see it, between carrying a bag of marbles and carrying a transistor radio?

WRITING TASK

Write an essay of your own design that reflects your consideration of the quotation, comments, and questions. Remember to use various patterns of development and details from personal experience and knowledge.

JOHN HOLT

From the very beginning of school we make books and reading a constant source of possible failure and public humiliation. When children are little we make them read aloud, before the teacher and other children, so that we can be sure they "know" all the words they are reading. This means that when they don't know a word, they are going to make a mistake, right in front of everyone. Instantly they are made to realize that they have done something wrong. Perhaps some of the other children will begin to wave their hands and say, "Ooooh! O-o-o-o!" Perhaps they will just giggle or nudge each other, or make a face. Perhaps the teacher will say, "Are you sure?" or ask someone else what he thinks. Or perhaps, if the teacher is kindly, she will just smile a sweet, sad smile — often one of the most painful punishments a child can suffer in school. In any case, the child who has made the mistake knows he has made it, and feels foolish, stupid, and ashamed, just as any of us would in his shoes.

Have you ever felt humiliated in a classroom? By a teacher? By classmates? Can you recall details of the experience and how you felt? Have incidents of this nature influenced how you feel about being in classrooms even now? How *do* you feel about being in classrooms? Comfortable? Uneasy? If allowed your choice, where do you sit? Why? Do you prefer an active or passive role as a student in a classroom? Do you prefer lectures or class discussions? Why? Can you recall particular classes at any level of your schooling that you either looked forward to or dreaded? Can you bring to mind details of the scene and specifics about how you felt while there? Do you agree with John Holt that having students read aloud is a poor teaching method? If you were a teacher at any level of schooling, what would you do differently than your teacher at that level did? Have teachers or have fellow students had more to do with your attitudes and behavior in classes? Have you ever done anything really stupid in a class? Can you tell about it without embarrassment? What punishments are the most effective? The least?

WRITING TASK

Write an essay of your own design that reflects your consideration of the quotation and questions. Remember to use various patterns of development and details from personal experience and knowledge.

CHRISTOPHER LASCH

The problem of women's work and women's equality needs to be examined from a perspective more radical than any that has emerged from the feminist movement. It has to be seen as a special case of the general rule that work takes precedence over family. The most important indictment of the present organization of work is that it forces women to choose between their desire for economic self-sufficiency and the needs of their children. Instead of blaming the family for this state of affairs, we should blame the relentless demands of the job market itself. Instead of asking how women can be liberated from the family, we should ask how work can be reorganized — humanized — so as to make it possible for women to compete economically with men without sacrificing their families.

How true is Lasch's statement that there is a "general rule that work takes precedence over family"? Is it equally true for men and women? Is the present pattern of work in our country the best we can devise? Could it be reorganized and rendered more human? Could it be made more meaningful for the workers? Could it be structured to allow both men and women greater flexibility in their lives?

Ask yourself questions such as these pertaining to your job or what you know about the demands of work in general. Then do some creative thinking about how our work lives could be better.

WRITING TASK

> **Write an essay of your own design that reflects your consideration of the quotation and questions. Remember to use various patterns of development and details from personal experience and knowledge.**

ROBERT M. LINDNER

Abroad in the world today is a monstrous falsehood, a consummate fabrication, to which all social agencies have loaned themselves and into which most men, women and children have been seduced. . . . "The Eleventh Commandment"; for such indeed has become the injunction: You Must Adjust! . . . this is the legend imprinted in every schoolbook, the invisible message on every blackboard. Our schools have become factories for the manufacture of robots.

e. e. cummings

to be nobody-but-yourself in a world which is doing its best, night and day, to make you everybody else — means to fight the hardest battle which any human being can fight . . .

Lindner's statement was written in 1956. Based on your experience, is it true today? What examples can you think of to support or deny his statement that "You Must Adjust . . . is the invisible message on every blackboard"? Why does he call the message invisible? Is "adjustment" a good thing for the individual and the society in spite of Lindner's attitude? What are some of the victories and defeats you have had in what Cummings describes as the battle to be "nobody-but-yourself"? Are you still fighting the battle or do you find it more comfortable to be "everybody else"?

WRITING TASK

> **Write an essay of your own design that reflects your consideration of the quotations and questions. Remember to use various patterns of development and details from personal experience and knowledge.**

ROBERT THEOBALD

Our key problem stems from the fact that we have made the value of a man synonymous with the economic value of the toil he performs; we fail to recognize that people should have a claim on resources even if they do not toil. The measure of destruction of our values is, I believe, shown in the fact that those living in an industrial society find it natural that people do not receive an adequate amount of food, clothing, and shelter even though there is surplus food in storage and the possibility of producing more housing and more clothing if we gave people the money to buy them. We can contrast this view with that of the so-called primitive societies; in many of those it was literally impossible to starve unless the whole community was starving. George Peter Murdoch, the celebrated anthropologist, described the reaction of one group of natives when he tried to explain the problem of the poor in Western countries. There was stark disbelief: "How can he have no food? Does he have no friends? How can he have no house? Does he have no neighbors?"

Do you agree with Theobald's statement that "we have made the value of a man synonymous with the economic value of the toil he performs"? Do we assume that people with high-paying jobs are somehow more worthy than others? What kinds of work or careers do you associate with high pay? With human worth? Are the two lists the same? What are some of the ways our culture tells poorer people they are less worthy? Have you ever seen people in your neighborhood doing acts of direct charity for more needy neighbors? Or is your neighborhood so homogeneous economically that you wouldn't be able to find a needy neighbor even if you looked? Are your own acts of charity largely done through contributions to organizations so you never see the recipients? If so, is faceless charity good or bad? How well do you know your neighbors? Have you ever known someone who had tremendous pride and dignity in spite of a low economic position? Does your own sense of personal worth require that you make a lot of money? How effective are government programs to help those in need? Have you ever had personal experience with welfare programs, unemployment insurance, or public assistance of any kind? If so, what are your thoughts about it?

WRITING TASK

Write an essay of your own design that reflects your consideration of the quotation and questions. Remember to use various patterns of development and details from personal experience and knowledge.

CHRISTOPHER LASCH

In an age of diminishing expectations, the Protestant virtues no longer excite enthusiasm. Inflation erodes investments and savings. Advertising undermines the horror of indebtedness, exhorting the consumer to buy now and pay later. As the future

becomes menacing and uncertain, only fools put off until tomorrow the fun they can have today. A profound shift in our
sense of time has transformed work habits, values, and the definition of success. Self-preservation has replaced self-improve-
ment as the goal of earthly existence. In a lawless, violent, and
unpredictable society, in which the normal conditions of everyday life come to resemble those formerly confined to the underworld, men live by their wits. They hope not so much to prosper
as simply to survive, although survival itself increasingly demands a large income. In earlier times, the self-made man took
pride in his judgement of character and probity; today he anx-
iously scans the faces of his fellows not so as to evaluate their
credit but in order to gauge their susceptibility to his own blan-
dishments. He practices the classic arts of seduction and with
the same indifference to moral niceties, hoping to win your
heart while picking your pocket. The happy hooker stands in
place of Horatio Alger as the prototype of personal success. If
Robinson Crusoe embodied the ideal type of economic man, the
hero of bourgeois society in its ascendance, the spirit of Moll
Flanders presides over its dotage.

How do you feel about Lasch's indictment of our society? Are we as
selfish and indifferent to moral niceties as he says? Can you relate his
attack to specific examples of situations and people you know? Or do
you think he overstates his case? What are the Protestant virtues? Do
you and those you know subscribe to them? Live by them? Or are they
old-fashioned now? Do you agree that in an uncertain world "only fools
put off until tomorrow the fun they can have today"? Have you had any
personal experiences with debt? Have you ever been seduced into buy-
ing something you should have waited for until you could afford it?
Does advertising ever make you feel you "need" something you really
don't? Does advertising have an influence upon our definition of "success"? Do we really live in a lawless, violent, and unpredictable society?
Can you think of ways our day-to-day activities reflect values formerly
confined to the underworld? What values are more important to you
than economic well-being? Are other people often trying to manipulate
you? Do you manipulate others? Who is Horatio Alger and what do you
think of the values attached to his name?

WRITING TASK

Write an essay of your own design that reflects your consideration
of the quotation and questions. Remember to use various patterns of
development and details from personal experience and knowledge.

MORTON HUNT

The record of man's inhumanity to man is horrifying, when one compiles it — enslavement, castration, torture, rape, mass slaughter in war after war. But who has compiled the record of man's kindness to man — the trillions of acts of gentleness and goodness, the helping hands, smiles, shared meals, kisses, gifts, healings, rescues? If we were no more than murderous predators, with a freakish lack of inhibition against slaughtering our own species, we would have been at a terrible competitive disadvantage compared with other animals; if this were the central truth of our nature, we would scarcely have survived, multiplied and become the dominant species on earth. Man does have an aggressive instinct, but it is not naturally or inevitably directed to killing his own kind. He is a beast and perhaps at times the cruelest beast of all — but sometimes he is also the kindest beast of all. He is not all good and not perfectable, but he is not all bad and not wholly unchangeable or unimprovable. That is the only basis on which one can hope for him; but it is enough.

Humans are very critical of humanity. Why is this so? Why are newspapers and newscasts so full of man's inhumanity to man? Why are history textbooks largely the records of conflict? Is anything accomplished by all this attention to our failures? Is kindness boring? Why not make a contribution to the record Hunt calls for, "the record of man's kindness to man"? When did you last see an instance of human love freely given? What examples come to mind of people helping other people? Do you know of instances where one human risked his comfort or life for another? Do you recall an incident where you made yourself feel good by showing thoughtfulness to another? How about recording the time your day was brightened by the smile or kind words of someone else? Can you do it? Can you make such a paper interesting? Can you make it real rather than sentimental?

WRITING TASK

Write an essay of your own design that reflects your consideration of the quotation and questions. Remember to use various patterns of development and details from personal experience and knowledge.

PART THREE

DAILY WRITING

This section includes eight week-long units of thirty-minute writing tasks. The writing you do will be free-flow, a form of prewriting. Besides giving you regular practice sessions, we're trying to show you that one way to find something to write about is to write. These thirty-minute tasks take no special skill or knowledge. For instance, one week you'll spend the thirty-minute practice sessions writing about your current life. The first thirty minutes you'll describe what's taking place in your life at the moment. For the next sessions you'll write about the contents of your wallet, purse, or medicine cabinet or about interesting activities and places. During the successive weeks, you'll write about such things as past experiences, world events, people you know, even dreams and fantasies — but for no longer than thirty minutes. Besides giving you daily practice at writing, the raw material you collect can serve as a resource for the formal assignments you'll be doing.

25 KEEPING A JOURNAL

To say it right out, this section is going to ask you to spend some time doing a great deal of writing. If you spend twenty or thirty minutes each day writing one or two pages in a notebook, your graded work will get better.

Twenty or thirty minutes! Every day?

Yes. A very simple command — *sit down and write* — but one that is hard to meet.

Too many forces compete for your attention. The obvious ones, family, work, friends, and other classes, have all staked out claims on your time. The less obvious ones seem to have come with the modern territory: disc jockeys and discos, soap operas, news broadcasts, political elections, political scandals, and so on. In this hyped-up age it may seem that you hardly have time to squeeze a drop of ink from a pen, let alone write daily in a journal.

One student journal writer describes her experience with the busy world this way:

> The outside world is so confusing. At times I feel I'm dreaming. I sense I'm in a forest — something from Grimm's fairy tales. I'm lost. It is night. All around me at unexpected moments creatures keep popping up out of the dark, whispering and screaming for my attention. I want to ignore them and find the path out, but some eerie fascination keeps drawing me deeper into the woods.

Like this writer, all of us at times feel the eerie fascination of the marketplace. Its pull is hard to resist. Besides, in the thirty minutes most of us spend struggling to fill a blank page, by merely flicking a TV knob we can take a fairy tale journey across America to see the destruction left by an earthquake, tornado, or torrential rains. In an instant we can be lifted to the Middle East to see the rubble of a village left from a terrorist attack. Carried to Finland we might hear a report on the efforts of the superpowers to avoid a rerun of Hiroshima and Nagasaki. We might see the World Tennis Championship or the World Series or the Academy Awards. We certainly would hear pitches for dog food, beer, cars, deodorants, or headache or hemorrhoid remedies. With all this going on, who has time to practice writing, you might ask. No doubt it would be easier to meditate in a typhoon. Still, to improve your writing you must practice. And practice. And practice.

Spend some time watching a child learn to roller-skate, ride a bike, or walk the top of a fence. After a week or month of skinned knees and elbows and a time of brooding frustration, the instincts take over, but only after practice. Soon the child, bent forward, arms flaying the air, legs rhythmically thrusting out and back, streaks down the sidewalk, the skates humming against the pavement. The young bicyclist will be cruising the neighborhood, popping wheelies, and leaping curbs. And the fence walker will move with the grace of a ballet star, arms balanced and eyes looking straight ahead, fixed on some vision of the Ringling Brothers' center ring. In many ways learning to write is like learning to skate, bike and fence walk — or like learning any other physical skill. The more you practice the less self-conscious you become of your performance. Practice helps you work in a natural way. Practice helps you move the pen across the page with ease. Writing daily in a journal is a good way to get that practice.

The kind of writing you will be doing daily is relaxed writing — some call it free writing. Whenever most students hear the word *writing* in an English class, they associate it with very proper forms of communication. That's a mistake. When you are doing free writing your work should be unbound, snaring fleeting hunches, half-remembered experiences, and images as soon as the mind shapes them. When you are doing formal writing, on the other hand, your work should be more controlled. Formal writing gets reports, essays, and research projects done; free writing helps you train to write reports, essays, and research projects. When doing free writing, you need not be concerned with grammar, logic, spelling, punctuation — the niceties of writing. Instead, you will work to capture the flow of your thought — limbering the writing muscles as sprinters might limber their legs before a race.

Where to Keep Daily Writing

Perhaps the best way to keep daily writing is in a large notebook. If you use a pocket-sized pad, you will not have room to stretch out; your writing will be cramped; you will quickly fill the pages. Soon you may be toting around several tiny volumes of daily writing — an awkward situation.

You might be tempted to use a calendar book, one of those appointment books that have the days divided into neat squares. While the calendar book may be fine for keeping records of assignments and appointments, it is too limited for free writing. After all, when your thought starts flowing, how can you contain it in a four-by-six-inch square that represents the space for that day's entry?

Better to use a regular ten-by-eleven three-ring binder. A ringed binder is more effective than a permanently bound book because the binder will give you more flexibility. Flexibility is what you want for your daily writing. You will often find time on your hands, perhaps while riding a bus, waiting for a class to begin, or just sitting in the cafeteria or library. You can use some of this free time to make an entry. If you have been storing your work in a binder, then there is no need to carry it with you. You can write an entry on any sheet of notebook paper. When you return home, all you have to do is snap open the rings and insert the new sheet or sheets. A permanently bound book lacks this advantage. You must lug it with you. You may also wish to develop a section with a specific focus, adding entries over a period of time. You can do that with a ringed binder; you cannot with a bound book. It is also a good idea to have a section where you keep old papers, written tests, book reviews and reports — all the writing you do in such classes as history, psychology, sociology, or geology. Often, just as practice writing in the form of a notebook entry becomes the spark to ignite a formal class assignment, an old paper can become the base for future work. A binder makes saving papers that might be reworked easy. Of course, the choice of a book to work in is yours, and you should feel comfortable with the one you pick.

Creative People and Journals

By this point you may have gotten the impression that free writing involves more than meeting a course assignment.

It may.

Without much searching in the library you would find that creative people from all fields have written regularly in diaries, journals, daybooks, and notebooks. For many, the entries not only allowed them to express themselves by keeping a history of their experiences, but also fed their life works.

If you take the trouble to search the library, you will find that Leonardo da Vinci, the great Renaissance artist, kept journal entries about his observations of birds and his theories of flight. And that nineteenth-century French painter Paul Gauguin kept a notebook that captured his memories, dreams, and thoughts on art. You would find that contemporary artist Claes Oldenberg consciously set out to generate his art from his own life and psychology. He developed a "scrapbook" of a fantasy city, and many of the details surface in his current work. Oldenberg has said, "Everything I do is completely original — I made it up when I was a little kid." He began by capturing it all in a notebook.

You would also find that psychologist Carl Jung kept a notebook he called the "Black Book." It numbers five volumes and traces his personal growth in both writing and art. The deep value of keeping a personal notebook is reflected in a comment from his autobiography, *Memories, Dreams, and Reflections:* "All my works, all my creative activity, have come from fantasies and dreams which began in 1912. Everything that I accomplished in later life was already contained in them, although at first only in the form of emotions and images."

And if you continued your search, you would find that modern photographer Edward Weston kept daybooks that chart the details of his life and the growth of his inner self and art; that an educator named John Holt kept a log of his experiences teaching elementary school children; that a young Jewish girl named Anne Frank kept a record of her life while hiding with her family from the Nazis; and that writers such as Gustave Flaubert, Henry James, F. Scott Fitzgerald, Anaïs Nin, Graham Greene, and Albert Camus kept diaries, journals, and notebooks at different times in their lives.

Journal Styles

Often a journal entry will be brief. Something — a gesture, an idea, an observation, or a bit of conversation — will capture the journal keeper's interest and will be recorded. For instance, Graham Greene in a journal published under the title *In Search of a Character* makes several brief entries dated February 10:

> The cows with the elegant snow-white birds — *pique-boeufs*, not egrets — which attend them like guardian angels. The birds are so sleek and smooth that their feathers seem of porcelain. Innumerable butterflies. . . .

> Names of Africans. Henry with a *y.* Attention, Deo Gratias. . . .

> Men playing mysterious game altering the number of beans that lie in rough troughs on a home-made board. . . .

> A coil of caterpillars brought home by a leper to sell or eat.

And under February 12 Greene briefly notes:

> The water at the bow of the pontoons the color of burnt sugar. . . .

> A first sentence perhaps: "Each day after breakfast the captain read his breviary in the deck-house. . . ."

> The approach to Bakuma and the excitement of Père Henri: "my home."
> "Not your prison?"
> "No. Yonda is my prison."

In other entries Greene, whose fictional characters often face a crisis of faith, becomes more philosophical. Again from the section dated February 10:

> How often people speak of the absurdity of believing that life should exist by God's will on one minute part of the immense universe. There is a parallel absurdity which we are asked to believe, that God chose a tiny colony of a Roman empire in which to be born. Strangely enough two absurdities seem easier to believe than one.

And under March 8 he records:

> Hinduism is a tropical religion: a reaction from indiscriminate slaughter, which only happens in the tropics. For every insect one kills in Europe, one must kill a hundred at least in tropical countries. One kills without thinking — a smear of one's napkin or the pages of one's book.

Greene's fleeting details, observations, and thoughts may not have been of immediate value beyond keeping him in the habit of writing and looking hard and close at himself and life. Yet by regularly making notebook entries while on a journey through Africa, he stored away enough to draw on for a novel he titled *A Burnt-Out Case.*

Of course, not everything that goes into a notebook will find its way into a future work. Indeed, writing daily in a notebook may seem to involve a series of waste motions. But there is one advantage. The material you collect will have a time to cool off so that later you can come back to it and begin to see how it might be used in another way.

Sometimes the entries will not be as brief as the ones from Greene but instead will be extended impressions recorded with care and in detail. Albert Camus must have made thousands of short and long entries in his notebooks. This excerpt published in *Notebooks: 1935–1942* influenced the shaping of situations and characters in his novel *The Stranger*.

> The old woman who dies in the old people's home. Her friend, the friend she has made over a period of three years, weeps "because she has nothing left." The caretaker of the little mortuary, who is a Parisian and lives at the mortuary with his wife. "Who could have told them that at seventy-four he would end up at an old people's home at Marengo?" His son has a job. They left Paris. The daughter-in-law didn't want them.
>
> Scenes. The old man finally "raised his hand." His son put them in an old people's home. The gravedigger who was one of the dead woman's friends. They often went to the village together in the evening. The old man who insisted on following the procession to the church and then to the cemetery. Since he is lame, he cannot keep up and walks twenty yards behind. But he knows the country and takes shortcuts that enable him to catch up with the procession several times until he falls behind again.
>
> The Arab nurse who nails down the coffin has a cyst on her nose and wears a permanent bandage.
>
> The dead woman's friends: little old people ridden with fancies. Everything was wonderful in the past. One of them to a neighbor: "Hasn't your daughter written to you?" "No." "She might remember that she does have a mother."
>
> The other has died — as a sign and a warning to them all.

You can see in this passage that Camus has captured an interesting situation, drawn brief portraits of the people there, suggested the setting, recorded snatches of dialogue, and responded to the entire entry by commenting on the fear that may be running through these old people, "The other has died — as a sign and a warning to them all." When he made the entry, he may not have had a hint that the "little old man" would become Perez in *The Stranger* and that the funeral would become the funeral of the central character's mother. How could he have known? This entry along with all the others are scraps from his daily experience. But by keeping them in a notebook, he had them handy when he needed them.

Of course, after an artist becomes successful the critic can analyze his notebook entries. Many critics like to do that. But notebook entries are not made for analysis. They are made to sustain the creative person in work and are written without concern for what future critics or the admiring public may think. So, like the artist, when you work in your notebook don't write as if some critic, whether an English teacher, a parent, or a helpful friend, is peeking over your shoulder. In your notebook you have one audience — yourself. If you wish to share your entries, that's your decision, but as a working principle, keep in mind that you're writing for you.

Guidelines for Practice

In order to get this practice rolling and to collect material to use in other assignments, in the next section we have sketched out several weeks of journal exercises. After that you are on your own. Meanwhile, here are some suggestions for working:

1. Keep all your writing in a single book, preferably a three-ring binder. The binder will give you the flexibility you need in shuffling and rearranging your work into sections.
2. Date all entries so that you will have a chronological history of your free writing progress.
3. Try to set aside a twenty- or thirty-minute block of time to complete each exercise. Write at least two pages — two authentic pages — but do not bloat the size of your writing strokes to fill the page. If you finish in less than two pages, write something else.
4. Write clearly enough so that you will be able to read the entry when you go back.
5. Always keep in mind that this is practice. Although the material can be reworked if you need it for a formal assignment, in your journal write it once. If you write a line or phrase you do not like, leave it and keep going.
6. Don't be concerned with mechanics. Don't stop to look up words. Don't stop to revise. Instead, write to capture the flow of your thought, the detail of experience.

26 FIRST WEEK: FREE WRITING

You have your notebook. You have set aside some time. You are ready to begin. For the first exercises you will be doing unfocused writing. The goal here is to write nonstop for at least twenty minutes. Don't stop to think or judge or arrange your thought — just write, letting the words pepper the page. This is free flow. This is a way to get your thought loose.

Some beginning writers get scared when set free. You may be like that. You might say, "I can't get it loose. I just shut my eyes and it's all a blank. No thought — except 'What shall I write about? What shall I write about?' Beyond that there's only a void, a big zero."

The problem is not uncommon with beginning writers, and probably it is not uncommon with professional writers either. But they have learned to live with it, knowing it will pass. So here is what you do: describe your "zero." If you are sitting in a quiet place, notebook open to a fresh sheet, pen ready to start recording, and nothing comes, describe the nothing.

Here is how one student started his unfocused writing:

> I can't think . . . mind's a blank. Eyes closed. See nothing but black . . . something purple, circles expanding in the black — reminds me of a lake I visited in the Cascades. A bowl. What was it? Devil's punch bowl. I tossed a rock as far toward its center as I could. The rings. . . .

Though this entry continues by discussing the circles floating toward shore, it starts off describing the color black many of us might see if our eyes are pressed shut. Then some purple comes in the shape of expanding circles; finally, the writer's mind begins to free-associate — that is, to make loose, spontaneous connections. His mind is becoming less constrained. It is opening up for imaginary flight. If you give yours the same opportunity, it will fly, too.

One goal to keep in mind before you start free writing is to be honest. To be honest does not mean you have to confess or to "come clean," as a detective in a thirties cop film might say. Instead it means to write the truth, the kind of truth with a little t, not a big T. The little-t truth has to do with firsthand experience; the facts of your life, your imagination, your dreams. It is a personal truth, the truth of your life experience. This truth is uniquely yours because it is filtered through your eyes and your mind. In your daily writing, work to corral your unique experience. Remember, too, that you should be less interested in recording your interpretation — the whys behind your experience — and more interested in describing it — herding its vast details onto the page.

There is another kind of truth to keep in mind while making entries in your notebook — the truth of the words you use. Of course, no words are untruthful in themselves; their falsity depends on how accurately or inaccurately they are used to describe experience. All good writers try to use words accurately by being as concrete and specific as their subjects allow them. But for beginning writers that may be hard.

This is the age of the marketplace, and there is little doubt that marketplace language, the language of advertising, politics, talk shows, and so on has affected our language. All of us have spent too many hours listening to the drone of disc jockeys, TV commentators, politicians, and show business personalities for our language not to be tainted. It is safe to generalize that much of this language, if not downright false in the way it presents experience, is certainly misleading and almost always general and vague. Consider the problem ad writers face in communicating with millions of people. The size and breadth of their audience forces them to be vague. They hope that by writing at the most general level they will get buyers in cities, towns, and hamlets across the nation to identify with a product and plunk down the cash to own it. They do not give buyers information; instead they try to give them feelings.

Often, the ad writer's vague language will creep into a beginning writer's prose. The beginning writer may be attempting to express a sincere feeling, but often the words smack of the ad writer's talent for saying very little.

Here is one student's first attempt at describing a trip to the beach:

> Yesterday I spent a delightful day at the beach. Whenever I feel lost or just want to be with friends I go to the cove and lie on the sand to collect my thoughts. The sky was a New England blue. Many of my friends were there. I have known some of them since elementary school. To see them makes me feel good. Some

were flying kites, some were playing volleyball. Everyone was having a good time. It picks me up to go.

This writer may wish to be sincere, but this piece is general and vague. Not much is being said except that the writer feels good going to the beach whenever he feels "lost." What does "lost" mean? The writer doesn't confront the feeling, but going to the beach will cure the condition because thoughts can be collected and friends are doing it. At the beach everyone has a good time. Consequently, the beach will pick him up. Perhaps the writer did not know he was writing an advertisement. Still, the point here is clear: the sooner you can break the grip the marketplace has on your writing, the sooner you will become a good, honest writer. ·

Here is part of another brief entry that deals with the beach. This student has tried to capture the detail of the experience in specific language. In itself the entry may seem unhinged from any point. But for notebook entries the goal is to practice and to collect raw material. This piece is fresh, unlike the first example, because the writer trusts what her eyes, ears, and nose tell her: she focuses on the actual experience, not on what she thinks about it.

> Walking across the sand. Hot. The sun eating at my back. The sand so hot I feel it burning through my sandals. Bodies scattered everywhere on towels, some lying, some sitting. All of them young. Only the young come to 39th street. They grease themselves up, streaks of silver reflecting off the grease coating their arms and backs. The beach has the smell of cocoa butter. The smell mixes with the music from portables.

In seven lines this writer has escaped the influence of the marketplace and packed her work with detail. Besides collecting some specifics she may use in a later piece, she has touched on a theme that could be expanded into a formal work — the contrast between the young and the old. In any case, she is collecting raw material and getting practice doing it.

WRITING TASK

Each day for the next five days write as fast as you can without interruption for twenty minutes. Keep the writing going. Don't stop. If you draw a blank, describe the blank — the zero, the nothing, or the void, whatever you might call it. You may be like many beginning writers and hear a little voice that seems to come from some mischie-

vous gnome riding on your shoulder. This devilish creature is never happy with anything you write. It nags at each word and carps over sentences and condemns each paragraph. This tiny creature is a pest. If you have a cranky gnome that tells you to give up, don't; there is a way to beat the gnome.

The gnome is a little like a pet. When you most want to do something, it will decide to rub up against your leg or screech or growl. But if you reach down and give it a couple of strokes, the chances are it will curl up in its favorite corner so you can finish your job. So the best way to deal with this pest is to give it a couple of strokes. You stroke it by recording what it says and by giving it credit for having said it. You might do it something like this:

> The grouchy gnome speaks, "You know you can't write. What are you doing it for? If I've told you once, I've told you a thousand times — YOU CAN'T WRITE! Now don't misunderstand me, I'm not saying you're dumb. Maybe you are, maybe you aren't. Who's to judge? BUT WRITE YOU CAN'T! So stop. Go do something you do well. Take a nap!"

If you hear a voice like this and you record it, you may find some new path to your creative depths. After all, in folklore a gnome is reputed to be a creature that lives underground and guards buried gold. Once you get past it you may be free to mine the tunnels of your imagination. In fact, by writing down its chatter you may be led to answer it; then you have a dialogue. Who knows what kind of honest encounter could come from that?

So the message for this week — for all the weeks of the term — is to keep your nose to the task. Keep writing. Keep the flow going. Once it's going, try to be specific. Remember, you are not working for perfection. You are practicing. So if you record a thought you dislike, leave it alone and continue to write.

After twenty minutes, stop. Reread the entry; if you have anything to add, add it. As a final check, see if you have dated the entry. You might also want to jot down the day and place: "Monday, September 21, 1980: Library."

27 SECOND WEEK: CURRENT LIFE

You spent the first week's practice doing unfocused tasks to help you capture bits and pieces of experience. This week will be slightly different. We'll give you more direction, and the exercises will focus on your current life. In the words of Henry David Thoreau, you will begin a "simple and sincere account" of your life. He writes:

> I, on my side, require of every writer, first and last, a simple and sincere account of his own life, and not merely what he has heard of other men's lives; some such account as he would send to his kindred from a distant land; for if he has lived sincerely, it must have been in a distant land to me.

The distant land Thoreau writes of is the land of the mind. Although we often work with common materials, none of us sees, smells, touches or hears the world as anyone else does. This is what makes each mind a unique landscape.

One writer, a mother who returned to college after a five-year absence, began to chart her immediate life in this fashion:

> I'm in a place where I never seem to get anything done; the laundry, dishes, trips to the market, birthday parties, term papers. Two children with runny noses, skinned knees and elbows — that damned skateboard — a midnight toothache. Why does it all happen at once? A cosmic question!
>
> The car breaks down; trip to the mechanic's: "Can't do it now, lady. Next Tuesday," he says. Why do I feel so weak around mechanics and hardware and paint salesmen? Real power.
>
> Walk to the bus. Thirty minutes to school. Books dropping, wind, clouds. The rain comes. Cold, cold days.
>
> Everything working against me.

Tuesday rolls around. Phone the mechanic and imagine him leaning back in a chair, puffing a cigar, his feet propped up on my gutted VW engine. He says, "Have it tomorrow morning. How's 'bout nine." He says it not like a question but like a command. He knows he has me trapped. Slam down the receiver and press down a scream — another day on the bus.

"Mommy, can I have a jelly sandwich" — it too is not a question it is a command: "GET ME A JELLY SANDWICH NOW!" Peanut butter, jelly, milk, cookie crumbs, gum balls — all smashed and ground into the floor. Need to scrape it off. Need a chisel.

Must read *Gatsby* by Friday.

Wednesday A.M. Back to the mechanic's: "That's $78.50." More than I had intended to spend. Oil, grease job — you bet, a grease job — brakes, spark plugs, points. "The points, lady, that's what's giving you trouble. That's why it won't start. Ought to have 'em changed at least once every two years." His cheeks, so smoothly shaved look like a barber with a straight razor did it; odd, always think of mechanics as grubby. A cynical smile — small sharp teeth under a lavish mustache. Teeth for chewing into my bankroll, teeth for biting into my time.

I need a vacation! Spring — a fantasy: I see myself flying over snow and landing in Bermuda, lying on some beach. White, white sand. Blue, blue sky. Blue, blue water. (With my recent luck, blue, blue sharks.) The sharks are in the surf. I'm swimming for the beach. Stroking toward safety. Why do I want a degree? I want leisure. I want escape. I wish I had a harpoon. The college is my white whale.

Overall this is a rough piece of writing, and well it should be. To be rough is the nature of free writing. No one was sitting on the writer's shoulder giving her commands about proper punctuation, spelling, and organization: those commands come with formal writing, not with practice writing.

The only direction she was given was to write nonstop for thirty minutes about her current life. She does it, not by sitting down and figuring it out, but by taking the first step on the exciting journey. She gets into the movement instead of analyzing whether or not what she writes will be correct. Potters do the same. They thrust their hands into the clay so that they can find out what shapes hide in their imagination. Critics have another method. They stand back and analyze the result to see if it has artistic value. The one group plunges forward and gets the job done; the other sits and calculates. Calculating is an important part of formal writing, but in free writing it can block the work.

So this writer has thrust herself into her life's flow. By groping around, she has captured the chaos and frustration that she feels is running through it by recording those fleeting thoughts and images that seem to swim just below the surface.

Often her catch is surprising. For instance, the encounter with the mechanic begins with a stereotypical image — a cigar-chomping bandit, who pridefully poses with his latest kill. The image then becomes more realistic — a meticulous man, who shaves his cheeks as carefully as a professional barber would. And finally, the image turns surrealistic — a cartoon character, perhaps a giant rabbit, who eats at her bankroll and her time as if they were hunks of lettuce.

And she uses specific words and phrases from her daily life — not clichés as they might be gleaned from advertising, but language that comes from looking at the particulars of her world. Here are a few words and phrases taken from the lists she compiles:

laundry	jelly
dishes	milk
trips to the market	cookie crumbs
birthday parties	gum balls
term papers	oil
runny noses	grease
skinned knees and elbows	brakes
skateboards	spark plugs
midnight toothache	points
peanut butter	

Specific words and phrases create a feeling that a work is made from more than straw and air. Snatches of dialogue help to make it seem real. People talking to us are part of our daily lives. Shreds of their talk hang in our minds: if lines from a recent conversation come to you while writing nonstop, record them. This writer quotes one line from her child and several from her mechanic:

> Can't do it now, lady. Next Tuesday. Have it tomorrow morning. How's 'bout nine. That's $78.50. The points, lady, that's what's giving you trouble. That's why it won't start. Ought to have 'em changed at least once every two years.

And she also includes fantasy. When you are practicing writing, your mind may want to drift. If so, follow it by recording where it goes. The writer's fantasy starts in an idyllic setting — "Lying on some beach. White, white sand. Blue, blue sky" — followed by a tug back to her real life — "Blue, blue sharks." Some of a writer's richest images may come from fantasies; be sure to record yours when they appear.

Finally, our writer has uncovered some provocative questions she may wish to explore in more direct ways. "Why do I feel so weak around mechanics and hardware and paint salesmen?" "Why do I want a degree?"

For us to overexplore a single journal entry may be a mistake if you take the entry and our comments about it as a model to emulate. If you ever feel that urge, don't give in to it. We offer the example and comments as possibilities, not as formulas. Don't, like Cinderella's half sisters, try to cram your feet into another's shoe.

WRITING TASK

What follows is a group of tasks, one for each day of the week, designed to focus your practice. Each exercise will lead you to write something about your current life. In another section you will do exercises designed to lead you into your life history, but in these exercises you are to capture some of the present — the now of your life.

As a reminder, be sure to set aside twenty to thirty minutes for uninterrupted writing. Keep the pen moving across the page for the full time, trying to fill at least two pages without worrying about punctuation, grammar, or spelling. Give yourself plenty of space so your entries will not be crowded. Write legibly enough so you will be able to reread the entry. Finally, be sure to date your entry.

One last suggestion. Before you begin to write, relax a moment. Close your eyes, or rest your head on the desk top. Feel your breathing. Let the breathing become rhythmical. Sometimes a minute or two of relaxation will let a busy mind clear. It will then be easier to focus and begin.

Monday: This entry is to capture where you are in your life. It may be a good idea to begin with a comment on your general situation as you sense it. For instance, in the example above, the writer begins with a broad comment: "I'm in a place where I never seem to get anything done." She then lets her mind sweep through her recent life. She records the specifics, the bits of dialogue, the frustrations, the questions, the fantasies — everything that comes to her.

You might also keep this thought in mind while you write: there is no reason to worry about whether or not what you record is true — true in a permanent sense. Indeed, if the woman who wrote the example had done the exercise the following week, the entry might have been completely different. Your goal is to capture the truth of the moment in as much detail as you can.

Now take a moment to relax. With your eyes closed, consider where you are in your life now. When the moment is right, begin to write your entry.

Tuesday: In yesterday's entry you described where you are in your current life. Today you are going to continue the process by recording impressions of where you live.

Where you live. If you think about the phrase, it may suggest outlandish possibilities. If you have read enough science fiction, recording impressions of where you live might lead you to the outer reaches of the solar system and back to earth. But if you have a less expansive nature, you might be content to focus on your country, state, county, city, neighborhood, or house. Or if you tend to be nomadic and wish to narrow the focus further, you might describe your van. And these are just the literal possibilities. There are metaphorical ways of looking at "where you live."

If you see yourself as a spirit temporarily housed in a body, where you live — for now — could be inside a bag of skin. But for this assignment, you can skip that kind of metaphysical chin rubbing. Try instead to keep your work simple. This exercise assumes that where you live means your immediate physical surroundings — maybe your room, house, or apartment complex, but certainly nothing larger than your neighborhood.

Keep in mind that your entry need not cover every aspect of where you live. Instead try to capture fleeting impressions and details. Let your mind loose, recording the associations it makes. Perhaps your mind will connect with other places where you have lived; work those details into your entry, but always come back to your immediate surroundings. Remember, be specific. Never let your mind linger for long in general statements such as this:

> I live in a pretty white house with a big lawn and some palm trees near the center of town. I like it here. The neighbors are . . .

Instead, get to the details and the associations they bring:

> My front lawn has gone brown from the drought, but it still has two fat palms about two stories high with drooping limbs. I used to swing on them when I was a kid: Ahhhhhh — Tarzan. People could hear my scream all over town (at least my mom said they could). Ahhhhhhh, ahhh, ahhhhhhhh! But now things are different. I've gotten older and the house . . .

Be specific. Capture the details. Now, for thirty minutes write about where you live.

Wednesday: Today you can begin to take the next step in exploring your current life by making a list of the personal items in your possession. Keep in mind that a list need not be limited to naming individual items but can also include brief descriptions of the items and associations you have with them. To start the writing session you might empty the contents of your wallet or purse on the desk. Arrange the items in whatever way suits you, then begin to study them. Take them in your hand. Read the writing on the ones that have writing. Smell the ones that have smells. Read the numbers on the ones that have numbers. Then, in your own time, begin to record your list. If exploring the contents of your purse or wallet doesn't capture your interest, go to the medicine cabinet or cosmetic table. Follow the same procedure by listing the jars, bottles, tins, and toothbrushes and any associations you have with these items.

As with this week's other entries, this writing session should last for around thirty minutes. Be sure to date the entry and to leave yourself plenty of space — don't crowd your entries.

Thursday: What are some of the activities you do? You attend classes, read, write papers, take tests; you drive, walk, bike or ride a bus to school; you sleep and roll out of bed in the morning; you talk with friends, teachers, parents; you may also hold a job. Many activities you do are commonplace; many, many people do them. The fact that people do them doesn't mean they're not important; they are. But you probably need less routine activities that add more meaning or pleasure to your life.

For today's writing you can begin by drawing up a list of activities you do or wish you did, not because you are forced to do them by the necessities of living but because you want to. Then from the list select one or two activities to write about. Record everything that comes to you: how it feels to do it; why you like it; how long you've been doing it. Record the associations you have with it; these might include the different times and places you've done it. While recording the entry, use specific language. This student entry about jogging starts off fuzzy, a way many writers begin, then goes past the general comments to the particulars of the experience:

> I like jogging because it makes me feel good. After I finish jogging, I relax. My body is limber — limber, reminds me of lumber. That's how I start in the mornings, my legs like pieces

of lumber — I lumber along. But after I run for a while, I feel limber, like a birch tree in the wind. I like the sound of my feet slapping the asphalt and the sound of breathing deep in my chest. I like to jog on cold mornings. Once there was frost on the grass. I ran across the park. Crunch, crunch, crunch.

Keep in mind that you are still working under the thirty-minute time limit — so work fast. Try not to spend time evaluating your writing; just write. Leave yourself plenty of space between and within entries. Be sure to date the entry at the top.

Friday: Where you are in your life now, the place you live, the items and activities that compose your current life — all these practice entries have helped collect experience that you can begin to use in your formal work. Start looking for opportunities to use them. Now, to conclude this week's daily practice, you will write about special places in your current life.

Once again, start by sitting quietly and letting your thought settle. Then begin to randomly list places that come to mind. These special places need not be your favorite spots, ones you associate with pleasure; they may also be places you associate with discomfort, such as a doctor's or dentist's office. Perhaps one or two places on your list will be secret places, spots you may visit for a moment or two when the world seems to be coming down around your shoulders, such as a rock overlooking a field, a window looking out to a yard or street, or a couch in a quiet place in your home.

The list you draw up may include places that are not so special but that you recorded because you listed as many as possible. Whether each place you record is truly a special place is not the point of the listing process. The listing process is to pull out a great deal of material in a short time. For example, here is a part of one student's list of special places:

the mountains: love the cool breezes that hum through the pines.

the beach: but not with people — people everywhere, an anthill.

restaurants: Salernos — ummmmm! El Torito, but only on Fridays between four and six. El Tapito: carnitas, jalapeños, flautas

I like: my shower
        the park in early morning
        sitting in the quad
        my granddad's garage — cans of old paint, rusted tools,

pipes, bicycle parts, at least a dozen alarm clocks — all waiting to be fixed.

Notice the phrases that follow some of the items on the list. They add the concretes; often they are lists themselves. This kind of random listing helps writers cover a great deal of territory so that they can find out what might be worth exploring more completely.

Now it is time for you to begin. During this practice session, take the first ten minutes to draw up your list of special places and record some associations you might have with the spots. Then after ten minutes, select one or two to write about more completely. Be sure to practice for the full time.

28 THIRD WEEK: PAST LIFE

Your notebook is beginning to fatten from collecting the scraps of your present life. In many ways your notebook may begin to work like an artist's sketchbook, except your practice is done with words rather than lines and curves. Artists practice figure drawing through a series of quick studies — fast sketches of arms, hands, fingers. They may sketch finger joints and nails. Other parts of the body will fill other pages — stomachs, chests, shoulders, and necks. An artist may have done heads and faces from several angles. No sketch is a finished piece, yet someone who flipped through all the pages would get an impression of a whole body.

The same is true of the entries you have made thus far. If readers were to scan them, though the entries are fragmented — works in progress — they would go away with a feeling for the whole. Of course, in the case of your notebook, the parts are not of a figure but of your life. Certainly you have not been consciously composing an autobiography, but only capturing a series of passing impressions and immediate associations that make up your life in motion — a view caught on the run. And finally, like artists working to develop their skill with form, you too have been practicing to become more limber at the writing craft.

During this week's thirty-minute writing sessions, you will practice by continuing to capture experiences from your life. This week's exercises will have a basic difference from previous ones: instead of dealing with the present you will deal with the past.

If you've watched your mind during the last two weeks of notebook entries, you have seen how it hops around. You may have wanted to keep it on a straight path, but it probably acted like a rabbit erratically skipping, stopping to nibble, then dashing off down a trail. No doubt you have already captured experiences and feelings from your past by following your rabbit mind. They are embedded in your previous entries. Do you recall the example used to illustrate the exercise asking you to describe where you live? It began:

> My front lawn has gone brown from the drought, but it still has two fat palms about two stories high with drooping limbs.

After the opening, this writer's mind starts skipping. He connects with the past, and for a line or two he's a kid again, swinging from vines like Tarzan.

> I used to swing on them when I was a kid: Ahhhhhh — Tarzan. People could hear my scream all over town (at least my mom said they could). Ahhhhhhh, ahhh, ahhhhhhhh!

He records the association with the past, then he returns to his original intent — to record the details of where he lives.

The point here is that the mind naturally leaps to the past. It acts like a time traveler who is not a prisoner of calendars and clocks. If you link up with past experiences, record them. This kind of practice writing is supposed to rouse associations. Memories and images should be hooking together from all parts of your experience.

Now, in order to keep the work going, this week's exercises will give you a way of nudging your memory so you can capture more details that may be of use to your formal writing. But first, here's how not to do it. Don't sit at your desk with your fingers clutching a pen and in cold blood start hacking out an autobiography. After about three minutes and forty-five seconds you'll feel as if some half-educated surgeon has cut open your skull, taken out your brain, and put it in the freezer.

Better to begin less directly. Better to let the mind do its skipping, nibbling, and dashing away. And then better to use that natural energy to sketch those parts of your past that seem to connect to your current life.

It can be done in two phases: first, by making a list of brief entries that span your life; and second, by taking the entries separately and enlarging them.

WRITING TASK

Monday: **Make a series of brief entries in the form of an extended list that spontaneously captures memories from your past. The key word is *spontaneously*, for the goal here is not to capture only the most important events in your life — although they may be on your list —**

but to let the memories and images from your past come uncalled. Their relative importance to the movement of your life is not your concern. After all, you are sketching — filling in pages with practice. By looking only at major landmarks, you may miss some rich detail in the general landscape. So work to create your list spontaneously and try to record each entry in no more than two or three lines. For example, here is a list of random experiences recorded by photographer Edward Weston in one of his notebooks under the heading "Notes from N.Y., 1922":

> Near the "penny bridge," a few steps from my room (Columbia Heights).
> Morning coffee with Jo from the purple cup sister gave me.
> The Hurdy Gurdy man who played to our window.
> The lone man who wandered by playing a softly quavering flute; 30 years ago. I must have heard the same man in Chicago. "God bless you sir for the money. I surely needed it."
> Almost daily I haunted the bridges, Brooklyn or Manhattan. One Sunday I walked over Williamsburg Br. at sunset — then down among the tenements on Rivington Street — memorable night.
> Two "specials" from Tina, each with $20.00 enclosed: "knowing that I would need money, that I must see Balieff's *Chauve Souris.*"

You may find deciphering these brief entries impossible. Sure, you can pick up some references to common places, but the experiences behind the entries belong to Weston. Of course, journal keeper Weston does his work for himself without being concerned if a reader can understand the entries. He drops a bucket into his experience and may be surprised at what it holds when he hoists it up. Yet no one else, while the details are in rough form, may even appreciate his catch.

Now here is a list of entries written by a student journal keeper. Like Weston's these also seem fragmented — written in a personalized code:

> – I remember walking to school on a cold morning. It had rained — puddles covered with thin ice. Mountains with snow.
>
> – Graduating from high school. The speech seemed like hours. Fear. Thought I could never do it.

- Running on the mountain trail. A trip with dad. A cabin. Fishing. Hated the smell on my hands.
- Living in the city. Once a man stopped me on the way to school. "Got a quarter, missy? Give me your lunch money." I ran.
- My first real date. Must have taken three hours to get ready. Spilled a coke in my lap.
- Flunked geometry — the end of the world. Thought all hell would break loose. Mom shrugged her shoulders. Dad said to take it over.
- Mom and dad divorced. Took me a year before I could say the word.
- Away to school. Mixed feelings. Couldn't wait to get out of the house. Yet scared.
- Bobby K. shot. Remember my mom weeping. Train going across the TV screen. I was 9. Didn't mean much to me.

This writer dips deeply into her past. In fact, the list appears to reach from very early memories to more recent ones. The list also includes the ups and downs of experience. Often, when making life history lists of this sort, writers tend to consciously exclude difficult times. But if the mind finds its own course, the list will include both good and bad memories. Finally, notice that the list goes beyond the personal by including a memory of Robert Kennedy's assassination. We all live in a society. Although changes, especially traumatic events, may be beyond our control, they still affect our lives. If these kinds of memories come to you, record them. Notice also that the writer quickly ties Kennedy's death to her personal world. That's natural. We see the world from our own situation.

Now, let's go back to see what this writer has done to complete the first step in recording material from her life. Her goal was simple. She had only to sit for a few moments in quiet and let the memories come to the surface. She did it by sending her thought into the past, as far back as she could. Then by letting it move forward across years of memory to the present, she randomly recalled a handful of experiences. She continued to sit quietly for a few more moments. Finally, after the strongest memories, the ones that held her interest, presented themselves, she recorded them in a few lines. She didn't judge if they were the most important. She didn't criticize herself for having any particular memory; she merely listed them on a sheet of paper in enough detail to recall them when rereading at another time.

For this first half-hour session develop a list of memories from your past. Begin by sitting quietly and directing your thought to the past. Then record in two or three lines a half dozen to a dozen of the strongest memories that come to you. They may not be big events in your life, but for the moment they will hold your interest. Be sure to write legibly enough to reread your entries, and leave plenty of space around them. And finally, after you finish the list, reread it and write the dates when the events took place.

Tuesday Through Friday: During the rest of this week's writing sessions, you will work by expanding four entries from your list. In a way each memory you've listed is like a doorway to your past. To write a brief entry is to open the door just a crack. To expand the entry is to swing the door open wide. Behind it will be a story or heaps of detail that you may have forgotten. This recalled detail can work as material for other writing. But even if you never use it, the writing practice will aid in limbering your style. The fear of confronting the blank page — if that fear is one of your hobgoblins — will lose some of its witchery.

But before you begin, here's another example that illustrates what you are supposed to be doing. Recall the list used to illustrate the last exercise. One entry dealt with the assassination of Robert Kennedy:

> Bobby K. shot. Remember my mom weeping. Train going across the TV screen. I was 9. Didn't mean much to me.

The writer selected this entry to expand. She sat quietly for thirty minutes and recorded the thoughts that came to her while focusing on the memory.

> March 7, 1978: Bobby K. killed
> I was nine then — I didn't know what being nine meant. I didn't know that it was a good time to be alive, a time to play, and laugh, and innocently cry. Crying was something you did when you got hurt or wanted your way. But looking back I can remember sensing the sadness my mother felt when Bobby Kennedy was shot. I didn't know about politics then. I only knew it usually took the TV away from me. Politics and the news. Neither were very much fun for me then. They're not now, either. I remember getting out of bed. My mother was

watching the news and she was crying. I asked her why — I was confused. It was the first time I had seen her cry and I didn't see her cry again until dad left — then they were both crying. She said that a great man had died — she didn't say "was shot" — only that he died. I put the "was shot" in later. I remember being upset at first because I knew to die wasn't good, but then because I was missing the programs I liked to watch — then I think it was Captain Kangaroo or maybe Soupy Sales. How stupid a kid is — no that's not fair, not stupid but innocent. That's the key. Maybe that was my first step out of innocence — the death of Bobby K. and my not knowing what it meant. After that my family began to break up. After that . . . there's a lot of after thats. They all seem to lead to where I am now, at college, and it seems that many, many people like Bobby K., only who are not so well known, are being murdered every day by bombs and bullets and clubs. Sometimes I wish I were nine again. Nine and just cuddled up in front of Captain K. Sometimes I wish I had never learned about Bobby K.

Did you notice how the entry begins with the focus then starts to skip and hop? It moves from the far past to the present and pauses at places in between. The writer doesn't linger with any one thought but records whatever comes to her in relation to the focus.

Does this entry have a point?

Does it have value for later work?

Does it serve only as practice?

Writers must answer these kinds of questions themselves. The piece is certainly rough, written without regard for the concerns of critics, who sometimes stick their noses into a writer's work at the wrong time. But whether or not an entry is valuable enough to be reworked is for each writer to judge.

Each day for the rest of the week, reread the list of memory experiences. Select the one you feel most curious about. Then for thirty minutes expand it by recording whatever comes to mind.

29 FOURTH WEEK: DAILY ACTIVITIES

In this week's writing sessions you will describe daily experiences from the inside or the outside. Feel free to do whichever you wish — or do both.

Though there are a couple of ways of going about it, a description of the day is an exercise close to traditional diary keeping. To do it writers sit down (usually in the evening) and describe the highlights of their experience from the time they crawled out of bed to the time they took up the pen. The danger in this kind of entry is that it can become routine and dull. A typical example might begin like this:

> John called this morning. We talked for two hours about which college he should attend. He went through the entire list — UCLA, U. of Arizona, Berkeley . . .

And so on.

If this entry were to continue in this fashion, it would give the writer practice — and that's what we want — but it would be lifeless.

Let's take the subject of lifeless writing a bit further. By this time you've probably found that writing comes more easily when your emotion gets involved. Emotion gives prose energy, and when yours comes into play, you may find it tough for the hand holding the pen to keep up with the mind shaping the words. You may even feel transported, as if you had leaped into another space. If you reach that state of deep involvement, great. Stick with it. Later, if you wish to integrate a journal entry into a piece of formal writing, you bring in the intellect to prune the overgrown first effort.

The problem you'll be facing in this task is how to pump life into routine entries.

It's easy: describe them from the inside. Get your emotion involved and expand your entries by including feelings and insights. Describe the emotional nuances, those subtle messages behind so many of your experiences, the ones you may seldom listen to. This is writing from the inside. Here is the above entry rewritten, after a routine beginning, from the inner perspective.

> John called this morning. We talked for two hours about which college he should attend. He went through the entire list — UCLA, U. of Arizona, Berkeley . . . the list seemed endless. And he had to go through the pluses and minuses of each one. I wanted to scream, to slam down the receiver, to escape. All those thoughts were running through my mind. Then I realized he was truly confused. I listened more carefully. He said things like, "Berkeley has a great name, but that town scares me. I like the campus, but there is something wrong with the feeling there. It's the town. And I don't want to live in a dorm." As I listened, and he went through a similar routine with each school, I realized he was scared. He didn't want to leave home. Then I realized something about myself. I was feeling scared, too. Maybe that's why I wanted off the phone — his fear was tugging at mine. Then I thought, well, why shouldn't we be scared? We were both born here and neither of us has lived anyplace else.

The writer has gone beyond routine practice. He has put his feelings into the picture. When recording the day's highlights, keep in mind that your life is made up of both external experiences and internal responses. Put yourself fully in the picture by including not only the details of what happens in the outer world but also the details related to the inside world. Feelings, insights — the emotional responses that connect you to your entries — add vigor to routine assignments.

While we are talking about emotions, let's take the discussion another step. Although our purpose in having you make daily notebook entries is to limber your writing style, sharpen your observation, and collect material to use in formal assignments, we want to mention that there is often a cathartic value in recording your feelings. You may tap intense feelings just below your awareness. If you do, continue to record. Some journal keepers find that recording their feelings not only leads to a sense of emotional release but also helps them to clarify their feelings and to learn from their experiences. So don't get edgy if an entry seems to take an unexpected turn. Just stay with it. Write it out.

Outside entries, on the other hand, involve describing something you saw that caught and held your attention. To write an outside entry, take the point of view of the detached observer, someone who is not part of the event yet captures it in writing as a photographer might snap a photograph. This kind of exercise is often associated with the professional writer who collects random material for a future work. Whatever you record as a detached observer doesn't need to be earthshaking, but it should be sufficiently interesting to make you pause when you see it. One notebook keeper recorded this entry describing a boy trying to fly a kite:

> *Sitting in the park:* A little boy about six was trying to fly a kite. He was in the center of a grassy area. His father sat nearby, smoking a pipe. The boy carefully laid out about ten feet of kite string. He then lined the kite up at the end. Next, while holding the stick with the excess string wrapped around it, he ran toward the trees, the kite bumping along behind him. Finally, he stopped and flopped on the ground to rest. A minute or two later he reset the kite and ran back toward his father. Finally, after several runs, the father took the pipe from his mouth and shouted, "There's no wind." The boy was again laying out the string and the now tattered kite. He stopped, turned to his dad and said, "Dad, I run and make wind."

This entry has been done from an objective viewpoint — from the outside. It has the quality of a documentary film that merely presents an event in a neutral manner. Whether you choose to record daily experiences as an outsider who is merely describing an event or as an insider who includes emotional responses, you will get practice putting experience into words.

WRITING TASK

For this week's thirty-minute practice sessions, record highlights of your day or interesting events you observed during the day.

30 FIFTH WEEK: DREAMS AND FANTASIES

This week will take your writing practice into another dimension. So far you've recorded unfocused entries and collected material from your current life and daily experiences. You've also collected memories. Now you'll collect experiences from another realm, from dreams and fantasies.

Dreams offer excellent material for those who say: "Nothing ever happens to me. My life is so uninteresting. I have nothing to write." Well, dreams are often full of excitement. They take dreamers into landscapes and situations they might never be able to imagine while awake. One notebook keeper recorded this dream:

> *The cave*
> I found myself in a strange land . . . a combination of wooded mountains and barren desert. All around me were pines, rivers, and lakes — there were even patches of snow. Yet the land was also a desert with volcanic rocks and ancient lava flows. I was walking through pine groves that seemed to be growing out of rock. It was hot, the sun like a desert sun. I came to a stream, and though I wanted to rest, I decided to move on — I felt I had an appointment, although I wasn't sure what kind. I crossed the stream, the cold water swirling around my calves. Soon I left the trees and began to walk across a wasteland, a place that looked like a moonscape. I wanted to turn back — to go to the stream — but I couldn't. I began to climb a hill with a steep grade that ended at the face of a cliff. Rocks kept slipping under my feet. Finally, when I reached the foot of the cliff, I noticed a cave and walked to its entrance. The mouth was so black it looked as if it had been painted on the rocks with tar. I became

uneasy. I wanted to go in; after all, I had come this far — or so I thought. But I couldn't bring myself to take the step into the darkness. I woke without entering the cave.

Is a dream seen or felt as intensely as the "real" experiences we record from our day? Though the setting seems to come from a mythic land, the writer's dream is described with all the intensity of a waking experience. She has concentrated on capturing the particulars of her dream journey, attempting to give us as full a picture as her writing skills allow. This picture not only is concrete but includes her feelings.

If you are one of those people who forgets dreams, that's fine. You can record fantasies. Some people call fantasizing "wool gathering" or "castle building in Spain" or "middle distance staring" or just plain "daydreaming."

Daydreaming has the quality of "tuning out," of taking a momentary leave of absence by stepping from the realistic world of objects, people, and tasks and into an imaginary space filled with private creations or re-created combinations from daily life — pictures in the mind's eye. Daydreaming! A trip to Araby with tales of a thousand and one nights.

A child dawdling over a math problem who begins to mumble about Darth Vadar and galactic wars, punctuating his thoughts with zooms from passing star ships; the history student who suddenly realizes she has read ten pages and can't recall doing it; the professor who falls into a profound silence while staring at the chalkboard — all are daydreaming. Even Albert Einstein, the scientist who described relativity, daydreamed. He once asked a friend, "Why is it I get my best ideas in the morning while I'm shaving?"

Einstein's question brings up an interesting point. People may need daydreams to allow the mind to relax in order for ideas to emerge. Most of us have used expressions such as "it came from the blue," "the idea just popped into my head," or "it suddenly hit me." These experiences usually come when the intellect has dropped its guard and the intuition begins to shape itself into the images of the imagination.

Daydreams come in two varieties, brief and extended. Brief daydreams are more like hunches and insights, yet they have the quality of stepping into another space. Whenever you have one, jot it down and add it to your notebook. Extended daydreams, on the other hand, may have recurred during our lives. These are the ones you especially want to record during this week's sessions. They offer more material for practice.

Here's an example of a recurring daydream written by a young man raised in the city:

Fly Fishing
Ever since I saw a film about Ernest Hemingway's life I have

wanted to fly fish. Not such a big wish, but one that is totally unrelated to my life. I've never even been to the mountains, let alone waded in a stream with hip boots. Still, I have this vision of myself like the guy who played Nick Adams (Nick Adams was supposed to be Hemingway) in the early parts of the film, pulling in a trout. My daydream usually goes something like this:

The scene — early morning. The sun coming through thick pines.

The action — I crawl from my tent, stretch, and breathe deep from the fresh mountain air. The world seems great. I kick a log on the fire, which has been smoldering all night, and toss on some chips. Leaning down, I blow on a few hot embers. The flames flare up. Then I decide to catch some fresh fish for breakfast. I take up the pole that has been leaning against a tree next to my fishing vest.

Of course, the piece continues to the end of the fantasy. One technique this writer uses is to bring the reader (even though for a notebook entry there may never be a reader other than the author) into the daydream with a brief opening statement that presents the background. That's fine. If you decide to record a daydream and you know its background, include it.

WRITING TASK

During your thirty-minute writing sessions this week, practice by recording dreams and fantasies. They need not be current — if you have dreams and fantasies that you recall from different times in your life, record them. While practicing, be as concrete as you can. Include details. Finally, be sure to keep to the task for thirty minutes. If you finish describing a dream or fantasy in less than thirty minutes, write another entry. Perhaps you will want to include your thoughts on the dream or fantasy. Also, after you have made the entry you may want to give it a title. Sometimes dream and fantasy entries have the qualities of brief narration. A title can highlight the main element.

A thought on style. Some beginning writers who re-create dreams or fantasies will do it in one of two ways. The first is a skimpy prose style that generates a breathlessness by using a personal shorthand very close to listing. The second is an inflated style that decorates the entry with ornamental flourishes to make it seem significant. The cave and fly fishing writers made neither mistake. Both used a direct and natural style. In your practice work, write directly and naturally.

31 SIXTH WEEK: PORTRAITS AND RELATIONSHIPS

Some entries never seem finished. Dreams and fantasies may come neatly packaged with beginnings, middles, and ends, but memories are seldom as tidy as dreams and fantasies. Often, by tugging on a thread of some distant experience you may begin to unravel large parts of your personal history. You record and record and record yet seem unable to reach an end. Thirty minutes pass. Soon you've worked into the early morning — when to stop?

Well, there is no true stopping place — there is only an arbitrary one determined by the thirty-minute time limit or by the feeling that it's comfortable to step out. You see, a journal is as open ended as life itself. We don't live a life neatly packaged like TV programs. We live an organic process. When we write about it — even for writing practice — we may get caught up in its intricacies.

If you're feeling uncomfortable about the open-ended nature of some of your entries, we suggest you return to them and add more detail. Or, as you already may have found to be true, the details you left unrecorded in one entry may surface in another. This week's practice will give you a chance to pick up some of the material you may have left unrecorded, for you will be writing portraits of people in your life.

To begin the portraits we suggest you develop a list of people from your past as well as your present. Keep in mind that these people should hold some significance for you. They should be people you've been emotionally connected to, not people who just casually passed through your life. It is that connection that will fuel these practice entries. Now, a way to develop the list is to return to those parts of your notebook where you collected details from your current life and where you expanded entries from your memory lists. Reread those sections and make a separate list of people who appear in them. Your list should be more than a simple record of names; it should also include some brief comments to locate the people in your life.

For instance, here are three entries from an extended list developed by one student:

> Martha K: See her often. Sometimes we walk down University where the sycamores drop their leaves. No real commitment, just comfortable with her. We sometimes have lunch — introduced me to lox and cream cheese on bagels.
>
> Old Ben: Vietnam. Playing with blocks, Tinker Toys. Fishing at the jetty. Taught me about death.
>
> John C: Three years together on the football team — left and right halfbacks. Everyone called us Heckle and Jeckle. "He's Jeckle," we both once said, while pointing at each other.

Notice that this partial list includes specifics. The writer does not slap a few general comments on the page and leave it at that. If he had, an entry might read like this:

> Martha K: A real swell person. I like to walk and have lunch with her.

But instead the writer has worked in specific details — "where the sycamores drop their leaves . . . introduced me to lox and cream cheese on bagels" — along with some general words that suggest the quality of the relationship — "No real commitment . . . comfortable." The use of specific detail makes writing come alive. This is not to suggest that general words don't have a function. They do. But when a piece of writing begins to sag, the chances are it can be shored up with specific detail.

After developing a list of people, the next step is to select someone from the list to use for your portrait. At first glance a portrait may suggest a physical description, but yours will be much more. Besides physical and personality impressions, you'll include some background information and describe some experiences you've shared with the person. If you are writing a portrait of someone from the past and the entry leads to recent experience that connects to those early points in your life, record those details just as you did in other entries.

So this kind of portrait goes beyond a limited physical rendering; it attempts to show an evolving relationship. Here's a portrait expanded from an entry on the writer's list above:

> I can remember playing and learning from a man I used to know as Old Ben. I'm not sure how he came to be called Old Ben, maybe because of his white, white hair that seemed to get

blown every which way whenever a breeze came up. And his face was wrinkled and a deep tan from spending a lot of years in the outdoors. His laugh, though, was young. Whenever something pleased him he would laugh at the sky. He had a way of lowering his upper lip when he laughed — I guess to cover his front teeth which were chipped and partly brown, as if rust was slowly taking them over.

When I first met him I was about seven. It was a tough time. My dad flew helicopters for the Navy, rescuing downed pilots somewhere off the coast of Vietnam. At that time I couldn't understand what war meant — sure, I saw war films on TV and played combat with neighbor kids, but it was all a game. Because my father was gone, my grandfather used to come to stay with me when my mom had errands to run. That's how I met Old Ben — he came with my grandfather. My grandfather didn't care much for children, or at least that's what I thought then, because he would always sit in an easy chair and read. But Ben was different. He would always want to get down and play with me. He loved to build with Lincoln Logs (I had an old set that belonged to my father) and Tinker Toys. I can remember trying to keep his constructions together from one visit to the next. I would try to copy them; that's how much I liked him. Of course, I would always fail. For some reason I would end up needing a particular piece that would be in the middle of whatever he built. So when I would try to work it free, all the other pieces would cave in around my hand.

Once Old Ben and I went fishing. When I think about him now, I understand — I guess I should say appreciate — how patient he was. Last summer I watched a kid fish with his dad. The boy must have been about the age I was when Ben took me. The boy couldn't let his line stay put — reeling it in, shouting for his dad to put more bait on the hook and then to help him cast it out. His father was trying to fish also, but the demands of his son didn't give him time to do it. Finally, the father got angry. He shouted something at the boy, then reeled in the boy's line and put the pole away. The boy cried, trying to choke back the sobs. Now when Ben took me fishing, he never tried to fish himself, he just sat on a nearby rock and smoked a pipe while giving me simple advice. And once in a while when my line got tangled, he'd get up to help. Whenever I fish I think of Old Ben.

But Ben taught me more than fishing and how to build with Lincoln Logs and Tinker Toys — he taught me about death. My father was killed in a crash — that's a whole other entry and I don't want to go into it now. Everyone in the family came to our house. I remember some woman, later I found out she was an old cousin, who was somewhere in her seventies, coming out of the crowd and leaning her powdered face to me — I can still smell the perfume — and saying, "It was the Lord's will. Your father is with the Lord."

Later, I asked Ben about what the woman had said. He kind of smiled, keeping the upper lip over his teeth. He said, "That probably made her feel good to believe it." Then I asked him what he thought death was. He said it was up to each person to decide for himself. And the only way to do it was to spend some time studying death.

The idea of studying death hit a curious note in my mind. About three years later I had a chance to do it: Ben gave it to me. He had a stroke and was sent to the hospital to recover. Of course he didn't — the stroke had paralyzed his right side and he couldn't talk. He couldn't even smile because half his face was paralyzed and his lip had a permanent lifeless droop. I used to visit him when my grandfather went. My grandfather would read aloud to Ben, never really noticing what was going on around him. While my grandfather was spending his time in books, I looked into Ben's eyes. They always seemed to be staring back at me and asking whether or not I was learning.

Notice that the entry goes back into the writer's life. It connects to some very important parts of his life — the separation from his father and the death of his father. The writer skirts these large concerns by focusing on Ben, but they lie behind most of the entry's detail. If the writer continues to keep a notebook, he will probably describe these experiences. Once you learn to trust free writing, you'll find that notebook entries often lead to the important experiences in your life. Your entries may not go directly to the target, but they get there in their own fashion, something like a boomerang tossed in one direction and coming back in another.

Notice also that in this portrait the writer gives more than a physical description and personality sketch of Ben. Certainly these descriptive facts are in the piece, but they speak beyond ordinary description by suggesting the deep relationship developing between the writer and Ben. It is easy to see that Ben becomes a surrogate father by serving as a sometime playmate, teacher, and model. He even becomes a teacher for the final lesson of life — death. The father's death took place unnaturally and at a distance. The writer could only participate in the rituals, which were probably marred by insensitive comments as suggested by the appearance of the aged cousin. Ben's death takes the writer beyond cosmetics.

Finally, notice that there is tension in this portrait — the entry is built on opposition. This is suggested by the implied contrasts between Ben and the grandfather. Although the writer does not develop the difference, in fact may not even be aware that it is developing as he writes, two conflicting views of life emerge. Ben wants to get into the boy's world: to play at building, to show him how to fish, and ultimately to teach him about death. We see the grandfather with his nose poked in a book. He seems uninterested and withdrawn. This kind of natural tension deepens the entry by helping the writer to capture a universal truth.

We may be overevaluating a notebook entry. That's not what practice in a notebook is for. Yet, if you find subjects in your daily writing that capture your interest, return to them with the idea that they can be expanded. Those interests that naturally emerge from practice are valuable to develop the emotion needed to give writing life. This portrait is still ragged, as most notebook entries are. But it offers raw material for an original paper.

WRITING TASK

Monday: **Spend your practice time today developing a list of people to use for possible portraits. You can go about doing it in two ways. First, you might draw together a memory list by sitting quietly and allowing your mind to roam throughout your life history. As the names of important persons come to you, jot them down. Another way to draw up a list is by browsing through your previous entries in order to find references to persons who may be important to you. Put these people on your list. Remember to add brief comments about the relationship and the experiences you've shared with them. In other words, this is to be an extended list, full of detail and observation.**

Tuesday Through Friday: **Each day select one person from your list. Spend your practice time describing the relationship you've shared with the person. Remember to include more than physical details. Include all that comes to you about the relationship.**

32 SEVENTH WEEK: SOCIAL ISSUES

So far the bulk of your practice writing has been done by focusing on the personal aspects of your life. By zeroing in on current activities, dreams, fantasies, memories, and people from your past and present, you were guaranteed subjects you knew well and had strong feelings about. These subjects acted as flywheels to keep your notebook entries moving. You will still be working with personal responses during this week's sessions, but the exercises will have a new twist. They will take you to places located beyond your personal domain.

Although we may wish to escape them, the reality of our lives doesn't let us isolate ourselves from issues of social importance. Questions about such issues as crime, poverty, abortion, ecology, energy, political corruption, industrial chicanery, and international terrorism often take up our emotional and intellectual energy. Since these and many other issues are part of the larger social fabric, we must deal with them, at least on a personal level.

Often these larger-than-our-personal-life issues — these "big issues" — are the ones beginning writers most want to confront in formal assignments. It makes sense. After all, the big issues are the backbone of most academic courses. They dominate sociology, psychology, history, anthropology, and literature. Their dominance may lead beginning writers to feel as if their personal experiences are not important. This attitude could be the reason many students choose to write about the Mafia controlling American politicians instead of vandalism in their own neighborhoods. Or to write about the moral implications of abortion instead of the effects of abortions on people they know. Or to write about the American way of death instead of the death of someone they know.

Although in short formal papers the big issues are too large to cover, they can give you the opportunity for writing practice. Using them as a center for daily writing gives you a chance to creatively explore your relationship to issues beyond your immediate influence. But first you need to find out what interests you — to identify your social concerns.

The way to begin is to start your first writing session by sitting quietly and making a list of issues beyond your direct influence, the ones that occupy your thoughts or conversations. Don't formulate a position. Don't be overly detailed. Merely jot down a word or two so you'll be reminded of the concern that lies behind the issue. Here's an example of one student's concerns:

> noise
> abortion? not so sure!
> terrorism
> cigarette smokers — all smokers
> language
> whales — ecology
> killing/battering children
> not killing murderers (execution): capital punishment
> trucks

Now no one told this writer what should be important. Her job was to sit quietly and let some concerns she has about issues beyond her control come to mind. She listed them very quickly. Then after she collected a handful, she took the exercise to the next step.

The next step is to reflect on the issues a little more. The writer returned to the list and recorded in a few phrases the thoughts she had about the entries. Here's what a few of her fleshed-out entries look like:

> Noise: Portable radios blaring at the beach and pools. FM blasting in clothing shops, beauty parlors, restaurants, the cafeteria — everywhere. I can't seem to get away. Like music, all kinds, but when it's played too loudly and blares from third-rate speakers, it isn't music, it's torture. Maybe my focus here is the inconsiderate people who play music in public places.
>
> Abortion: For some reason abortion is on my mind. Have no clear feelings about it. Just confusion. Hasn't touched my life.
>
> Smokers: Tie in with music. Smoking in public places inconsiderate. I feel rage when around a smoker in a restaurant. They can kill themselves, but I don't want them fouling up my air. What about cars? Smog? The smog from cars is killing.
>
> Language: Never thought about language until I took a critical thinking course. Whenever I hear a politician speak, I feel stu-

pid — rather, I used to feel stupid — now I know better. Many of them use vague, deceptive language to fool the people — and that's me, a people. I want to get on the politicians' cases. And TV also.

Remember, first draw up a brief list, then flesh out each item with your general observations.

Once the list is complete and the observations have been added, you'll select one item at a time to extend. Just as you've done in other journal keeping tasks, you'll write everything that comes to mind during the practice time. As an illustration, here's an expanded item from the above list. Notice how the writer lets her mind drift with the subject. She includes details from the current news, history, and films.

> Terrorism: Should have written it with an exclamation point. But what do I truly know about terrorism? Very little. But to write a notebook entry I don't have to know anything. I just need to feel something about it, and I need to write my feelings.
>
> – A kid in a vacant lot. Several of us. Billy K. had matches and firecrackers. Was near the 4th, hot, hot summer. Billy stuffed a firecracker into an anthill, lit the wick. Boom! The ants began to swarm. Lit several more. Boom! Boom! Boom! Ants going crazy. Then he lit some weeds and began to fry the swarming ants. I watched, yet knew something was wrong with doing what Billy was doing.
>
> – Remember *Experiment in Terror,* film on TV with Glenn Ford as the cop. A heavy breather terrorized a young woman and her sister.
>
> – Films of Nazi Germany concentration camps (the word "concentration" seems out of place, the Nazi politicians/propagandists). The Uris novel, forget the title. Jews escaping to Israel before it was Israel.
>
> – Middle East, highjackings, assassinations, burning buses, exploding bombs. Death. Red Brigade, kidnaping, S.L.A., Patty Hearst — victim or criminal. What is all this adding up to? My thoughts are expanding but seem so confused. How do I feel about terrorism? Fascinated — sickened.
>
> Somehow it's all mixed in with people wanting change. If change doesn't come, the terrorists attack — beat the opponent to the ground, make a midnight call — "if you value your life" — or blow up a plane or school or movie theater. Stupid. I think of the opening scenes from *The Wild Bunch.* The gang shooting up the town parade. Many slaughtered. The innocent, that's what

cuts me. Children or just happy folks, everyday people, destroyed by some crazies who come out of nowhere. Boom! For no real reason.

Glancing at this example you can sense the difficulty the writer has in dealing with a large subject like terrorism. She doesn't have a great deal of information about terrorism, so once she lets her mind go, thoughts of her past come up, associations she has with terrorism from childhood. The childhood memory of terrorizing the ants echoes the sense of helplessness with which the piece ends.

WRITING TASK

Monday: **Begin by listing the big issues in your life. Then, once the list is complete, flesh out each item by adding your general observations.**

Tuesday Through Friday: **Each day spend your practice period by expanding one item from your list of big issues. Let your mind roam freely. Collect the associations you make with the issue.**

33 EIGHTH WEEK: SELF-REFLECTION

You have been practicing for several weeks by exploring a subject close to you — your life. We hope you are beginning to sense the scope of self-exploration. People, places, memories, feelings, objects, events, books, films, music, dreams, even unharnessed thought — all fall into that vast, partially charted territory called your life. We also hope you have made some discoveries about yourself. One of the side benefits of pursuing daily writing in a notebook is the self-examination that comes with accumulating a record of your life experiences.

If you were to ask around, you would find that educators disagree on what kinds of knowledge people need to learn to get through life. Should they master the classics? Foreign languages? Should they be able to recite math formulas and scientific principles?

The issue becomes more confused when you stumble across scholars and scientists who have not mastered all the important classics and who have forgotten the simple principles of geometry and physics — and are all doing just fine, thank you. But the educator reasons that these are rogues — the talented, the gifted, the intuitive — people who don't fit into the common scheme of things.

So the debate rages. You don't need to listen long to discover two views. The first supports practical education, one that stresses the nuts and bolts of living today. The second supports a more ethereal education, one that points to the wisdom in ancient texts as keys for unlocking life's predicaments.

But there is a neutral zone where weighty thinkers can meet and proclaim in a single voice (probably because none of them can build a course around it) that one kind of knowledge is indispensable: self-knowledge, the kind that comes from self-examination. During this last week of daily writing tasks we want to lead you a few steps down the path of self-examination, or as we prefer to call it, self-reflection.

Now self-reflection has nothing to do with parading what you consider to be your hang-ups onto the page. You must have acquaintances who like to lead now-I'm-going-to-tell-you-the-truth-about-you sessions, which are made up of an hour's worth of slander disguised in pseudo-analytical jargon. This is not the kind of reflection we suggest. After all, if insensitive criticism and verbal harassment could lead to a deepening of our self-knowledge, the chances are we would all be perfect. We aren't. And self-slander won't help us gain insight into our lives.

Instead of making a direct assault on yourself, you'll follow a more gentle course by merely rereading your entries and recording any responses or insights you have.

Once, after considering the course of his life, P. D. Ouspensky, an esoteric philosopher, wrote:

> There exist moments in life, separated by long intervals of time, but linked together by their inner content and by a certain singular sensation peculiar to them. Several such moments always recur to my mind together, and I feel then that it is these that have determined the chief trend of my life.

"The chief trend of my life," a very large phrase that holds some meaning for Ouspensky, but perhaps not for you. Nevertheless, the point is clear. Before he could gain this insight, Ouspensky had to collect his experience, reflect on it, and somehow come to conclusions about where he had been and where he was going. He actively examined his life.

Novelist Anaïs Nin, after years of keeping diaries, reflected on her recorded experiences:

> In the early diaries I speak of my feeling that I am playing many roles demanded of woman, which I have been programmed to play. But I know also that there is a part of myself that stands apart from that and wants some other kind of life, some other kinds of authenticity. R. D. Laing [a contemporary psychiatrist] describes this authenticity as a process of constantly peeling off the false selves. You can do this in many ways but you can also do it by looking at it, for there is so much that we *don't* want to look at.

Both Ouspensky and Nin talk about the broad insights self-examination has brought them, the former of the intuitive threads connecting his experiences, the latter of her awareness of a self behind the social roles she plays and the difficulty in reaching that self.

Reflecting on notebook entries need not always lead to deep insights. Often a thought will come that's related to your current life. Or you may feel as if you have re-experienced what you've already described. You may then want to extend it. After rereading a dream, one student wrote:

> Reread the cave dream. The whole experience came back to me, almost as if I were in the dream again. When I finished I felt I was still standing at the cave's mouth. Afraid, unable to move, just staring into the darkness. This is crazy, I thought, why am I scared of going in there. Then I began to imagine I went in. I told myself there was no reason to be afraid of the unknown. Unknown! The word sounded in my mind like a scream. Unknown! That's what the cave was. So I imagined I walked into the darkness. I had to put my hands in front of my face the cave was so black. I felt my way around a turn and there was a blue light ahead — a soft hazy glow. In a moment I was at the edge of an underground pond — more the size of a lake than a pond. It was beautiful. It seemed to glow. It was worth the journey through the dark. This entire imaginary journey took only a second, but I saw some truth in it. It told me that I'm often too timid when I face something I don't know or understand. Thinking the word "unknown" made me realize I'm frightened of it, but if I move ahead with some caution, it will be okay.

The sequence of this entry is simple. The writer reflects on the dream, which led her to again face the dream dilemma — to enter or not enter the cave. She suddenly realizes what the dream suggests to her — the unknown — then does in fantasy what she was unable to do while dreaming. She finally gains the insight that facing unknowns in her life needn't frighten her.

Whether or not her insight will have any lasting significance is not the point. What's important is that she's looked at a part of her life and come away with a message. She's been engaged in self-reflection.

WRITING TASK

During this final week of directed journal entries spend each thirty-minute session both rereading previous entries and recording your responses to them. You may reread several entries before you have a response. That's fine. The appropriate way to do this task is the way that works best for you.

34 CONTINUING WORK

We hope the several weeks you've spent in daily writing practice have not only perpetuated some good writing habits but also improved your writing fluency. We also hope you've accumulated a pool of material to draw from and use in more formal assignments. If you use your journal material in this fashion, you'll be in the company of many other writers who have done just that.

If Henry David Thoreau had not kept a journal, would we have the marvelous record of his life at Walden Pond? Any reader who wishes to make the effort can discover how Anaïs Nin's *Diaries* and Albert Camus's *Notebooks* fed their works. Even world statesman Winston Churchill — the man who led the British Empire through its grimmest years during World War II — claimed he was able to write his six-volume history of those years because of wartime diaries and journals.

Of course, it may be hard for you to see yourself as a Thoreau, Nin, Camus, or Churchill. But along with them and others who have kept personal records of their lives and times you may feel the satisfaction that comes with this sort of self-expression. Disclosing the self to the self, telling a private tale held in the heart, charting the soul's inner territory — these may be the deeper values of journal keeping. By this time we hope you've touched these values.

If you've been hooked on this mode of self-expression, you may be just beginning your journal work. Perhaps you've also found a direction. If so, keep writing in whatever way suits you. But if you wish to continue and have no direction, we have some suggestions.

Logs

A log is similar to a diary. It is used less to explore aspects of a life, as you have been doing in this section's writing tasks, and more to record important day-to-day details. It holds one danger: often a log can become routine and boring to keep up. In order to avoid a dull routine we suggest you focus your log.

Use one part to keep track of an important activity. Though you may also use the log to record interesting details along with the activity, the primary focus will be on the activity.

What is an important activity? You need to answer that question yourself. One thing is certain. Since you are a student, we assume you value your education. You may, therefore, wish to record your educational progress. Or to be more specific, you may want to record progress in a particular subject area or course.

But more than likely education is not the only important activity you have. You may have several. Exercise, art projects, hobbies, business, a household to run, even relationships with friends and family could be important activities in your life. You must decide for yourself. Keep in mind, too, that your list of important activities also changes over time — one might last no longer than the time it takes to complete a research project, while another, such as mastering a musical instrument, might last for years.

Arnold Bennett, early twentieth-century novelist, used his journal to log the progress he made while writing *The Old Wives' Tale.* The following selected excerpts from Bennett's journal also include details from his life, especially details of his walking excursions into the French countryside. Study Bennett's entries along with our comments to see how he kept a log.

> *Wednesday, October 9th.*
> Yesterday I began *The Old Wives' Tale.* I wrote 350 words yesterday afternoon and 900 this morning. I felt less self-conscious than I usually do in beginning a novel. In order to find a clear 3 hours for it every morning I have had to make a time-table, getting out of bed earlier and lunching later. This morning I calculated that I could just walk to the Croix de Montmorin and back in an hour. I nearly did it this morning without trying, in heavy rain. Tomorrow I may do it. A landscape of soaked leaves and thick clouds and rain — nothing else. But I like it.

Did you notice how Bennett also includes his inner responses — "I felt less self-conscious than I usually do in beginning a novel" — and specific physical details from his walk — "A landscape of soaked leaves and thick clouds and rain"?

Read a couple more entries, watching the focus, the inner responses, and the specifics.

Thursday, October 10th.

A magnificent October day. I walked 4 miles between 8:30 and 9:30, and then wrote 1,000 words of the novel. This afternoon we penetrated into the forest with our bicycles and without a map! Had to walk miles, got lost gloriously, and at last reached home after 2 hours 40 minutes of labour. Far off, in an unfrequented path, we came across 3 old women sitting in the hedge and discussing mushrooms.

Wednesday, October 16th.

I have written 7,000 words of the first chapter of the novel, and am still far from the end of it. Regarding it objectively, I do not see that it is very good, but from the pleasure I take in doing it, it must be.

Nothing but rain. I walked 4 miles in 59 minutes this morning in the rain. And this afternoon I went with Marguerite to Moret in pouring rain. A promenade on a thoroughly bad day in autumn is the next best thing to a promenade on a fine late spring morning. I enjoy it immensely. I enjoy splashing waterproof boots into deep puddles. Now it is dark, and I write this by my desk-lamp (after only 1½ pages my eyes feel fatigue) and it is still raining on the window.

Again, Bennett records his inner responses — "I do not see that it [the novel] is very good, but from the pleasure I take in doing it, it must be." He also makes some observations about the weather and his walk. The closing details relate to his working conditions and add reality to his entry. By embodying inner responses, observations, and some specific details, these entries go beyond a limited log of Bennett's work activity.

He continues this practice:

Monday, October 21st.

Today I finished the second chapter of my novel. I seem to be rather uneasy as to its excellence. The date of the first part worries me, as my own recollections don't begin till 10 years later than 1862. However, the effect of the novel will be a cumulative one.

Lately I have been overworking, in spite of all the resolutions to the contrary. I rise at 6:30 or so, and after reading Italian, one hour's walking, etc., I begin on the novel at 9:30 and work till 12:30. Then my afternoons are often taken up with articles. I had meant to keep my afternoons quite free of composition. Nevertheless, my health, thanks to walking 4 miles in an hour each morning, is simply admirable, and I sleep well. But my eyesight is weakening.

And notice in the next selection the opening comments on nineteenth-century novelist Stendhal. Bennett has read Stendhal's journal. He momentarily regrets having taken care, unlike Stendhal, in proper sentence construction when vivid, fragmented impressions would have served him as well. He then follows with a paragraph of fragmented details that capture the rain and forest before he returns to logging the progress of his novel.

> *Wednesday, October 23rd.*
>
> In reading Stendhal's unpublished journal in the *Mercure de France,* it seemed to me that in *my* journal I wasted a great deal of time in the proper construction of sentences. Quite unnecessary to do this in recording impressions.
>
> Still much rain. A perfect baptism of damp this morning in the forest, though not actually raining. The forest all yellow and brown. Leaves falling continuously. Horse-chestnuts quite yellow. Sound of water occasionally dislodged from the trees by wind.
>
> I have written over 2,000 words of the third chapter yesterday and today. I planned the chapter perfectly yesterday morning in the forest.

Finally, one last selected illustration:

> *Saturday, October 26th.*
>
> The forest is now, for me, at nearly its most beautiful. Another fortnight and the spectacle will be complete. But it is really too close to our doors for us to appreciate it properly. If we had to walk 5 miles instead of 500 yards in order to get into one of these marvelously picturesque glades, we should think we were exceedingly lucky in being only 5 miles off and not 50. On the whole a very wet month, with, on days free from rain, heavy persistent fogs lasting till afternoon. The sound of voices is very clear in the forest in this mushroom weather. I have learnt a little about mushrooms. I have tremendously enjoyed my morning exercise in the mist or rain. But mushrooming only interests me when the sport is good.
>
> In general, slightly too much work. 18,000 words of *Old Wives' Tale* in 2 weeks 4 days.

A work log, a collection of inner responses, observations, and specific details from his walks and the weather — all these make Bennett's entries interesting and vivid. We offer them as illustrations. They can be guides for you to follow if you choose to keep a log of your important activities. Of course, after starting your log, you will find your own way.

Extended Portraits, Imaginary Conversations, Unsent Letters

You may also keep your practice going by writing more portraits. If you've already written portraits of the people collected in your first listing, you might begin a new list and then continue the descriptive process. On the other hand, you may wish to extend the portraits you've already completed.

Since the people you've listed are emotionally important to you, you've probably found that a single portrait for each one doesn't truly capture the relationship. After all, relationships are complex, and to get at that complexity in writing may take several sessions.

In order to do it, we suggest you begin by rereading one of your portrait entries. Then write another descriptive entry. This time you might focus on one aspect of the relationship or on one event the two of you shared. Keep this up for several sessions, at least until you feel the relationship has been adequately fleshed out. We suggest, as with every entry, that you date these descriptions and that you keep them together in a portrait section. Remember to continue to record memories, physical details, feelings — all the stuff that comes to you while practice writing.

After you've fully described a person and the relationship, try writing an imaginary conversation with the person. These conversations are not necessarily transcriptions of actual conversations nor are they attempts to imagine what the person might say if the person were with you. These conversations are merely you letting yourself record an inner dialogue between yourself and the other person.

Sometimes these conversations will deal with feelings that have never been expressed in the relationship — deep feelings of love or intense concern; anger or gnawing frustration; perhaps even fearful feelings. Other times they might revolve around an issue or event. You may record an imaginary conversation during which you ask for advice or give it.

To begin an imaginary conversation, review your previously written portraits and then write a brief introduction that expresses the reasons for holding the conversation — nothing formal, just a relaxed explanation to set the scene. Next, address the other person in a way that seems natural. Write down what you say and what the other person says in script form — the way a playwright might record dialogue.

What follows is an imaginary conversation between a young man and his uncle. The young man begins with a brief opening statement in order to focus the conversation, then records the dialogue that follows.

> Uncle Pete was always important to me, yet I've never told him how important. I don't know why I haven't. Maybe because

I haven't had the chance or maybe because I'm just now beginning to realize how much he means to me.

Me: Well, Pete, I'm in college now. Bet you didn't think I'd
       get here.
Pete: I knew you'd get to where you wanted to go. You were
       the most determined toad I've ever seen.
Me: Toad! You used to always call me toady, ever since you
       read me *Mr. Toad's Wild Ride,* or is that the name of the
       Disneyland attraction?
Pete: I hope you're not majoring in history. You aren't one
       for facts. Or at least one for getting them straight.
Me: I used to sit on your lap and you'd read. And I can
       remember thinking of you as my father. I knew you
       weren't but —
Pete: That was when your dad was overseas — Korea. Your
       mother let me stay there while I got settled in Los An-
       geles. She is the best sister a man could have.
Me: I still remember the stories you used to tell me about
       the two of you growing up in Vermont. I always wanted
       a younger sister after hearing them. I wanted to live in
       the snow, too. You made me feel so good by telling
       them to me. I guess I felt lonely then and you made
       me . . .

And so on.

If you decide to continue practice writing by recording imaginary
conversations, you may find that they often circle back over the relationship as you've recorded it in the portraits. That's fine. Let them circle.
Eventually, they will reach where they set out to go.

If practicing by recording imaginary conversations isn't for you, yet
you would like to address a significant person in your life, we suggest
you write an unsent letter. The purpose is to give yourself a chance to
record what you're feeling in another format. There is no need for you
to bother with including a formal salutation; just get the letter under
way in a fashion with which you feel comfortable. (And don't worry
about sending the letter. Ultimately to send it is not the purpose.)

Here's the start of one student's unsent letter addressed to her room-
mate:

Clare: I'm tired of picking up your nightgowns, shoes, stockings,
sweaters, skirts, pants, books, papers, pencils, pens — everything. Tired! Tired, Tired, Tired, T-I-R-E-D! DOG TIRED!
This isn't working for me, but it must be working for you. You
leave messes like an unhousebroken, six-foot pigeon. And I'm

not cleaning up your cage anymore. You think I'm your mother, maybe. A mother I'm not. A zookeeper I'm not. What I am is . . .

The content of unsent letters and imaginary conversations comes spontaneously. We suggest, therefore, you give them plenty of space, recording whatever comes to mind.

Drawings and Photographs

When you first started journal keeping, we said that undirected writing — free writing —is a good way to loosen the writing process. We also said a journal is much like an artist's sketchbook, a place where writers can practice sketching fragments of their lives in words just as artists do with lines. Well, writers sometimes like to draw squiggles and curlicues, perhaps even figures from dreams or caricatures of people from their lives. They often like to decorate the margins of books and note paper.

What do these images mean? Who knows? We only know that to doodle doesn't take much artistic talent. In fact, doodling seems to grow from an urge totally separate from artistic drives. It seems to come from a need to meditate. There is a strange compulsion in some writers to let the hand follow the uncharted direction of the mind and create images in the process.

If you are a writer who finds yourself doodling, fine. Keep it going. Do it on scraps of paper or in the margins of lecture notes. Then paste the doodles into your journal. The next step is to describe them — describe all that they suggest to you. Ask yourself what the images mean. Explain where they come from. Write your responses under the doodle.

By writing about your drawings, you'll not only be practicing, but you'll also be exploring your inner nature. Here's how one writer responded to her doodles of a snake image:

> This is mister Snake. To some people he may seem dangerous, but to me he's the source of deep wisdom. Sometimes when I catch myself drawing him I am daydreaming about some problem I face. In many ways drawing him is like talking to a wise man — someone who knows the answer I need. I guess that's a dialogue because my drawing him makes me feel as if I'm having a conversation. He doesn't always give me a straight answer, snakes are like that. They speak with forked tongue. So I have to decipher his message. It is usually very secret, for snakes are secret things. This snake, my old friend, knows many of my life's secrets. He'll never reveal them. Just ask to see.

When this writer set out to write a response to her doodles, she didn't know what would come out; she merely started writing while focusing on her drawing.

A variation of the doodle exercise involves the use of photographs. This exercise can take a couple of forms. You might write a response to a photograph you see in a book or magazine. Or you might write a response to a photograph or photographs from your personal experience. We suggest you paste the photographs into your journal. If that isn't possible, write brief descriptions of the photographs as part of your entries.

What follows is part of a philosophical response to a photographic slide of Salvador Dali's *Persistence of Memory:*

> This morning in art history I saw a slide of a Dali painting. A crazy thing. It was filled with melting pocket watches — pocket watches that looked more real than real watches. These watches were melting in a desert wasteland with some strange trees in the background. One watch had thousands of ants crawling out of it. Another was melting over a strange ameba-shaped object covered with hair and with a tongue hanging out of an opening.
>
> The painting reminded me of words from an old song: "Time, time, time — what's to become of me . . ." And I began to wonder about how time worked in my life. Time is a funny thing to be thinking about, but I can't get the thought out of my mind. I wonder how time works. I know I live in time that moves forward, that is, I was born, I went to grammar school, junior high school, and high school. I know all this education has led to college, but in my mind I can be in all these places at once. Time in my mind seems to melt together.

While this writer chose to write about a photograph of a well-known painting, the following writer chose to record his responses to a series of childhood photographs. Over a period of weeks he spent thirty to forty minutes each day recording his inner responses to pictures of himself as a child and pictures of family members. His response to a photograph of himself as a baby being held by his father starts like this:

> When I look at this picture, I feel very strange. I know the man standing next to the birch tree is my father and I know the baby he holds wrapped in a blanket is me. But for some reason I can't emotionally accept the thought. My father seems so young, not any older than I am now, and I find imagining him at my age is difficult.
>
> Did he feel at 22 what I feel?

At that age he had a child — me. It makes me feel he had his life under control. But here I am at 22 without an idea of what I'll be doing four years from now.

My father now, compared to the picture, seems so much older. So changed. Once he was thin, athletic. Now he has a paunch and looks as if he never sees the sun. His hair, once full and wavy, is now thin. His face was smooth, now wrinkled.

At this moment I wonder if somewhere there exists a photograph of him and his father. I wonder if he has ever compared himself to his dad's image. Where does this lead, this photographing, this photographing of fathers and sons?

Where?

Back, back, back. And forward — into the future. The never-ending future. But somehow I feel there's knowledge to be gained from studying these images.

And so on.

The key to responding to images, whether drawings, paintings, or personal photographs, is to avoid trying to figure out what you are going to write before you write it, but instead to focus on the image and just write — write as an artist sketches.

Off Days

Writers have off days — days when the words don't seem to come in the right patterns. That's to be expected. Writing, like any other activity, depends on energy. On some days there are larger supplies than on others. If you have an off day, we suggest you do some simple exercises to keep yourself writing — exercises that don't require much mental effort.

One activity you might do is copy word for word a poem or a piece of professional prose you admire. The copying doesn't require much thought, since all you have to do is make sure you get the right words in the right order. But the copying will help you develop a feel for the English language. Good writers make good teachers. Use them as models.

Another activity you might pursue on an off day is writing random lists. These lists can serve as a kind of doodling with words. Be sure to center them — focus on a single aspect of your life.

To get started, here are a few ideas. List the joys and sorrows of your life and add the details you associate with each up or down experience. You might also center another list around fears — all kinds of fears: childhood fears and adult fears. Try centering on a particular period of your life and make a memory list or try centering on a relationship and make a list of its key events. You could also center a list around trips you've taken or music and books you like. No matter how you center your list, be sure to include some details, and always work in a spontaneous way.

On an off day one writer decided to write a memory list of his senior high school year. Read the first few entires.

> Playing ball: remember the photo in the *Daily Pilot*. Gil pitching the ball to me, the field open all the way to the goal posts. Fumbling. Ugh!
>
> Sally: two dates — wham. In love. Walks on the beach. Empty, empty sands. A month later, tears. Living in Denver.
>
> John: knew John since the 6th grade. Big John — 6'4". All black hair and white teeth. A friendly bear. Joined the Marines.
>
> Reminds me of: trip to big bear, Big Bear John — must be a connection. First time in the snow. The whole gang staying in Brenda's cabin. Took hours to clean it up. But the snow, white powder that seemed to float down, gently falling and collecting on the window ledges.

On off days this kind of practice will keep your hand moving across the page. You may also find that one entry begins to develop into a longer piece. If that happens, you're no longer having an off day.

Polishing

You have done most of your journal work spontaneously. We have suggested that by firing words onto pages you'll improve your fluency. We're not alone in this assumption. Many writers make the same claim. But there may come a time when an entry captures your attention, one that might not fit into a formal paper, but one you'd like to polish. If that's ever the case, use your journal as a place to polish the piece. Your journal, then, will be serving another purpose. It will be a workbook for you to practice writing techniques. In the journal you can work on a piece until you get it exactly the way you want it.

If you decide to practice by polishing interesting pieces, keep each draft. You'll then have a record of the piece's evolution. What follows is the evolution of a descriptive piece that began as a journal entry. The writer introduces the original entry this way:

> I made this entry after taking a long walk along the beach to one of my favorite spots, the end of a pier. It was late at night. I felt lonely. Sometimes when I feel this way, a walk clears my mind. When I returned home, I immediately sat down and described what impressed me.

What follows is her first entry:

>   Tonight I was feeling lonely so I took a walk on the beach. It was really a dark night without any moon, but the stars were bright and looked like tiny diamonds against the black sky. As I walked, I heard the crash of waves and saw how white the foam looked in the darkness. I felt how cold the damp sand was and knew I should have worn shoes. Up ahead I saw the pier. Its pilings reminded me of a huge skeleton. Soon I reached it and began to walk toward the end. I was still alone and I felt strange out there alone. Near the end I started to turn back, then I saw a man who interested me. He was bent over a bucket, putting bait on a hook. I watched him stand up. He lifted the pole over his head and tossed his line into the night. The hum from his line spinning from the reel sang in the darkness, and then I heard the sinker splash in the water.

About the first revision, the author says

>   After several weeks, I guess because I like the pier so much, I decided to rework this entry. My first goal was to edit it and communicate the sense of loneliness I had been feeling. For the first revision I cut out some useless words and phrases and concentrated on adding detail to reflect my mood.

What follows is a revision of the original entry:

>   The other night I was feeling lonely, so I took a long walk on the beach. It was a dark night without a moon, but the stars were bright and looked like cold diamond chips tossed against the sky. As I walked, I heard the waves crash and saw how white the foam looked. Ahead, I saw the pier. Its pilings reminded me of a huge skeleton. Soon I reached it and began to walk toward the end. I felt strange alone in the night. Near the end I started to turn back, then saw a man bent over a bucket, putting bait on his hook. I watched him stand up. He lifted the pole overhead and tossed the line into the night. The line spinning from the reel sang; then I heard the sinker splash.

About the second draft, the writer says

>   I wasn't happy with my revision. For one thing, it seemed choppy. I was trying to cover too much space in a short piece and the sentences didn't work together — no rhythm. The words I had added didn't create a mood; they seemed artificial.

I also found that the part that most interested me had to do with the fisherman. He was a lone fisherman just as I was a lone walker. Then I had the thought that he was also a night fisherman just as I was a night walker. In many ways we were both "fishing" — I didn't know if fishing could be used this way — in the night. Who knows, just as I walked the night to collect my thoughts, he might fish to collect his. The idea of "fishing" the night appealed to me.

I also got interested in the whole act of baiting the hook and casting. These acts seemed almost like a ritual or part of a dance. I also liked the idea of reaching the pier's end. This man was casting into the darkness beyond the end of things.

I decided to try to capture these thoughts and feelings, but to do it without editorializing — without directly saying what I was feeling. I also wanted to play with my sentence rhythms and end with the word "splash." For me splash says the end. Above all, I wanted to create a picture, something a reader could see, but also something packed with suggestion.

Are the elements the writer wanted to capture in this final draft? Study it to see:

The other night I walked to the end of the pier. The planks felt rough beneath my feet, while the sound of the surf slapping against the sand faded. There was no moon, but overhead the stars glittered like diamonds flung into the sky. By a lamppost that marked the end, I saw a figure move. It was a night fisherman bent over a bucket. He had a hook in one hand and a small squid in the other. Slowly, carefully, he worked the hook into the squid's back; then he stood. With the pole held overhead, he began to cast: his body near the rail, one foot forward, arching back and whipping the pole, the line humming from the reel. I saw the sinker sail beyond the lamplight and heard it splash somewhere in the darkness.

About her final draft the writer says

Well, I didn't end on the word "splash," but I feel the phrase "splash somewhere in the darkness" conveys more. "Darkness" to me means more than night and hooks back to "night fisherman," which I hope suggests more than merely trying to catch a halibut. All in all, I feel the piece suggests more than it states. That was what I wanted to do — to suggest.

Although there is a great deal more that can be done in a journal, we hope we've given you enough to keep you working.

PART FOUR

INDEX FOR WRITERS

This book is mainly a collection of tasks designed to teach you the process and structure of good writing. But there's more to say about writing than can be said through the use of tasks. Consequently, we've included this section to give you additional information about basic principles (such as coherence, unity, and point of view) as well as standard conventions (such as punctuation, capitalization, and agreement). We've also included more information about editing and revising and several examples of various kinds of introductions and conclusions you can use in your essays. All the material is arranged alphabetically for easy reference. Your instructor may guide you to particular entries as you need the information, or you may independently study the information. In either case, you'll be able to demonstrate what you've learned by integrating the knowledge into your work.

INDEX FOR WRITERS

Abbreviations

The best advice we can give you on the use of abbreviations is don't overdo it. What is acceptable is a matter of convention that depends on both subject matter and tone. Technical and medical writing typically include more abbreviations than general writing. And so does very informal writing — notes, lists, and memoranda, for example. The more informal the writing, the more acceptable it is to abbreviate. But for general writing of the kind you do for most college courses, the list of acceptable abbreviations is rather brief. If in doubt, don't abbreviate. You will seldom be criticized for writing the complete word.

1. Use abbreviations for titles and degrees used with complete proper names.

Mr. Samuel Needham	Gen. Edward Wymer
Mrs. Patricia Sandoval	Thomas Rich, D.D.S.
Ms. Sarah Glidden	Gloria Smith, D.V.M.
Dr. James Heard	James Hanson, M.D.
Prof. Susan Nelson	Bullard Ralph, Jr.
Rev. George L. Butler	Leslie Norman, Ph.D.

Don't abbreviate titles when you write them by themselves; instead spell them out.

The general will arrive by tank at dawn.

not

The gen. will arrive by tank at dawn.

The professor kept dropping the chalk.

not

The prof. kept dropping the chalk.

2. Use abbreviations for well-known companies and agencies. Periods are not needed.

IBM (International Business Machines)

CBS (Columbia Broadcasting Company)

FBI (Federal Bureau of Investigation)

UNESCO (United Nations Educational, Scientific, and Cultural Organization)

If the name is not well known but you plan to use it repeatedly in a fairly long paper, write the full name the first time and show the abbreviation in parentheses. Then use the abbreviation throughout the remainder of the paper.

Dwayne Merry, Ph.D., has taken the first steps toward his goal of establishing the Society for Cultural Interchange (SCI). The SCI will dedicate itself to . . .

3. Use abbreviations with times and dates when the reference may be unclear in your paper.

12:40 a.m. (*or* A.M.)

5:21 p.m. (*or* P.M.)

540 B.C. (B.C. follows the date)

A.D. 2980 (A.D. precedes the date)

If the reference to date and time are clear within the context of your paper, you don't need to include B.C., A.D., a.m., or p.m.

In 1980, the year of my twenty-first birthday, the sky fell dark at 10:05 on the morning of September 21.

4. In general writing, don't abbreviate

Personal names: Robert (*not* Robt.) Johnson

Units of measure: three feet (*not* ft.) long; two inches (*not* in.) high

Names of countries: France (*not* Fr.)

Names of states: Virginia (*not* Virg.)

Names of streets: Longfellow Boulevard (*not* Blvd.); the boulevard (*not* blvd.)

Subjects in school: political science (*not* poli. sci.)

Divisions of a book: seven chapters (*not* ch.); Chapter (*not* Ch.) 3

Days of the week: Sunday (*not* Sun.)

Active and Passive Voice

Good writing is vigorous and direct. In nearly all circumstances, the active voice achieves vigor and directness better than the passive voice.

Active	*Passive*
Jennifer softly squeezed his hand.	His hand was softly squeezed by Jennifer.
Arnie bought a fancy collar for his dog.	A fancy new collar was bought by Arnie for his dog.
Ruth slammed the ball over the centerfield fence.	The ball was slammed over the centerfield fence by Ruth.

In all these examples, the second sentence shifts emphasis from the doer (Jennifer, Arnie, Ruth) to the receiver (hand, collar, ball). The receiver actually becomes the subject of the sentence.

As a practical definition, then, we could say that if the subject *performs* the action of the verb, the sentence is in active voice:

I stabbed the mailman.

If the subject *receives* the action of the verb, the sentence is in passive voice:

The mailman was stabbed by me.

More precisely, the passive voice is formed by combining a "to be" verb (is, was, were, are, am, been, being) with the past participle form of a transitive verb (for example, seen, thrown, purchased):

He is seen	They are seen
He was seen	They were seen
He has been seen	They have been seen
He will have been seen	They will have been seen
He is being seen	They are being seen
He was being seen	They were being seen

There's no need to consult this list or memorize a definition of passive voice, though. Just remember that when the subject of the sentence is the doer of the action you have active voice.

In most situations you should use active voice. Why? For several reasons. Active voice sentences are usually briefer and more economical and therefore more direct:

Trinkets cluttered the shelves. (4 words)

Many trinkets had been placed on the shelves. (8 words)

Active voice emphasizes the doer of the action and is therefore more specific:

> Greg will always remember his years in the Army.
>
> Greg's years in the Army will always be remembered. (by whom?)

Active voice is more forceful:

> Hank pushed Rodney against the locker.
>
> Rodney was pushed against the locker by Hank.

At times, though, the passive voice is legitimate and useful.

Sometimes the doer of the action is obvious or unimportant and the passive voice is appropriate:

> He was elected senator five times.
>
> The high-rise apartment building will be completed by June.
>
> When Sanders became president of Farley Motors the decision to seek government contracts had already been made.
>
> Crosswalks should be painted at all intersections.

Sometimes the doer is not known:

> The windshield had been smashed and peanut shells had been thrown into the gas tank.
>
> Paxton's Liquor Store was robbed last night.

Sometimes you want to emphasize the receiver of the action:

> He was wounded by shrapnel.
>
> My car has been ruined!
>
> The entire block was flattened by the explosion.

But appropriate situations for the use of passive voice occur far less frequently than situations which call for the active voice. Carol Havens in "The Sky's the Limit in a Solar Balloon" writes in active voice, but twice in the following excerpt she uses passive construction.

> When Frederick Eshoo climbed into the gondola of his hot-air balloon and floated aloft over Albuquerque, New Mexico, at dawn, *the only sounds that could be heard were Eshoo's own cheers.* He had good reason for jubilation, beyond the normal exhilaration a hot-air balloonist feels on lifting off. For Eshoo was piloting a unique balloon, his own invention, which rose to an altitude of 12,500 feet and stayed up four hours, 10 minutes and 17 seconds, using the most economical of all fuels — the heat of the sun's rays.

Eshoo, an Iranian paper manufacturer and inventor who claims to be the Middle East's only balloonist, spent more than two years designing the balloon and testing materials that would make it an effective solar collector. He named the balloon Sunstat — a yoking together of the sun and aerostat, the technical term for a hot-air balloon — and he sees it as a harbinger of a new generation of aircraft and space vehicles whose *flight will be powered by the sun.*

The first passive construction — "the only sounds that could be heard were Eshoo's own cheers" — is appropriate because it emphasizes what is heard rather than who hears it. The hearer would be anyone witnessing the event at Albuquerque, but the important thing here is the relative silence of the scene and the personal triumph of the inventor. If the writer had said "none of the observers said a word" the event would appear trivial or the audience hostile. If she had said "he cheered in triumph" the sentence would emphasize the character of the man rather than the awesomeness of the scene.

The second passive construction — "flight will be powered by the sun" — is appropriate because the key idea here is the flight of aircraft and space vehicles, not the behavior of the sun.

The point is that selective use of the passive voice is effective.

And now, before we conclude our discussion of active and passive voices, we are going to yield to the temptation to show you an effective piece of writing which uses the passive voice almost exclusively. The subject matter is brain surgery, and Roy C. Selby, Jr., uses the passive voice to keep the focus on the process itself, excluding mention of either the patient or the surgeon.

A curved incision was made behind the hairline so it would be concealed when the hair grew back. It extended almost from ear to ear. Plastic clips were applied to the cut edges of the scalp to arrest bleeding. The scalp was folded back to the level of the eyebrows. Incisions were made in the muscle of the right temple, and three sets of holes were drilled near the temple and the top of the head because the tumor had to be approached from directly in front. The drill, powered by nitrogen, was replaced with a fluted steel blade, and the holes were connected. The incised piece of skull was pried loose and held out of the way by a large sponge.

Only one sentence here is in active voice. But don't let the excellence of Selby's paragraph divert your attention from the main point of this section: use active voice unless there are compelling reasons to believe that passive voice would be more appropriate.

Agreement

Agreement involves the correspondence of one word to another in person, number, or gender. A verb must agree with its subject:

Each day at 5:45 p.m. Harold ate two bags of peanuts. (The verb *ate* and the subject *Harold* agree.)

A pronoun must agree with its antecedent:

Wallace loaned Houston his camera. (The pronoun *his* agrees with its antecedent *Wallace*.)

Subject/Verb Agreement

Here are some guidelines to review if you have been making errors in subject/verb agreement.

1. Subject and verb should agree even when words intervene.

   Martha Tanner, who worked as an anthropologist in the Amazon, *has written* a book on South American tribes.

   Collecting stamps, once his teen-age hobby, *dominates* his professional life.

2. Two or more subjects linked by *and* require a plural verb.

   Corned beef and prime rib *are* his favorite meat dishes.

   "Cherrylog Road" and "Looking for the Buckhead Boys," no matter how often he reads them, *bring* him great pleasure.

   If the subjects refer to a single person or thing, the verb should be singular.

   The owner and manager of the store, Mr. Stevens, *decides* who will be hired. (Since the owner and manager is one person, the singular verb *decides* is required.)

   If *each* or *every* precedes a singular subject joined by *and,* use a singular verb.

   Each tree and each brook *is* important.

   Every comma and semicolon *is* to be exact.

3. Use a singular verb when two or more singular subjects are linked by *or* or *nor*.

   Jones or Smith *is* to pick up the package.

   Neither stroking nor striking *is* likely to change his thinking.

   A problem may arise if you have one subject that is singular and another that is plural. In that event, the verb should agree with the subject it is closest to.

   Neither Ralph nor the Snows *are* coming.

   Neither the Snows nor Ralph *is* coming.

4. Use a singular verb with most indefinite pronouns. Pronouns like *anybody, anyone, anything, each, either, everybody, everyone, everything, neither, nobody, no one, one, somebody, someone,* and *something* do not refer to specific persons or things. Most indefinite pronouns are singular in meaning, and you should use singular verbs with them.

> Something *has been nagging* me all week.
>
> Anyone *is* allowed to use the language lab.
>
> Someone *is* knocking at the door.
>
> Everybody *is* getting into the act.

Some indefinite pronouns, however, like *all, any, none,* and *some,* may be either singular or plural. When using them, select the verb form appropriate for the particular situation.

> All the students *are* to bring their lunches. (*All* refers to students.)
>
> All of the class *is* nervous over the final. (*All* refers to class.)

5. Generally, use a singular verb with a collective noun. Collective nouns are singular in form — administration, army, audience, class, committee, crowd, faculty, family, government, public, squadron, team, and so on — but possibly plural in meaning. Most often you'll use a singular verb with a collective noun.

> The committee *stands* firm.
>
> The class *meets* from three to five each afternoon.
>
> After dire predictions from sociologists, the family *is* still surviving.

Sometimes you'll need to use a plural verb because you are referring to individual members within a group.

> The committee *have split* into factions.

However, to use a plural verb with a collective noun often sounds awkward. We suggest, therefore, that you rewrite to avoid this kind of awkwardness.

> Committee members *have split* into factions.

6. Use singular verbs with nouns plural in form but singular in meaning.

> Measles *is* one childhood curse.
>
> Billiards *takes* concentration to play well.

7. Use a singular verb with the title of a work or with a word written as a word when either is used as a subject.

> *Games People Play is* required reading in Psychology 100.
>
> *Persons is* often misused for *people.*

8. Use singular or plural noun and verb — whichever are appropriate — with the expletive *there*.

> There *is* only one right answer.

> There *are* sixteen right answers.

Pronoun/Antecedent Agreement

Problems with pronoun agreement are easy to clear up. Begin by remembering that the antecedent of a pronoun is the noun or pronoun it refers to. Then remember that a pronoun and its antecedent must match.

> John did well on *his* project.

> The students did well on *their* projects.

Sometimes sentences are more complicated than these; then the relationship between pronoun and antecedent is harder to trace.

> Since the *students* requested the second *test,* I gave it to *them.*

Keeping the pronoun/antecedent relationship is usually easy. There are only three places where writers seem to run into trouble.

1. Generally use a singular pronoun with such antecedents as *anyone, each, everybody, none, no one,* and *something.*

> Something ominous made *its* presence felt in the mansion.

> Each of the women likes *her* teacher.

> Everybody on the men's volleyball team gave *his* opinion about the match.

In these examples the gender of the pronouns is clear. But often when you use an indefinite pronoun, the gender won't be clear. Although indefinite pronouns refer to no particular gender, by tradition you would use a masculine pronoun to match an indefinite pronoun.

> Everybody in the neighborhood did *his* best to clean up the park.

Clearly the neighborhood would be made up of both males and females, but traditional usage calls for the masculine pronoun, a tradition that unfairly excludes females. Some writers would solve the injustice by using a plural pronoun.

> Everybody in the neighborhood did *their* best to clean up the park.

Other writers would use both masculine and feminine pronouns.

> Everybody in the neighborhood did *his or her* best to clean up the park.

Even though this is colloquial, it is unacceptable in written form to most authorities. The use of *his* and *her* in this way seems cumbersome. Instead of using either solution, we suggest you substitute a sentence of this sort.

People in the neighborhood did their best to clean up the park.

2. Use a plural pronoun with two or more antecedents joined by *and;* use a singular pronoun with two or more singular antecedents joined by *or* or *nor.*

The dog and cat fought until *they* collapsed in the flowerbed.

Beth and her friends enjoyed *their* holiday.

Did either Joe or Tom pay *his* bill?

Neither Jill nor Jan will give up *her* claim.

If one of the antecedents joined by *nor* or *or* is singular and the other is plural, the pronoun should agree with the nearer antecedent.

Neither the speaker nor the respondents made *their* points clear.

3. Use a plural or singular pronoun with a collective noun, depending on whether the collective noun is used in a plural or a collective sense.

The team held *its* yearly awards dinner last night. (*Team* is used as a single unit.)

The committee is trying to explain *its* behavior. (*Committee* serves as a single group.)

The band put away *their* instruments. (*Band* acts as a group of individuals.)

Apostrophe

Errors in the use of apostrophe are common among beginning writers. But the situation isn't hopeless, because the apostrophe has only three main uses — to show contraction, to show possession, and to form plurals of numbers, symbols, and words.

Apostrophe in Contraction

Contraction is shortening a word or word group by dropping a letter or syllable. When you form a contraction, you'll usually join the contracted word to another word and use an apostrophe to show the omission.

it is	it's	you have	you've
you will	you'll	of the clock	o'clock
do not	don't	they are	they're
cannot	can't	you are	you're

Apostrophe in Possession

The possessive case shows ownership. Possession may be shown with an "of" phrase — the performance of the troupe — but more often it will be shown by adding an apostrophe and *s* to the word — the troupe's performance. Seems simple, doesn't it? But it's not quite that simple. There are several guidelines you must be aware of when you form the possessive case.

1. Add an apostrophe and *s* to show possession by singular or plural nouns or indefinite pronouns not ending in *s*.

Tom's book	Connie's car	Someone's hat
Men's club	Children's school	

2. Add an apostrophe and *s* to show possession by singular words ending in *s* unless the addition of an *s* makes pronunciation awkward.

the boss's desk	Lois's career
Charles's homework	Moses' life

3. Add only an apostrophe to show possession by plural words ending in *s*.

   the Smiths' car

   the writers' convention

4. Add an apostrophe and *s* to the last word in a compound or group to show possession by the compound or word group.

   mother-in-law's story

   everyone else's dream

5. Add an apostrophe and *s* to the last word in a word group that shares joint possession.

   Tom and Bill's radio

   Flora, Carl, and Hank's family

6. Add an apostrophe and *s* to each word in a group that shares individual possession.

   Tom's and Bill's cars

   Flora's, Carl's, and Hank's families

Apostrophe with Plural Numbers, Symbols, and Words

Whenever you form a plural out of a number, symbol, or word, add an apostrophe and *s*.

The second graders are learning to count by 3's.

His name has three m's.

I'm working for straight A's.

He bores me with his what's and why's.

Never use apostrophe and *s* with possessive pronouns (*his, hers, ours, its, yours, theirs* and *whose*). Those words are already possessive.

This cabin is theirs.	not	This cabin is their's.
Whose balloon is this?	not	Who's balloon is this?
What is its name?	not	What is it's name?

Generally, avoid using apostrophe and *s* to form the possessive of an inanimate object unless using an *of* phrase sounds awkward.

The door of the shed	not	The shed's door

However, a word expressing time or amount usually forms the possessive by adding apostrophe and *s* to the singular and only the apostrophe to the plural.

an hour's notice	a day's work
several weeks' time	a dollar's worth
fifty cents' worth	two years' delay

Brackets

You'll find little use for brackets in general writing, but in academic writing you'll find four specific uses for them — usually when you are quoting someone else.

1. Use brackets with *sic,* a Latin term that means "thus it is," to indicate an error that you let stand in a quotation. Often the error will be a misspelling:

   Susanne Singer writes, "Muddled thinkers who confuse the slogans of ad writers with concrete comunicatiom [*sic*] are doomed to live out their lives as puppets of well-paid hucksters."

2. Use brackets to correct a garbled quotation so that it reads clearly:

   In a tape-recorded interview, one coal miner reports, "I used [to] work twelve hours [daily] in the hole. Then [I'd] come home and cough till midnight."

3. Use brackets to clear up the relationship between antecedent and pronoun that may be clear in the complete text but unclear in the excerpt you're using:

   Top athletes understand the importance of slowly letting their bodies cool following a strenuous event. "After running a marathon, she [Helen Case] jogs another mile before doing thirty minutes of leg stretches."

4. Finally, use brackets to include important facts or to correct mis-information in a quotation:

> Gadzbar claims, "In 1975 at the age of twenty-three [according to birth records, he was thirty-four in 1975] I encountered an Indian mystic who altered my world view."

Capitals

The guidelines for capitalization are constantly changing; however, there are certain ones that writers rigidly follow. We'll give you those along with the suggestion that you consult a dictionary to see if a particular word you wish to use needs to be capitalized.

1. Capitalize the first word of every sentence or word or phrase used as a sentence.

> Carl sprinkles his papers with fragments.
>
> Why?
>
> Latent hostility.
>
> Watch out!

2. Capitalize the first word in a full quotation.

> The speaker states, "What we call a symbol may be an object, a name, a picture, or even a mental image that carries emotional significance for us."

Don't capitalize the first word in a quotation after an interruption.

> "What we call a symbol," the speaker stated, "may be an object, a name, a picture, or even a mental image that carries emotional significance for us."

3. Capitalize the first word in every line of poetry.

> To see a world in a grain of sand
> And a heaven in a wild flower,
> Hold infinity in the palm of your hand
> And eternity in an hour.
>> — William Blake, "Auguries of Innocence"

However, if the poet does not follow this convention, follow the poet's style.

> anyone lived in a pretty how town
> (with up so floating many bells down)
> spring summer autumn winter
> he sang his didn't he danced his did.
>> — e. e. cummings,
>> "anyone lived in a pretty how town"

4. Capitalize the first word of a sentence that follows a colon if you want to stress the sentence.

> The future invites us like an unworked mine: The eighties will yield wealth.

5. Capitalize the first and last words and every important word in a title. Do not capitalize articles, conjunctions, and prepositions of fewer than five letters.

> *The Maltese Falcon*
>
> *All That Jazz*
>
> "The Love Song of J. Alfred Prufrock"
>
> *Atlantic*
>
> "How to Get Through the Day"

Don't capitalize *the* unless it is part of the title.

> I read the *Atlantic*.   not   I read *The Atlantic*.

Remember, too, that the convention holds for titles that include colons but with a slight twist: also capitalize the word — even if it is a preposition, an article, or a conjunction — that follows the colon.

> *The Uses of Enchantment: The Meaning and Importance of Fairy Tales*

6. Capitalize the pronoun *I* and the interjection *O*.

> No matter how hard I study, I seldom do well in math.
>
> Thank you, O Lord, for this opportunity.

Don't capitalize *oh* unless it begins a sentence.

> Oh, I seldom do well in math.
>
> I studied math for two hours, but oh, how I failed the test.

7. Capitalize proper nouns, proper adjectives, and words used as essential parts of proper nouns. Don't capitalize common nouns. This convention may confuse you. To keep a clear head remember that proper nouns name specific persons, places, or things; that proper adjectives derive from proper nouns; and that common nouns name general categories of persons, places, and things.

Proper nouns	*Proper adjectives*	*Common nouns*
Freud	Freudian	psychologist
Shakespeare	Shakespearean	writer
Harvard	—	university
Nebraska	Nebraskan	state
Germany	German	country
Australia	Australian	continent

Specific persons, things, places

Norman Mailer	the Pacific Ocean
Judy Jernigan	Oak Creek Canyon
Tom Wert	the Washington Monument
the South	New York City
the West	Europe
the Northeast	Asia

Historical events, documents, periods, movements

the Civil War	the Middle Ages
the French Revolution	the Declaration of Independence
the Roaring Twenties	

Days of the week, months, holidays

Friday

May

Thanksgiving

Organizations, associations, government departments, political parties

Postal Service	Democrats
Department of the Interior	Republican party
Big Brothers of America	Peace and Freedom party
Young Men's Christian	20/30 Club
Association	League of Women Voters

Names of educational institutions, departments, courses, student classes, degrees

Huntington High School	the Social Science Department
Reed College	B.A. (Bachelor of Arts degree)
Math 54	Junior Class

Religious terms, religions, religious followers

God	Buddhism, Buddhists
Allah	Islam, Islamites
Holy Ghost	Hinduism, Hindus
the Virgin	Taoism, Taoists
the Christ Child	Christianity, Christians
Judgment Day	Judaism, Jews

Races, tribes, nationalities

Indian	French
Iroquois	Chinese
Negro	Mexican

Names of stars and planets

the Big Dipper

the North Star

the Milky Way

Mars

8. Capitalize common nouns when used as parts of proper nouns.

Fairview Road

Third Street

Mayford Park

Atlantic City

9. Capitalize titles when they come before proper names but generally not when they follow a name.

Professor Tamara Adams   *but*   Tamara Adams, professor of English

President Smith   *but*   William Smith, president of Edna College

10. Capitalize abbreviations that indicate time, divisions of government, national and international organizations and businesses, and call letters of radio and TV stations.

A.D.	FHA	NBC
B.C.	YMCA	IBM
A.M. (or a.m.)	NATO	
P.M. (or p.m.)	KTTV	

11. Capitalize the pronouns *he, his, him, thee, thou,* and *thine* but not *who, whom,* and *whose* when referring to the Diety.

God is a mystery; we cannot know who He is or what He is.

12. Don't capitalize geographical directions unless they refer to specific regions.

General directions	*Geographical regions*
west	the West
east	the East
south	the South
northeast	the Northeast

13. Don't capitalize seasons and academic years or terms.

spring	freshman year
summer	junior year
fall	fall quarter
winter	spring semester

14. Don't capitalize the names for relationships unless they are used instead of the proper name or with the proper name.

my father	My father lived until he was seventy-nine.
my uncle	I used to go swimming with Uncle Harry.
my mother	Mother played the flute, guitar, and piano.
my aunt	Give the book to my aunt.

Clutter

We subscribe to the notion put forth by Neil Postman and Charles Weingartner in *The Soft Revolution* that "If an idea cannot be expressed in language that a reasonably attentive seventh-grader can understand, someone is jiving someone else."

Plenty of jiving goes on. Advertisers, militarists, scientists, medical doctors, politicians, and even educators do it. For instance, what does it mean when an educator writes, "The ultimate goal is to motivate the client toward the successful completion of a quality educational experience"; or when a politician states, "Hope may be the one human factor absent from today's democratic landscape"; or when a physician announces, "The terminal infection began in the abdominal area then metastasized and permeated the entire system"?

No doubt these sentences hold some concrete information, but to get at it would be something like eating an eight-inch-thick ring of fat to reach the meat. Well, we'll start chewing.

Perhaps the educator means, "We want students to finish the course." The politician, "Things are dreary." And the M.D., "The cancer spread from the stomach through the rest of the body."

We're driving toward the idea that much of the writing we read is unnecessarily confusing. There's no need to use a difficult word where a simple one will do or three words where one accurate one will work better. It all adds up to cluttered writing, and cluttered writing leads to confusion.

You can cut out intensifiers, words such as *very, really, quite, totally, completely, definitely,* and *so.* In "Getting Started" we said these words carry over from speech habits. When speaking, people use them with vocal stress:

The REALLY terrible storm ripped across the bay and TO-TALLY destroyed business buildings and homes when it hit shore. The result was VERY disastrous: SO MUCH wreckage, SO MANY helpless people, SO MANY lost dreams. To see it was REALLY disturbing.

In writing, stress comes from using powerful words, not from using vacant intensifiers. In fact, intensifiers seem to "deintensify" by distracting from more muscular words. To see what we mean, reread the passage with the intensifiers cut out:

> The terrible storm ripped across the bay and destroyed business buildings and home when it hit shore. The result was disastrous: wreckage, helpless people, lost dreams. To see it was disturbing.

Once you've cut out the intensifiers you can clearly see what you've said. Sometimes you'll want to revise by adding more detail because you'll sense some empty spaces, and sometimes you'll want to revise to create a better rhythm.

In the case of the example, the second sentence seems almost telegraphic, moving forward with quick bursts of information:

> "The result was disastrous: wreckage, helpless people, lost dreams."

It could be revised by adding detail and by creating a more rhythmic movement:

> The result was disastrous: wreckage floating in the flooded streets, helpless people clinging to each other on high ground and rooftops, and lost dreams that seemed to have been carried away on the winds.

Maybe the phrase "lost dreams that seemed to be carried away on the winds" is too "poetic" for such a concrete passage. Okay, one more revision would take care of it.

You should cut statements that suggest modesty, phrases such as *I think, I feel, I believe, in my opinion,* and *it seems to me.* What do phrases like these tell readers that they don't already know? You wrote whatever they're reading; therefore, the piece must reflect your opinion, right? So cut modesty.

Also cut hedging. Sometimes you'll need to qualify your points; there's no doubt about that. But when it's overdone, you're hedging. You'll find yourself using words and phrases such as *for the most part, more or less, somewhat, rather, as it were,* and *virtually.* You may even write a passage like this:

> In my opinion the registration procedures at this college virtually require more discipline to complete than academic courses. For the most part, it seems to me, each of us is subjected to standing hours in lines that twist from steamy registration bungalows into the cement quad beneath the blazing sun. I feel the situation is not only unhealthy but also somewhat inhuman.

Do you feel the power in this passage? It's there, but hard to sense because of the excess language. After we cut the modesty and hedging, the energy comes through:

> The registration procedures at this college require more discipline to complete than academic courses. Each of us is subjected to standing several hours in lines that twist from steamy registration bungalows into the cement quad beneath the blazing sun. The situation is not only unhealthy but also inhuman.

Now the passage has more impact and reads faster. Often speed and power result from cutting clutter from your prose.

Let's consider prepositions dangling from the ends of verbs that need no excess growth.

> Beth called and said she would be arriving down from San Francisco Friday.

> We need a strong leader to head up student government.

> Don't be nervous; face up to the danger.

> I'll be there if I can free up some time.

Why use *down* with *arriving*? Better to write,

> Beth called and said she would be arriving from San Francisco Friday.

And why use *up* or *up to* with words such as *head, face,* and *free*? Better to write

> We need a strong leader to head student government.

> Don't be nervous; face the danger.

> I'll be there if I can free some time.

Are we nitpicking? Maybe, but remember a nit is a tiny parasitic insect that irritates its host. When a reader goes through a passage full of these verbal nits, he may not know what's irritating him, but he'll be scratching his scalp and complaining.

Roundabout phrases can also clutter your prose. Your goal is to write in a simple, clear style. Your words should be easily understood, and your sentences should move with some speed. But some writers, either out of ignorance or a sense of self-importance, impede clarity and speed by using several words when one or two will do. These circumlocutions muddy the verbal waters. Readers have to strain to see through the murk. As an example, read this handout distributed to members of a history class.

> Prior to taking this course you should have completed History 100 in order to be prepared to meet the basic entrance requirements of History 110. It is often the case that after several weeks

into the term students will come to the realization that they have not given proper consideration to the required prerequisite. If this is true in your case, make contact with me for the purpose of discussing the problem.

We have one major fear in offering this as an example. You have probably read so much writing like it that you may think it's high-quality stuff. Well it isn't. It's prefabricated junk — chunks of stock phrases strung together by a thin thread of thought. For instance, what does "prior to taking" mean in plain English? "Before," that's what it means. And what does "in order to be prepared to meet" mean? It means "to meet." And "to come to the realization that" means "to realize" or "to see." These phrases are roundabout ways of saying simple things. The writer needs to cut them out and cast them away. Once that's done, the writer will see other ways of making the passage even clearer. The first step, as you know by now, is to cross out the offending phrases and write in other words to keep the continuity.

> *Before*
> ~~Prior to~~ taking this course you should ~~have~~
> *take*
> ~~completed~~ History 100 ~~in order to be prepared~~
>
> to meet the ~~basic~~ entrance requirement ~~of~~
> *often,*
> ~~History 110.~~ ~~It is often the case that~~ after
>
> several weeks, ~~into the term~~ students will ~~come~~
> *see/realize*
> ~~to the realization that~~ they have not ~~given~~
> *completed*
> ~~proper consideration to~~ the ~~required~~ prerequi-
> *for you*   *call*
> site. If this is true ~~in your case,~~ ~~make con-~~
> *to discuss*
> ~~tact with~~ me ~~for the purpose of discussing~~ the
>
> problem.

The editing done and the continuity established, all the writer has to do is revise the passage for simplicity and clarity.

> Before taking this course you should take History 100 to meet the entrance requirement. Often, after several weeks, students will see they have not completed the prerequisite. If this is true for you, call me to discuss the problem.

The passage is no longer murky. It's simple and to the point. But be on guard, because many of these wordy phrases have crept into our daily communication. You as a writer need to be aware of them or they may muddy what you try to say. To help you, here's a list of circumlocutions with shorter and clearer ways of saying the same things.

come to the realization	realize, see
of the opinion that	think
present with	give
for the purpose of	for
in the nature of	like
along the lines of	like, similar to
concerning the matter of	about
prior to	before
subsequent to	after
in connection with	by, in, for
during the course of	during
in the event that	if
for the period of a week	for a week
in connection with	by, in, for
with respect to	about
with reference to	about
with regard to	about
in the amount of	for
regardless of the fact that	although
at this point in time	now
at that point in time	then
at any point in time	whenever
on the occasion of	when
in case of	if
in view of the fact that	as, since
for the reason that	as, since
with a view to	to
make contact with	call
it is often the case that	often
in as much as	since
the fact that	that
for the simple reason that	because

due to the fact that	because
despite the fact that	though, although
regardless of the fact that	though, although
on the occasion of	when, on
give consideration to	consider
have need for	need
make an adjustment in	adjust
is of the opinion	believes
give encouragement to	encourage
make inquiry regarding	ask
comes into conflict with	conflicts
give instruction to	instruct

And more, many, many more. These phrases hatch faster than anyone can crush them. They creep into the most diligent writer's prose. But don't be discouraged. We want to give you encouragement to ward them off regardless of the fact — which is often the case — that the language of public figures, college professors, and news reporters often comes into conflict with the value of clear, pointed writing. Don't be taken in. Fight clutter in your work.

The verb "to be"

One problem beginning writers share comes from using forms of the verb *to be*. Often they add clutter to your writing. Here are some examples of what we mean:

> Max Ernest was sixty-three and knew madness and death were before him.

> The sun was setting. The few clouds that were on the horizon were orange.

> Hemingway's "The Killers" is a story which is dominated by the feeling of impending violence.

When you reread a passage you have written, mark the various forms of *to be* and see if you can revise the sentences. Usually you'll be able to cut out some unnecessary words and use a stronger verb. Here are the sentences revised:

> At sixty-three Max Ernest saw only madness and death lying before him.

> The setting sun turned the few clouds hanging over the horizon orange.

The feeling of impending violence dominates Hemingway's "The Killers."

Now these sentences are direct and clear; moreover, they read quickly.

For further illustration, study the following student example while watching for *was* and *were* structures.

The motorcycles were sweeping into the park like 1000-pound bees. The lead rider was a huge man and was hunched over the handlebars. His face was behind a mirrored visor that was reflecting a minature and distorted image of the road that was stretching before him.

A good piece of description, but it could be sharper. Concentrating on eliminating *was* and *were* structures, the writer revised it.

The motorcycles swept into the park like 1000-pound bees. The lead rider, a huge man, hunched over the handlebars. His face was hidden behind a mirrored visor that reflected a miniature and distorted image of the road stretching before him.

The revision reads more quickly and carries more punch. The writer kept a *was* structure but added *hidden* to make the sentence stronger. That's fine; after all, we are not recommending that you restructure every sentence with a form of *to be* in it. We only suggest you restructure the ones that use it unnecessarily. Remember, we can't give you rules for editing and revising, but only suggestions. What to restructure is up to you.

There are/There is

Sometimes when you reread a passage you'll find sentences built on *there are* and *there is* patterns. We don't want to tell you not to use this pattern — it's an effective one — but we do want to tell you how to use it. *There are* and *there is* patterns simply assert the existence or presence of something; they do nothing more. The secret is not to abuse the pattern by asserting the obvious.

There are differing opinions regarding women's liberation.

There is a rift between America's Democrats and Republicans.

There is conflict over who is responsible for the oil crisis.

To assert the existence of differing opinions, rifts, and conflicts regarding such controversial issues in this fashion is to waste a pattern that you can use more effectively to stress a fact that may be significant in your paper. In other words, save it to announce real news.

There are more women than men enrolled in auto shop.

There is only one answer to this problem.

There are only two qualified candidates out of two hundred applicants.

More women than men enrolled in auto shop! One answer to a problem! Two qualified candidates out of two hundred applicants! This is news. News should be highlighted before the particulars are presented. *There are* and *there is* work this way.

But when something is beside the point, the pattern is useless:

> There is an old investment formula that says when the little man buys, sell.

If such a formula is commonly understood, why highlight it? Instead merely write

> An old investment formula says that when the little man buys, sell.

These are subtle differences compared to the way many beginning writers abuse this pattern. Often they unconsciously sprinkle their work with *there are* and *there is* sentences. Many times, while writing in this mental state, they'll also stir in some *it is* or *it was* patterns. To see what we mean, read the following passage:

> There are two types of characters in fiction: flat and round. It is the flat character who has only one outstanding trait, such as the drive of the relentless cop or the push of the power-hungry politician. It is the round character that is more complex, usually fleshed out with many traits and in a variety of detail. Often there is one trait that dominates the others, but the round character will be more fully drawn than the single-faceted flat character.

This is lazy writer's prose. The whole passage needs to be revised by reworking the sentences to eliminate *there are* and *it is.* Here's one way to do it:

> Flat and round characters dominate fiction. A flat character usually has one outstanding trait, such as the drive of the relentless cop or the push of the power-hungry politician. The round character is more complex, usually fleshed out with many more traits and in a variety of detail. Sometimes a dominant trait will stand out from the others, but even so the rounded character will be more complex than the single-faceted flat character.

If you find you write sentences using *there are* and *there is* ineffectively, rework them. Soon you'll find they will seldom appear in your rough drafts. Your first efforts will be sharper.

Coherence

One problem you need to avoid is the sense that your sentences seem disconnected — that they are running on watered fuel, spurting and coughing into action. When this happens coherence has broken down;

your sentences aren't working together. Sometimes the flow is broken because you have tacked an irrelevant sentence onto your prose; this is a unity problem and can be corrected by simply cutting the offending statement. A coherence problem runs deeper; the parts belong but have not been properly joined.

As is usually the case in writing instruction, the problem is much easier to show than to explain. Take a look, therefore, at this example to see what we mean.

> Nowhere can I relax more than at my favorite lake. I like a lake with clear skies and fresh water. At the beach, salt water always makes me itch and the smog is often terrible. There's privacy at my lake with no more than a handful of campers scattered throughout the pines and meadows. The beach is usually packed, and I go away feeling more like an egg in a carton than a human being. I like fishing for trout, cooking the trout for breakfast, hiking the trails, cooking trout for lunch, napping in the shade, reading, cooking even more trout for dinner, and sleeping under the stars. Sometimes I go to Harry's, a beer bar that serves down-home meals and country sounds. After about ten days at my lake and Harry's, I'm ready for another semester.

Do you feel the disconnections, the spaces between the sentences? Reading it is almost like being led on a tour by a guide who has your nose between his fingers. Who yanks your head from side to side while rapidly declaring, "Look at this — Now this — And this!" Who makes no connections. Who doesn't show the relationships between sites. Who just yanks and announces. That's pretty much what this writer does to us. He hasn't smoothed our way. He hasn't connected his sentences. To write coherently a writer has to learn to blend sentences together. Often this means supplying more information for the reader so that the relationships are clear.

Now read the rewritten draft of the above paragraph. The writer has supplied the connections and filled in the empty spaces.

> Nowhere can I relax more than at a lake I visit each August outside of Cedar City, Utah. I like the lake with its clear skies and fresh water more than the beach near my house with its smog and salty sea that leaves my skin itchy. My lake offers privacy with usually only a handful of campers scattered throughout the pines and meadows; the beach is usually packed, and I go away feeling more like an egg in a carton than a human being. My days at the lake move in nice circles: fishing for trout at dawn, cooking trout for breakfast, hiking the trails, cooking trout for lunch, reading and napping in the shade, cooking trout for dinner, fishing for trout at dusk, and sleeping under the

stars. Two or three evenings during my vacation I break the circle by going to Harry's, a beer bar that serves down-home meals and lots of country sounds. After about ten days of my lake and a few evenings at Harry's, I'm ready for home and another semester.

We can follow the writer's thought; the sentences connect. He has successfully rewritten the paragraph to make it coherent. One way he has achieved coherence is by filling in some empty spaces with more information. We as readers now know where the lake is located, why it's so important to him, and how he sees the time he spends there moving in circles. Since we haven't the power to mind-gaze, we need this kind of information to follow his point.

He has also achieved coherence by combining sentences, using subordinate clauses and phrases and punctuation techniques to tie them together. For instance, in the first draft he wrote

> I like a lake with clear skies and fresh water. At the beach, salt water always makes me itch and the smog is often terrible.

After examining the ideas in these two sentences, he sees clearly that they relate through contrast. He decides to make them cohere by combining the ideas around "more than" to clearly show the contrasting relationship. He also uses a *that* clause to pack more information into the new sentence.

> I like the lake with its clear skies and fresh water more than the beach near my house with its smog and salty sea that leaves my skin itchy.

Later he uses a semicolon to show another contrast. First he writes,

> There's privacy at my lake with only a handful of campers scattered throughout the pines and meadows. The beach is usually packed, and I go away feeling more like an egg in a carton than a human being.

In the revision he ties these thoughts together:

> My lake offers privacy with usually only a handful of campers scattered throughout the pines and meadows; the beach is usually packed, and I go away feeling more like an egg in a carton than a human being.

We've offered these opening examples and comments to awaken you to the importance of writing coherently. Guiding a reader through your writing is not a matter of catch-as-catch-can. It takes careful thought. You must anticipate the reader. But once you begin to think through what you're saying and develop a sense of a reader peering over your shoulder, you'll keep your writing coherent without too much effort.

There are some mechanical tactics writers use to keep their work coherent — transitions. As we said in Getting Started, transitions serve as guideposts to direct the reader's attention. Let's study some of the standard transitional techniques. They will help you guide your reader.

When you give directions, develop illustrations, pack your writing with difficult information, or shift in a new pattern, you'll need to take some care in drawing your reader along. At these times we suggest you use obvious transitions. Plain ones. Ones that give a clear signal. You can select from a stock of standard ones. Here are a few listed by how they function.

Similarity	likewise, similarly
Difference	but, however, still, yet, nevertheless, on the other hand, on the contrary, in contrast, at the same time
Addition	moreover, and, in addition, equally important, next, first, second, third, in the first place, in the second place, again, also, too, besides, furthermore
Illustration	for example, for instance, to illustrate
Time	soon, in the meantime, afterward, later, meanwhile, earlier, simultaneously, finally
Direction	here, there, over there, beyond, nearby, opposite, under, above, to the left, to the right, in the distance
End	in conclusion, to summarize, finally, on the whole
Restatement	in short, in other words, in brief, to put it differently
Result	therefore, then, as a result, consequently, accordingly, thus

Author, educator, and U.S. Senator from California S. I. Hayakawa uses a few overt transitions to keep his reader awake while reading this paragraph.

> *To cite another example,* students trying to express themselves in writing may write poorly. In order to improve their writing, says the English teacher, I must teach them the fundamentals of grammar, spelling, and punctuation. *By thus* placing excessive emphasis on grammar and mechanics while ignoring the students' ideas, the teacher quickly destroys student interest in writing. That interest destroyed, the students write even more poorly. *Thereupon* the teacher redoubles his dose of grammar and mechanics. The students become increasingly bored and rebellious. Such students fill the ranks of "remedial English" classes in high school and college.

Hayakawa is sparing in the use of overt transitions. But because they offer an easy way to link sentences, beginning writers tend to overuse them. We suggest you guard against this mistake. Too many on the other hand's, moreover's, futhermore's, and in contrast to's have about the same effect on a reader that a mistuned bass has on a music lover.

Also be sure you use the proper transition to connect your thoughts. Each one must be used in its proper sense:

> We could go to the mountains; on the other hand, we could go to the desert.

Why "on the other hand"? The phrase announces a contrast — usually an extended one. Since no real contrast exists the writer should have written

> We could go to the mountains or the desert.

Repeating key words and phrases — much more subtle than using mechanical transitions — will also help to keep your writing coherent. One of the simplest tactics is to interweave pronouns along with the subject. This kind of repetition keeps the reader's attention focused. Conservationist Cleveland Amory uses this technique in discussing coyote survival behavior:

> In such situations, the *coyote's* only hope lies in *his* cleverness. And stories of *coyotes* outwitting hunters are legion. *Coyotes* will work in teams, alternately resting and running to escape dogs set upon them. *They* have even been known to jump on automobiles and flat cars to escape dogs. And *they* have also successfully resisted bombing. Lewis Nordyke reports that once when a favorite *coyote* haunt in Texas became a practice range for bombing, the *coyotes* left — temporarily. Soon *they* were back to investigate and found that the bombing kept people out. *They* decided to stay. Meanwhile, *they* learned the bombing schedule and avoided bombs.

In "The Death of Marilyn Monroe" Diana Trilling repeats personal pronouns to maintain coherence in a paragraph that compares Ernest Hemingway with the actress:

> Of Ernest Hemingway, for example, I feel, much as I do of Marilyn Monroe, that *he* was unable to marshal any adequate defense against the painful events of *his* childhood, and this despite *his* famous toughness and the courage *he* could call upon in war, in hunting, in all the dangerous enterprises that seduced *him*. *He* was an innocent man, not a naive man, though not always intelligent. Marilyn Monroe offers us a similar paradox. Even while *she* symbolized an extreme of experience, of sexual knowingness, *she* took each new circumstance of life, as it came

to *her* or as *she* sought it, like a newborn babe. And yet this was what made *her* luminous — *her* innocence. The glow was not rubbed off *her* by *her* experience of the ugliness of life because finally, in some vital depth, *she* had been untouched by it.

Any repeated key word or phrase — not just pronouns — or any synonyms that carry the meaning of a key word or phrase can serve a transitional function. But remember, the word or phrase must be *key* — one that carries the meaning of the passage.

Poet Erica Jong uses this technique in a paragraph from "The Artist as Housewife." She says a major difficulty the female poet faces is "to raise a voice." She then links the idea to authenticity, a word she repeats throughout the passage.

> The main problem of a poet is to *raise a voice*. We can suffer all kinds of kinks and flaws in a poet's work except lack of *authenticity*. *Authenticity* is a difficult thing to define, but roughly it has to do with our sense of the poet as a mensch, a human being, an author (with the accent on authority). Poets arrive at *authenticity* in very different ways. Each poet finds her own road by walking it — sometimes backward, sometimes at a trot. To achieve *authenticity* you have to know who you are and approximately why. You have to know yourself not only as defined by the roles you play but also as a creature with an inner life, a creature built around an inner darkness. Because women are always encouraged to see themselves as role players and helpers ("helpmate" as a synonym for "wife" is illuminating here), rather than as separate beings, they find it hard to grasp this *authentic sense of self*. They have too many easy cop-outs.

Besides obvious mechanical and repetitive transitional techniques, writers sometimes use transitional sentences to maintain coherence. Sometimes these sentences serve as resting points for readers by gathering up what has been said and pointing to what will be said. Jessica Mitford in a paragraph from *The American Way of Death* uses this technique:

> The next step is to have at Mr. Jones with a thing called a trocar. This is a long, hollow needle attached to a tube. It is jabbed into the abdomen, poked around the entrails and chest cavity, the contents of which are pumped out and replaced with "cavity fluid." This done, and the hole in the abdomen sewed up, Mr. Jones's face is heavily creamed (to protect the skin from burns which may be caused by leakage of the chemicals), and he is covered with a sheet and left unmolested for a while. *But not for long — there is more, much more, in store for him.* He has been embalmed, but not yet restored, and the best time to start the

restorative work is eight to ten hours after embalming, when the tissues have become firm and dry.

Writers also use parallel structure — structures that repeat word patterns — to generate cohesiveness in their writing. The movement of parallel structures creates a rhythm that builds expectations in the reader. Lionel Casson in a passage from *Ancient Egypt* uses simple parallel structure to stress how far back Egyptian history goes. Casson opens with a brief topic sentence, then writes three sentences that repeat a pattern: *It was, It flourished,* and *It was viewed.*

> Egypt was ancient even to the ancients. It was a great nation a thousand years before the Minoans of Crete built their palace at Knossos, about 900 years before the Israelites followed Moses out of bondage. It flourished when tribesmen still dwelt in huts above the Tiber. It was viewed by Greeks and Romans of 2,000 years ago in somewhat the same way the ruins of Greece and Rome are viewed by modern man.

In more sophisticated hands parallel structure can penetrate the psyche by going beyond a mere technique for organizing information and shaping an emotional cohesiveness for the reader. Joan Didion reaches for this impact in the opening paragraph of *The White Album.*

> *We tell* ourselves stories in order to live. The princess is caged in the consulate. The man with the candy will lead the children into the sea. The naked woman on the ledge outside the window on the sixteenth floor is a victim of accidie, or the naked woman is an exhibitionist, and it would be "interesting" to know which. *We tell* ourselves that it makes some difference whether the naked woman is about to commit a mortal sin or is about to register a political protest or is about to be, the Aristophanic view, snatched back to the human condition by the fireman in priest's clothing just visible in the window behind her, the one smiling at the telephoto lens. *We look* for the sermon in the suicide, for the social or moral lesson in the murder of five. *We interpret* what we see, select the most workable of the multiple choices. *We live* entirely, especially if we are writers, by the imposition of a narrative line upon disparate images, by the "ideas" with which we have learned to freeze the shifting phantasmagoria which is our actual experience.

So far we've illustrated transition as a way of maintaining coherence within paragraphs. But we want to point out the importance of connecting paragraphs. The standard tactic is to use a transitional word or phrase to make the connection. You've probably noticed that several paragraphs we've used as illustrations obviously connect with paragraphs that came before them. Hayakawa's begins "To cite another example"; Trilling's "Of Ernest Hemingway, for example"; Amory's "In such situations." All are using obvious transition as they glide from paragraph to paragraph. Sometimes writers will close one paragraph with a sentence or phrase that sets up the paragraph that follows. X. J. Kennedy uses this technique in an essay titled "Who Killed King Kong?"

> Why does the American public refuse to let King Kong rest in peace? It is true, I'll admit, that Kong outdid every monster movie before or since in sheer carnage. Producers Cooper and Schoedsack crammed into it dinosaurs, headhunters, riots, aerial battles, bullets, bombs, bloodletting. Heroine Fay Wray, whose function is mainly to scream, shuts her mouth for hardly one uninterrupted minute from first reel to last. It is also true that Kong is larded with good healthy sadism, for those whose joy it is to see the frantic girl dangled from cliffs and harried by pterodactyls. *But it seems to me that the abiding appeal of the giant ape rests on other foundations.*
>
> Kong has, *first of all,* the attraction of being manlike. His simian nature gives one huge advantage over giant ants and walking vegetables in that an audience may conceivably identify with him. Kong's appeal has the quality. . . .

We don't want to leave you with the impression that writers select one method of transition and use it exclusively. If you glance back at Kennedy's piece, you'll see he uses repetition and parallel structure as well as an overt transitional phrase. Most writing is webbed with transitional techniques. The following illustration is an excerpt from "Prediction as a Side Effect" by Isaac Asimov. Words and phrases which provide coherence have been underlined and keyed as follows:

P = pronoun
R = repetition
S = synonym
T = transition
* = pronouns not marked because there is no previous noun to which they refer

In the 1650s, the French duellist, poet, and science-fiction writer Cyrano de Bergerac (yes, he really lived, nose and all) wrote a tale of a trip
　　　　　　　　　　　　　　　　P
to the Moon. In it, his hero thought of various ways of reaching the
　　　　　　P
Moon, each logical after a fashion. One way, for instance, was to strap
R　　P　　　　　　　　　　　　　　　　T

vials of dew about his waist. The dew rose, when the day grew warm and turned it to vapor. Might it not draw the man up as well, once it rose? (The idea was wrong, but it had the germ of the balloon in it.)

Another of Cyrano's notions was that his hero might stand on an iron plate and throw a magnet up into the air. The magnet would draw the iron plate upward, together with the man upon it. When the iron plate reached the magnet, both would tend to fall down again, but before that could happen, the voyager would quickly seize the magnet and throw it up again, drawing the plate still higher and so on. (Quite impossible of course, but it sounds so plausible.)

And a third idea was to use rockets.

It* so happens that now, three centuries after the time of Cyrano, we* do use rockets to reach the Moon. It is the only method by which we can reach the Moon, at least so far and for the foreseeable future.

The first man to show that this was so in the scientific sense was Isaac Newton, in the 1680s, and we still use his equations to guide our astronauts in their flights. However, as it* turns out, the first to consider the use of rockets was not Newton, but the science-fiction writer Cyrano, thirty years before Newton.

Colon

The colon has several common uses, none of which will give you much trouble. For instance, the colon is used to separate subtitles from titles, for subdivisions of time, for parts of biblical citations, to separate a word or phrase from additional material, and to separate the salutation from the text in a formal business letter.

Title from subtitle

>*Origins of the English Language: A Social and Linguistic History*

Time

>2:31 p.m.

>12:51 a.m.

Biblical citation

>Luke 3:4–13

Word or phrase from additional material

>For rent: three-bedroom house

Salutation from text in a formal business letter

>Dear Ms. Randolph:

>Dear Mr. Templeton:

These standard uses of the colon are not very troublesome. You probably already use the colon in several of these ways without much thought.

But the colon is also used after an introductory statement to signal that more will follow. Here are five ways you can use it.

1. Use a colon to introduce a series:

>She narrowed her vacation choices to three sites: the Greek islands, the Irish countryside, or the Swiss Alps.

>No matter how social historians of English look at their task, three dates stand out in the evolution of the language: 450, when the Germanic tribes invaded and occupied Britain; 1066, when the Norman French invaded and conquered England; and 1607, when English speakers colonized America.

2. Use a colon to introduce a statement or series preceded by *the following* or *as follows:*

>Agreeing with Orwell, many linguists see the relation between language and thought as follows: a person's thought depends on the quality of a person's language, and, in turn, the quality of a person's language depends on a person's thought.

3. Use a colon to announce a long or formal quotation:

>The author uses the weather to set the scene of his story: "I hear thunder roll through my neighborhood, and from where I sit before the front window, I see the wind lash leaves from the eucalyptus trees and swirl rain down through the branches and

around the street lamps, the drops, like fragments of shattered mirror, splashing into pools of light reflected from the pavement."

4. Use a colon to announce a second main clause that explains the first:

His intention is clear: he is determined to become President no matter how far he must distort the truth.

Keep in mind that when the material that follows a colon is a complete sentence, you may begin it with a capital or a lower-case letter. The choice is yours. Remember, though, whichever you decide to use — capital or lower-case — use it consistently throughout a paper.

5. Finally, use a colon to introduce a final appositive:

Only one person is capable of handling the job: Elma Bowen.

A single trait gives man the power to dominate the kingdom of earth: speech.

In either of these examples, we could have used a comma or a dash instead of a colon. Keeping in mind that the comma is less formal than the colon and that the dash is more dramatic than either, select the one that best suits your tone.

Comma

By clearing up any errors you may be making in using commas, you will probably be clearing up a high percentage of your total mistakes in punctuation. Mastering commas isn't too difficult, for commas are generally used in nine main ways.

1. Use the comma to separate main clauses in compound sentences. The comma should be placed before any connective — *and, but, or, nor, for,* and sometimes *yet* or *so* — that links the clauses.

The man in the front of the boat gave hand signals, and the boy at the tiller steered by his directions.

Most of us who were raised in cities yearn for elbow room, but few of us ever venture farther than our city limits for quick glimpses of open space.

When the compound sentence has brief main clauses, the comma is optional.

The dance lasted hours and we exhausted ourselves.

or

The dance lasted hours, and we exhausted ourselves.

My feet hurt so I sat down.

or

My feet hurt, so I sat down.

2. Use the comma to set off some introductory elements. When you begin a sentence with an adverb clause, a long prepositional or verbal phrase, a transitional word or phrase, or an interjection, use a comma to separate it from the main clause.

Introductory adverb clauses begin with words such as *when, after, as, because, since, if, unless, although.* The following adverb clauses require commas:

After she returned from Paris, Barbara moved into a loft and began to paint.

If you hope to get a well-paying job, you had better develop some marketable skills.

If an adverb clause comes at the end of a sentence, it does not need to be set off by a comma.

Barbara moved into a loft and began to paint after she returned from Paris.

You had better develop some marketable skills if you hope to get a well-paying job.

If an adverb clause is short, there is no need for a comma:

When I dance she laughs and the cat hides.

If you write a long prepositional or verbal phrase at the beginning of a sentence, separate it from the main clause with a comma:

In the early morning near the river, runners gather each Sunday for the Hash House Run.

Exhausted from hours of study, Joan closed her books and collapsed on the sofa.

To run successfully for a congressional seat, Hannah Becker expects to spend at least $100,000.

If you write a short prepositional or verbal phrase at the beginning of a sentence, you should omit the comma:

In scientific writing accuracy sometimes overwhelms style.

Facing east Ronald saw the sun rising above the hills.

When you begin a sentence with a transitional word or phrase, you will usually separate it from the main clause by using a comma:

Finally, I would like to point out the difficulty in funding a new student center.

On the other hand, the film treated a subject never before handled in cinema.

You should also set off interjections and direct addresses with a comma:

Great Scott, the world seems destined to self-destruct!

Sarah, why haven't you written?

3. Use commas to separate words, phrases, and clauses cast in series — three or more items of equal importance.

The colors of Old Glory are red, white, and blue.

William Faulkner, Flannery O'Connor, and Truman Capote are American writers with roots deep in the experience of the South.

In the trunk she found a faded dress, several dim photographs, two Easter bonnets, and a loaded pistol.

Sometimes he would become so emotional that he could relieve the tension only by running through the neighborhood, bursting spontaneously into song, or hammering relentlessly against the old workbench at the rear of the garage.

Some writers omit the comma before *and* and *or* when either is used in a series. We suggest you make a practice of including the comma so that you will not mistakenly lead a reader to believe the last two items go together:

For the picnic he brought cake, apples, mustard, sourdough bread, ham, and eggs.

is clearer than

For the picnic he brought cake, apples, mustard, sourdough bread, ham and eggs.

Whenever you join each item in a series with *and* or *or,* don't use any commas:

The kitchen has no working oven or garbage disposal or dishwasher.

The wind swirled leaves from the ground and bent the treetops and swept the clouds east.

4. Use the comma to separate coordinate adjectives that modify a noun, a pronoun, or any word serving as a noun.

The tall, lanky, big-footed youth sauntered through the doorway.

You can spot coordinate adjectives easily. If you can rearrange the adjectives without changing meaning or replace the comma separating them with *and,* then they are coordinate. If you can't make either of these alterations without changing meaning, then they aren't coordinate and shouldn't be separated:

> My uncle holds a Midwestern Populist view of economics.

> She walked down the dimly lighted inner corridor.

5. Use commas to set off nonrestrictive clauses, phrases, and appositives. These nonrestrictive modifiers are used to give interesting information, additional details, or further description, but such additions are not essential to the meaning of the sentence.

> Janice Smith, who graduated from Johns Hopkins in 1978, published an anthropological study this year. (Nonrestrictive clause)

> He rubbed his eye, circled by a bruise, and moaned. (Nonrestrictive phrase)

> The Cliff Palace, a quaint but rickety hotel on the Maine coast, provides vacationers monthly room and board for less than six hundred dollars. (Appositive)

Restrictive modifiers give information essential to the meaning of the sentence and should not be set off by commas.

> I left the book that has my notes written in the margin at the library. (Restrictive clause)

> The woman teaching the only class in poetry writing won the Most Outstanding Teacher award. (Restrictive phrase)

> The novelist Norman Mailer has been more successful writing nonfiction than fiction. (Restrictive appositive)

How can you tell if a modifier is nonrestrictive or restrictive? One way, which works for most instances, is to read the sentence without the clause, phrase, or appositive. If the sentence still makes the same sense, the modifier is nonrestrictive and should be set off by commas.

Our earlier examples of sentences with nonrestrictive modifiers do make sense when the added clause, phrase, or appositive is left out:

> Janice Smith published an anthropological study this year.

> He rubbed his eyes and moaned.

> The Cliff Palace provides vacationers monthly room and board for less than six hundred dollars.

If leaving out the modifying clause, phrase, or appositive leaves a sentence that does not make sense or is confusing, the modifier is restrictive and should not be set off by commas:

I left the book at the library. (Which book?)

The woman won the Most Outstanding Teacher award. (Which woman?)

The novelist has been more successful writing nonfiction than fiction. (Which novelist?)

Occasionally, a sentence will contain a modifier that can be either nonrestrictive or restrictive, depending on the intended meaning.

The students, in the back of the room, applauded wildly.

With commas setting off the modifier, this sentence means that all the students, who incidentally sat in the back of the room, applauded wildly.

The students in the back of the room applauded wildly.

Without commas, this sentence means that some students, those in the back of the room, applauded wildly.

If you write such a sentence, it's up to you to be aware of the possible confusion it might create for a reader and punctuate it appropriately. Remember not to set off restrictive appositives — appositives that give readers information they need.

The novelist Norman Mailer has been more successful writing nonfiction than fiction.

My brother Tom will be in Pittsburgh next week.

John the Baptist was an early Christian prophet.

6. Use commas to set off parenthetical expressions. Parenthetical expressions interrupt the flow of the sentence. Often they are transitional and serve to guide a reader's attention. Words and phrases such as *however, therefore, consequently, furthermore, accordingly, on the other hand, in the first place,* and *for example* serve this function.

Serious mystery writers, for example, try to re-establish sense in the senseless world of murder.

They are, consequently, destined for a life of struggle.

Gold, on the other hand, has a value that will not only endure but also increase over the years.

At other times parenthetical expressions will take the shape of afterthoughts or supply some additional information.

At eighteen, some fifty years ago, he struck out for Nevada in a broken-down Model T without a spare tire.

7. Use commas to avoid confusing readers. In order to maintain clarity, you will sometimes need to use a comma where one is not required.

> When sixty-five, executives of many major American companies are forced to retire.

> After eating, the cat curled up and began to purr.

8. Use commas to separate phrases that express contrast.

> He is a confused man, not an immoral one.

> His lips utter fire, but fail to burn.

> It was Jane, not Jan.

9. Use commas to separate absolute phrases. An absolute phrase is a parenthetical construction that modifies a whole sentence but is not attached to it by a connecting word. An absolute phrase will usually begin with a noun or pronoun and be followed by a participle.

> John ran through the rain, his feet pumping up and down in the puddles.

> Their faces calm, the drivers sat behind the wheels and gunned the engines.

> The film was dull, two hours stuffed with unremitting clichés.

10. Use commas according to established convention.

Salutations of informal letters:

> Dear Beth,

> Dear Fred,

Dates

> September 21, 1980 (*but not in* 21 September 1980)

Place names

> New York, New York

> Murphy's Bar and Grill, Chicago, Illinois

Addresses

> 2701 Fairview Drive, Costa Mesa, California 92626 (Don't use a comma to separate a state from a zip code.)

Numbers

> 345,678

> 78,632,112

Keep in mind that commas in numbers always set off groups of three digits and begin from the right. Also remember that in four-digit figures the comma is optional.

> 2,341 or 2341

Omission of understood words

This book belongs to Bob; this one, to Carol.

Burning Star does best at the start; High Prancer, in the stretch.

Comma Splice and Run-On

You probably already know that comma splices and run-ons are serious writing errors. But they are simple to correct. If you've joined two sentences with a comma, then you've written a comma splice:

Barbara French collects curios from around the world, William French collects maps of New England.

If you've joined two sentences without any punctuation mark, then you've written a run-on (sometimes called a "fused sentence"):

Barbara French collects curios from around the world William French collects maps of New England.

As you can see, there is very little difference between comma splices and run-ons. Both can be corrected in one of four ways.

1. Make two sentences.

Barbara collects curios from around the world. William collects maps of New England.

2. Use a semicolon. You may write a comma splice or run-on because the thoughts you're trying to express are closely related. Writers use semicolons to show close relationships between the thoughts in two sentences.

Barbara collects curios from around the world; William collects maps of New England.

Primitive people have myths that reflect group consciousness, modern people have television.

Primitive people have myths that reflect group consciousness; modern people have television.

American adolescence ended at the Pacific Ocean American maturity started with a turn toward the Atlantic.

American adolescence ended at the Pacific Ocean; American maturity started with a turn toward the Atlantic.

3. Use a coordinating conjunction. The ideas in the sentences must be closely related, and the coordinating conjunction must be preceded by a comma.

Barbara collects curios from around the world, and William collects maps of New England.

When you use a coordinating conjunction to repair a comma splice or run-on, be sure to select the one that reflects the proper relationship between your ideas: *and* shows complementary relationships; *but* and *yet* show contradictory relationships; and *or* and *nor* show alternate relationships.

4. Use a subordinate structure. When one idea is more important than the other, you can subordinate the less important idea in a dependent clause by using a subordinate conjunction or relative pronoun.

Emphysema's ultimate effect on the body is deprivation of oxygen; it kills by suffocating.

Since emphysema's ultimate effect on the body is deprivation of oxygen, it kills by suffocating.

Houston plays a gold-plated flute he got it as a gift.

Houston plays a gold-plated flute, which he got as a gift.

Common Word Mistakes

Accept/except

The word *accept* is always a verb meaning "to take," "to receive," or "to agree to."

Gladys accepted the gift graciously.

Eventually Tony accepted the fact that he would never make the team.

The word *except* is usually used as a preposition meaning "but."

Everyone except Charley arrived on time.

Affect/effect

Affect is a verb meaning either "to influence" or "to pretend."

Your refusal will not affect my plan to go.

He affected nonchalance to hide his sense of insecurity.

Effect usually means "result" and functions as a noun.

What was the effect of your disagreeing with him in class?

Sometimes *effect* serves as a verb that means "to cause to occur," "to bring about," or "to make."

His legislation effected an important change in the way we spend our tax money.

All right

All right should be spelled as two words. The one-word spelling *alright* is never acceptable in formal or informal writing even though it may be seen in printed conversations, advertising copy, or comic strips.

A lot

Always use two words — *a lot,* not *alot.*

Amount, number

If you are referring to something usually measured or weighed but not ordinarily counted, use *amount.* If you are referring to something which can be counted, use *number.*

> They poured a large amount of concrete.
>
> The chef's first duty was to bake a large number of pies.

Its, it's

Its is a possessive pronoun. *It's* is a contraction of "it is."

> The dog scratched its hind leg.
>
> It's raining in the mountains.

Less, fewer

If you are referring to something that is usually measured or weighed but not counted, use *less.* If you are referring to something that can be counted, use *fewer.*

> Americans are using less sugar now.
>
> Americans are buying fewer new cars.

Lie, lay

You can use the word *lie* to declare, "He told a white lie to excuse his missing a car payment." Or you can use it to say, "No matter how often I confront him, he continues to lie behind my back." These uses of *lie* probably don't give you any trouble. But when it serves as a verb that means "to recline," you might confuse *to lie* with *to lay,* which means "to place."

Perhaps the reason these verbs are often confused is that the past tense of *to lie* (meaning "to recline") is the same as the present tense of *to lay* (meaning "to place").

to lie (to recline)	to lay (to place)
lie	lay
lay	laid
lain	laid
lying	laying

Now let's put them into action. First sentences using *to lie* ("to recline").

> Don't call — I plan to lie down for an hour.

Yesterday, Pam lay in the sun for three hours, turning her skin from white to pink.

I had lain in bed for two hours before the phone rang.

His clothes were lying on chairs, the bed, and floor.

Now study the uses of *to lay* ("to place") in sentences. Notice that forms of *to lay* take objects — that is, something must be laid and that something, except in cases of the most controlled sentences, will come after the verb.

Lay the book on the table.

Yesterday, I laid carpet from morning until evening.

She has laid her pen down and is now traveling for more experience to write about.

Laying painful experiences to rest is difficult.

Their, there, they're

Their is a possessive pronoun showing plural ownership. *There* indicates a place or serves as an expletive (as in *There* are three men on deck). *They're* is a contraction for "they are."

Where is their house?

The house is over there.

They're at the house.

To, too, two

To means "toward," "until," and is also used before a verb, as in "to dance." *Too* means "more than enough" and "also." *Two* is the written form for the number 2.

They went to the theater to see *Jaws*.

His tennis game is too good for the other players.

Give me two dozen eggs.

Whose, who's

Whose is a possessive pronoun. *Who's* is a contraction of "who is."

Whose sock is this?

Who's the one walking the dog?

You're, your

You're is a contraction of "you are." *Your* is a possessive pronoun.

You're not as young as you used to be.

This is your book.

Conclusions

Like introductions, conclusions come in variety; no single one serves all purposes. Your only obligation is to design one that naturally follows from the entire paper and clearly ends it. Avoid writing a conclusion that seems tacked on, and never — never, never, never — write one that raises a new question or apologizes for not covering the subject.

In college writing, the most common practice is to restate the central point and then summarize the subpoints in order to reinforce what has come before. Too often the summary method seems mechanical, but it can be effective if the writer handles it in an interesting way. A summary conclusion does have one strong advantage because it clearly links with the rest of the essay. The following paragraphs from a student paper that deals with investing in the stock market illustrate the summary method. Although we've left the discussion out, you can easily see what it covered.

The introduction:

> If you have any cash stuffed in jars or mattresses or just lying around in some passbook account, lazily accruing 5¼ percent interest, you would be wiser to fling it on a crap table. A crap game would give better odds at coming out ahead, for, as sure as a mouse with enough time will eat a pound of cheese, double-digit inflation will nibble your money away. At least on the crap table, although you would be bucking tremendous odds against winning, you would have a sporting chance. And there is always the payoff and the high you would get from watching the dice skip and jump over the green felt. But if you are too conservative for the Vegas thrill, then you might want to try the stock market. Even though the market is at an all-time low, it has some advantages for the cautious investor. First, you get paid for playing in the forms of dividends. Second, you get tax breaks. And third, there's better than fifty/fifty odds the market will rise.

Now the concluding summary:

> Is the market a good risk? It's clearly better than rat-holing your money or even stashing it in a savings account. Moreover, you get paid for playing, taxes work to your advantage, and the market, like an angry drunk pushed to the floor, will rise.

Besides the summary method there are several other standard ways writers use to write conclusions.

1. A writer may use the conclusion to deepen the dimension of an essay. One student ended a paper on being robbed and threatened at pistol point by shifting from the external details of the experience to an implicit psychological fact. Notice the following writer's use of questions to put the reader in a reflective mood.

> And what does it mean when somebody holds you up? Just the loss of a few dollars? Or just the loss of a wallet and some mementos — a few peeling photographs, worn identification cards, tattered ticket stubs? Yes, it means that. And it means more. It means you have become part of that chosen group that no longer feels safe after dark to walk the neighborhood streets.

Although the writer draws a fresh inference from the whole paper, she does not raise a new issue. She has, instead, highlighted an implicit aspect that ran beneath the surface of the entire essay.

2. A writer may also conclude an essay with an anecdote — a brief story — that puts the central idea in clear perspective. Nora Gallagher closes with this method in an article that deals with homosexual rights.

> A group of citizens tried to remove a gay group's name from a Bicentennial plaque. They met with resistance from City Councilman Leon Mezzetti, who said, "I wouldn't necessarily want the gays teaching my children, but the rules were that for 50 bucks you got your name on the plaque. And the gay people, God bless 'em, are following the rules. . . .
>
> "This is America. You can't change the rules after the fact, or you may as well tear the plaque down."

3. A writer may conclude by drawing a lesson that links the subject to the reader's condition. Tom Wicker in "Kennedy Without End, Amen" explores the significance of John Kennedy's brief term as president. Wicker adds a new dimension to his essay by linking the lessons Kennedy learned to the reader's learning process.

> In his life, I wrote those many years ago, "he had had his dreams and realized them," but he learned also the hard lessons of power and its limitations. After his death, the rest of us began to learn those lessons, too. The shots ringing out in Dealey Plaza marked the beginning of the end of innocence.

4. A writer may conclude with a quotation that deepens the meaning of an essay. One student who wrote a description of her creative process used a quotation from Joseph Campbell to knot the threads of her thought.

> At best my artistic process seems haphazard, a kind of inner blindman's bluff that finds its expression in chaotic collages. My groping and stumbling used to bother me until I came across a passage in Joseph Campbell's "The Inspiration of Oriental Art." He writes, "There is an important Chinese term, *wu wei, not doing,* the meaning of which is not *doing nothing,* but *not forcing.* Things will open up of themselves, according to their nature."

A writer may find that a quote is especially effective to end an interview or profile. Michelle Arnot concludes an article on the pleasures of massage that highlights the methods of New York masseuse Joan Witkowski.

> If you're not getting rubbed the wrong way, you may well become addicted. Joan finds that her vacations cause panic among her clients. "I have to sneak away," she reports. "But it's always nice to come back. It's great to feel needed."
> Or kneaded.

These samples are just a few of the many ways writers use to end essays. Notice, also, how methods tend to overlap. One has a quotation, but the quotation is a definition. Another holds an anecdote, but the anecdote includes a quotation. Several use questions. Whatever label is placed on a method isn't important. What is important is to write a conclusion that echoes the entire essay.

By the way — and we save this by the way for last in order to burn it into your mind — never, absolutely never, write "The End" after an essay's conclusion.

Dangling and Misplaced Modifiers

You run the risk of confusing your reader unless modifiers (words, phrases, or clauses used as adjectives or adverbs) clearly relate to the words they modify.

Sometimes the problem occurs because the modifier is misplaced — put in a position within the sentence that makes it appear to modify something it doesn't. Misplaced modifiers are sometimes confusing and sometimes nonsensical.

> Mr. Sheridan kept a record of all the money he made in his bureau drawer.
>
> She gave the candy to the neighborhood children that didn't turn out right.

The solution for this kind of misplacement is to reposition the modifier.

> In his bureau drawer Mr. Sheridan kept a record of all the money he had made.
>
> She gave the candy that didn't turn out right to the neighborhood children.

Other times the problem occurs because a modifier is left dangling with no word or phrase to modify.

> Walking along the country road, the sun rose gradually over the hilltops.
>
> While ordering hotdogs, "The Star-Spangled Banner" played over the loudspeaker.

These sentences seem to say that the sun was walking along the country road and that "The Star-Spangled Banner" ordered hotdogs because the writers have left something out — in these two examples, the pronoun *we*. Such sentences need to be revised to make the parts fit properly together.

> As we were walking along the country road, the sun rose gradually over the hilltops.

or

> Walking along the country road, we saw the sun rise gradually over the hilltops.

> While we were ordering hotdogs, "The Star-Spangled Banner" played over the loudspeaker.

or

> While ordering hotdogs, we heard "The Star-Spangled Banner" played over the loudspeaker.

Dash

Be cautious with dashes. When used properly they can be dramatic; when used improperly, tiresome and confusing. In a typed paper, you can make a dash by striking the hyphen key twice without spacing.

1. Use dashes to dramatize parenthetical elements.

> Harold ran — given the heat, slouched — six miles to come in last.

> Judge Sarah Riley sentenced Tom O'Keeffe — the treasurer of Local 1918 and once the friend of local politicians — to five years at Soledad prison.

2. Use dashes to dramatize appositives.

> Halfway through the party Phil Lambert — the man in the black cape and tuxedo who kept trying to bite Sam's neck — fell from the balcony into the tulip bed.

> He has only three vices — vice, vice, and vice.

> One love dominates my dreams — food.

3. Use a dash to separate a series that comes at the beginning of a sentence.

> Aching feet and ankles, throbbing shins, clicking knees, and crumbling hip joints — these are the physical joys that come with running on asphalt and cement.

4. Use a dash to show a break in thought.

> I don't know — it's just that — okay, I'll donate twenty dollars.

He said, "You don't like it."
"It's too —"
"Too colorful?" he asked.
"Too — well, too skimpy."

When using the dash in this way, be sure to omit the period or the question mark.

5. Use a dash to precede an author's name after a direct quotation that has not been introduced or after one that stands separately from the text.

"If I had the use of my body I would throw it out the window."
  — *Samuel Beckett*

Success is counted sweetest
By those who ne'er succeed.
To comprehend a nectar
Requires sorest need.
  — *Emily Dickinson*

Editing and Revising

Sometimes students have the idea that editing and revising has something to do with pleasing a minor deity who presides over the uses of grammar and punctuation: each pronoun must be scrutinized to be sure it agrees with its antecedent; each comma, to be sure it is properly situated. A writer must be concerned with grammar and punctuation, no doubt about that. And we suggest you buy a good writer's handbook, perhaps one your instructor recommends, to help you with those concerns. But grammar and punctuation have more to do with rules and memorization than with editing and revising. To edit and revise properly, writers must evaluate each word, phrase, sentence, and paragraph of their work. It is a thoughtful process, not one governed by rules. When writers edit and revise a passage, they have no authority to guide them, no handbook to fall back on. They are alone.

We've already talked a little about editing and revising in Part One, Getting Started, and we suggest you review that section if you feel the general concepts have slipped away. But now we want to illustrate the process in more detail and to give you more information about doing it. We hope the information will ease the discomfort that sometimes comes from traveling without an authority.

If you're like most beginning writers, even some professional ones, you'll have a tough time accepting the idea that your prose isn't sacred. You've strained for ideas. You've found words to capture them. Nudged the words into sentences. Shaped the sentences into paragraphs. You've lavished time and energy on the whole creation. Why, you might ask, should I have to tinker with it any more?

Why indeed?

Your rough draft, like those of most writers, probably isn't much more than a scrawny chicken inflated to pass as a Thanksgiving turkey.

We're not suggesting you planned the deception. You didn't. It's only natural for you to do it because it's easy to slip into the illusion that every word, every sentence, every paragraph has a clear meaning. You want to be clear. You wrack your brains to be clear. But, unfortunately, the writing situation works against you. Surrounded by darkness, a single light illuminating the desk, you scribble over the page, trying to hold the reader in mind and trying to keep a firm grip on a line of thought. But somewhere deep in the imagination a seductive voice whispers. You become infatuated with the words and images it sets free. Ideas take off and soon you're floating in restless associations, the whole time writing under the illusion that your thought is clear. And it is — at least to you. But remember, except in your journal entries, you're writing for a reader. You must keep a grip on the reality of what goes down on paper.

That's where editing and revising comes in. It's okay to get lost in nocturnal associations as long as you examine them in the light of day. The act takes some courage. After all, to give up an illusion is hard, especially the illusion that you've been communicating clearly to another person — in this case, the reader.

To get started isn't too difficult, for it merely involves reading and rereading a rough draft as if you stood in someone else's shoes — the reader's. As you read, keep an eye out for words, phrases, and sentences that should be deleted, recast, combined with others, or replaced with more accurate ones (for example, a phrase such as *keep an eye out;* visualize the phrase — isn't it a horrible image?). With a pencil cross out the offending material. Rewrite between the lines or in the margins.

The problem in illustrating the editing and revising process comes from the fact that it happens all at once, not in a nice orderly pattern. We wish we could demonstrate it by the numbers — you know what we mean: first, take up a pencil; second, sharpen the pencil to a fine point; third and fourth, return to the desk and with the rough draft before you begin to . . . but editing and revising doesn't work that way. The process is in part intuitive, a kind of faith healing. Before the intuition can come into play, you must see how the process is done and collect some information about how to improve what you've written in a rough draft.

By way of beginning, we want to offer a passage published a few years ago in *Playboy.* What! Edit and revise a piece of professional prose? Why not? If you can see flaws in published writing, you may begin to see them in your own work. The passage is a reminiscence, and the author captures some details from his early years.

It begins very young up in the country whether you are raised on a big farm or in one of the small villages, which, though they often double as county seats, rarely number more than 1000 souls. There is a lumber mill down by the tiny river that manufactures crossties for the railroad systems, and the creosote the ties are treated with pervades the air. It is the smell of the town, depending on the wind: fresh-cut pine and creosote. In the center of the town there's a rather ugly yellow-brick courthouse, plain Depression architecture. The village is in northern Michigan and does not share the quaintness of villages in New England or the deep South, being essentially historyless. There are three baronial, rococo houses left over from the hasty passing of the lumber era, but most dwellings are characterized by their drabness, simply places for the shopkeepers to hide at night.

Confused? Absolutely! And your confusion doesn't come from our having lifted this single passage from a longer article. It comes from the author writing by midnight oil and failing to scrutinize the result in the sunlight. Truly, we don't know what this man is talking about. The intelligence behind the passage seems to be floating in a sea of personal associations. He seems to have no regard for a reader. For instance, what does "It" in the first line refer to? Moreover, what does "It begins very young up in the country" mean? Also notice how the writer begins by talking generally about villages and country but soon shifts to a particular village, one with a yellow-brick courthouse and three baronial, rococo houses. What are "baronial, rococo houses," anyway? What do they look like, really? Junk description like this often makes inexperienced readers feel stupid.

Since we wanted to find out what this passage was all about, we stripped it down, tore away the feathers to get to the meat. Where we could, we replaced difficult words with simple ones; we cut, rephrased, and combined. We worked with the intent of making the passage simple and plain. We weren't trying to clear up all the confusion; we only tried to edit away the decoration to see if anything could be saved and revised. Here is the result. We suggest you read it through, then reread it along with the marginal comments to get an idea of why we changed what we changed.

It begins ~~very~~ young ~~up~~ in the country	*How young is "very" young? Why "up"? These two words say little. No need for them.*
whether you are raised on a ~~big~~ farm or in ~~one~~	*How big is a "big" farm? Ten acres? A thousand? Since no perspective for big is given, there's no need for it.*

~~of the small~~ villages~~, which, though they often~~

~~double as county seats, rarely number more than~~ *of*

1000 ~~souls~~ *or less.* There is a ~~lumber~~ mill ~~down~~ by the

stream *makes*
~~tiny river~~ that ~~manufactures~~ crossties ~~for the~~

pine
~~railroad systems~~, and the smell ^*of* creosote and ^

fills
~~ties are treated with pervades~~ the air. ~~It is~~

~~the smell of the town, depending on the wind:~~

~~fresh-cut pine and creosote~~. In the center of

an
town there's ^~~a rather~~ ugly yellow-brick court-

built during the
house, ^~~plain~~ Depression ~~architecture~~. The

village lacks
~~village is in~~ northern Michigan ^~~and does not~~
history and *feeling* *of*
~~share~~, ^the quaint~~ness of villages in~~ ^New England
and Southern villages
~~or the Deep South, being essentially historyless~~.

mansions
There are three ~~baronial, rococo houses~~ left

over from ~~the hasty passing of~~ the lumber era,
homes
but most ~~dwellings~~ are ~~characterized by their~~

drab~~ness~~, ~~simply~~ places for ~~the~~ shopkeepers

to hide at night.

The phrase "one of the small villages" is too many words to say "a village." Keep your prose concise. Village implies small. The information about the county seat doesn't seem to serve any purpose.

"Souls" carries a connotation unnecessary to the passage. Delete "lumber." Lumber mill is implied by other detail. No need for "down."

A tiny river is a "stream." "Makes" is almost always better than the inflated "manufactures." Remember simple is better. "Crossties" are used for laying track; no need to say so.

This whole section is awkward; it needs reworking.

All this stuff can be dropped or combined with other sentences. It's repetitive.

Why "rather"? It doesn't do anything, really. "Ugly"? Readers should be able to see that for themselves.

"Plain Depression architecture" is awkward for "built during the Depression."

This needs reworking. Awkward structure.

What does "essentially" mean? Does this writer know? We don't think so. He's just mumbling to himself. "Historyless" is an awful misuse of language. The writer means without historical significance.

"Mansions" will serve for "baronial, rococo houses." No need for the "hasty passing."

"Homes" is simpler than "dwellings." In all your writing years you'll probably never need the phrase "characterized by." Always delete it. Always try to avoid sticking "ness" on the end of any word. Is there a need for "simply"? We don't see one.

Here's what the passage looks like with the changes incorporated:

It begins young in the country whether you are raised on a farm or in a village of 1000 or less. There is a mill by the stream that makes crossties, and the smell of creosote and pine fills the air. In the center of town there's a yellow-brick courthouse built during the Depression. The northern Michigan village lacks history and the quaint feeling of New England and Southern villages. There are three mansions left over from the lumber era, but most homes are drab, places for shopkeepers to hide at night.

Now, what do we have left? Not much — a limp balloon that sputtered from our fingers, made two turns about the room, then fluttered to the floor. We hope by our letting out the wind from this inflated passage you can see some of its problems. Can you?

Can you see the piece lacks unity? The writer didn't set the focus. He allows us to stray.

Can you see that the point of view is fractured? The passage should have been written from the "I" perspective, not the "you."

And the coherence? Can you see how the thought seems to skip and flop? The writer has tried to move from a general comment on rural northern Michigan to a particular description of one village. He fails to do it coherently.

Finally, we hope you can see how the sentences seem crippled. The writer has built them on *there is* and *there are* patterns, the thoughtless writer's short cut to description. These sentences need reworking.

With the editing done, we brazenly revised this writer's work; after all, under the writing teacher's blue pencil no one's prose is sacrosanct. We'll begin, as we suggest you begin when doing your own revisions, with the focus. This author's focus isn't clear. The focus must be made clear to achieve some kind of unity throughout the passage. Although the passage is confusing, we guessed from the first sentence that the writer was saying something about being young and becoming aware of the limited opportunities in his environment, which turns out to be Michigan:

> It begins young in the country whether you are raised on a farm or in a village of 1000 or less.

He also wants to speak to the condition of all young people, not just himself — hence the use of the general "you." Keeping these thoughts in mind we rewrote the sentence this way:

> Like so many from rural northern Michigan, while still young I became aware of how little my village offered.

This revision solves another problem besides focus and point of view disruptions. The writer mentions growing up on a farm, then promptly drops any details of farm life. By using "rural" we suggest farm and country life but allow for a smooth movement to the particular village that dominates the rest of the passage.

Once the opening sentence was set, we went after the rest of the passage. We reordered the details with a concern for coherence, restructured the sentences, maintained the "I" point of view, and, since the passage echoes insignificance, waste, and a drab life, added a few words to capture that tone. Here's the result:

> Like so many from rural northern Michigan, while still young I became aware of how little my village offered. My village had fewer than one thousand. It had neither significant history nor the quaint feeling of many New England and Southern villages. On its outskirts a stream flowed and carried away the waste from a mill that made crossties and filled the town with smells of creosote and pine. In the town center stood a yellow-brick courthouse that was built during the Depression. Near it sat three decaying mansions left over from the booming lumber era surrounded by drab homes, places for shopkeepers to hide at night.

This may not be the way the author would have rewritten this passage, but at least it is clear. Keep in mind, though, that editing and revising is not the reader's job; it's the writer's. In other words, it's yours.

You may be more concerned with writing information-centered pieces. No matter. The general approach to editing and revising holds up. Begin by rereading as if you stood in your readers' shoes. Ask yourself questions readers might ask you if they were present. "What does this sentence mean?" "Why have you repeated yourself?" "Why is this part muddled?" "Are you trying to confuse me with this word?" "What's your point, anyway?"

Exclamation Point

Be sparing in your use of the exclamation point. To overuse it is to create an immoderate, perhaps hysterical tone that exhausts most readers.

1. Use exclamation points after emphatic statements and commands.

   Horses couldn't drag me to that reunion!

   Be at my door at 7:08 p.m. exactly!

   He roared, "Give me the change!"

   "Off the roof!" Casey yelled.

   Don't use exclamation points after mild commands.

   When you finish the book, lend it to me.

   Come over sometime.

2. Use exclamation points after interjections.

>   Wow! The party lasted ten hours.

>   Can they win the relay? No!

Fragments

Sentence fragments are groups of words that have been written as sentences: each begins with a capital and concludes with a period, question mark, or exclamation point but is not really a sentence. Sometimes writers consciously use fragments for dramatic effect. "Oh my god! I got an A on the final." More often they attach them to sentences. "Oh my god — I got an A on the final!" But when writers write fragments unconsciously, they mar their prose.

>   The *Grapes of Wrath* touched my life. Because Steinbeck vividly portrayed a struggle my grandparents went through.

Many fragments, like the one above, follow sentences. Often they will be subordinate clauses introduced by words such as *although, because, if, since, until, while, that, which,* and *who.* Although a subordinate clause has a subject and predicate, it can't stand as a sentence. Fixing a fragment of this sort is fairly easy. Merely attach it to the preceding sentence or rewrite it so it can stand as a sentence.

>   The *Grapes of Wrath* touched my life because Steinbeck vividly portrayed a struggle my grandparents went through.

>   Faced with the prospect of not having enough money to buy food, the elderly poor must live each day in fear of slow starvation. Which some psychologists claim kills more of them than disease.

>   Faced with the prospect of not having enough money to buy food, the elderly poor must live each day in fear of slow starvation, which come psychologists claim kills more of them than disease.

>   Faced with the prospect of not having enough money to buy food, the elderly poor must live each day in fear of slow starvation. Some psychologists claim this fear kills more of them than disease.

>   Driving is still a cheap way to travel. Even though fuel prices have skyrocketed.

>   Driving is still a cheap way to travel even though fuel prices have skyrocketed.

Sometimes writers mistakenly treat verbal phrases as sentences. A verbal phrase begins with an infinitive (to dance, to sleep), a past participle (danced, slept), or a present participle (dancing, sleeping) and must always be part of a sentence. You can correct a fragment of this sort by combining it with a sentence or by rewriting it as a sentence.

We last saw Jane and Tom several hours after the game. Dancing in the street while the night poured rain.

We last saw Jane and Tom several hours after the game, dancing in the street while the night poured rain.

We last saw Jane and Tom several hours after the game. They were dancing in the street while the night poured rain.

Start your paper now. To have it ready by next Friday.

To have your paper ready by next Friday, start it now.

Start your paper now. Then you'll have it ready by next Friday.

Writers may also mistakenly treat prepositional phrases as sentences. Prepositional phrases begin with words like *toward, to, through, under, beneath, in, within, inside, over, above, outside, beside, behind, on,* and *about.* Generally, prepositional phrases can be attached to sentences but can never stand as sentences. Correct a fragment of this sort by combining it with the sentence that comes before or after it.

The newspapers carried the story. About the mayor hiring his son-in-law as a consultant for the city.

The newspapers carried the story about the mayor hiring his son-in-law as a consultant for the city.

It took three trips to Asia, two years of library research, and a mild heart attack. For Phillips to complete his study.

It took three trips to Asia, two years of library research, and a mild heart attack for Phillips to complete his study.

On days like today, when the sun is bright and the air is fresh and cool. I like to ice-skate on the pond at the edge of the woods.

On days like today, when the sun is bright and the air is fresh and cool, I like to ice-skate on the pond at the edge of the woods.

Sometimes writers treat appositive phrases — phrases that rename or describe nouns — as sentences. But, like subordinate clauses, verbal phrases, and prepositional phrases, appositives cannot stand as sentences. They must be combined with other sentences or rewritten.

The company is looking for a new sales representative. A person with a warm personality and an understanding of business.

The company is looking for a new sales representative, a person with a warm personality and an understanding of business.

Several popular weekend sports require exceptional hand-and-eye coordination. Handball, racketball, tennis, and squash.

Several popular weekend sports require exceptional hand-and-eye coordination — handball, racketball, tennis, and squash.

Hyphen

You can use the hyphen to divide words, form compounds, and attach prefixes and suffixes.

1. Use hyphens to indicate word breaks at the right-hand margin.

   Through storytelling the old communicate a family's history.

   Be sure to divide words only between syllables. Whenever you're unsure of the syllabication of a word, check a dictionary. The syllable break will usually be indicated by dots:

   com•mu•ni•cate

2. Use a hyphen to join two or more words that serve as a single adjective before a noun.

   That one-legged Easterner became a tobacco-chewing, rip-roaring broncobuster.

   Since taking a course in crafts, Beth has finished some well-designed cabinets.

   The twenty-year-old real estate tycoon will lecture tomorrow night.

   When the compound adjective comes after the noun, don't use a hyphen.

   Because she took a course in crafts, Beth's cabinets are well designed.

   The real estate tycoon, who is only twenty years old, will lecture tomorrow night.

3. Use hyphens to form certain compound words:

mother-in-law	deep-freeze
cross-reference	good-bye
clear-cut	half-moon

   Some compound words are hyphenated, and some are not, so check your dictionary for accuracy.

4. Use hyphens when spelling out numbers 21 through 99 and when writing fractions:

twenty-one	one-half
seventy-nine	three-fourths
two hundred ninety-nine	one three-thousandth

5. Use hyphens between prefixes and capital letters.

un-American	post-Civil War
pre-Nixon	non-South American

6. Use hyphens between words and the prefixes *self, co, all,* and *ex* (when it means "formerly"). Use a hyphen with the suffix *elect.*

   self-control   co-worker

   ex-student   all-world

   president-elect

7. Use a hyphen between a capital letter and a word that serves as a suffix.

   U-turn   T-shirt

   X-ray   F-sharp

8. Use hyphens to avoid doubling vowels and tripling consonants.

   anti-intellectual   re-evaluate

   bell-like   wall-less

9. Use "suspended hyphens" for hyphenated words in series.

   My mother-, father-, and brother-in-law all graduated from Locklin High School.

10. Use a hyphen to avoid ambiguity.

    re-creation (something   versus   recreation (a diverting
    created anew)   activity)

    re-count (to count again) versus   recount (to narrate a past
                                        experience)

Introductions

When you write an introduction, you must clearly state or strongly imply the central point, and you must shape the beginning so that it leads naturally into the discussion. At the outset of a draft, you will be wise to write an introduction that flatly states, no matter how awkwardly, the central point. Later, once the entire draft is written, you can rework the beginning or throw it out and create a more vigorous one.

Also, since an introduction must lead the reader into the discussion, don't back up too far to get a running start. For instance, if your subject is neighborhood vandalism, you would be unwise to start with a history of the Mafia.

Your introduction should also be appropriate and interesting. The kind you write will depend on the kind of essay and reader you envision. An essay written for an academic course would have a more formal introduction than one written for a student magazine. Here's a never rule: never write an introduction that reports the rigors you underwent writing the essay.

To write an interesting introduction is almost always to write in concrete language and specific detail. If your prose limps along, the reader's interest will wane. Avoid general, imprecise language, like this:

What do you buy when you buy an airline ticket? If you are going to fly in an airplane, it is important to know what you are guaranteed. If you read the fine print on the ticket, you will see you are not guaranteed much.

This introduction does little but present the subject and allow the writer to get twenty-eight extra words into the paper. He would show more consideration for the reader if he would merely start with the last sentence and toss out the first two. There are any number of effective ways to try to hook the reader's interest. All of them would use concrete language and specific detail.

What do you buy when you buy an airline ticket? What does it entitle you to, and what are the airline's legal obligations to you? What's their responsibility if they cause you to miss a connection or blow a hotel reservation? Next time you're sitting in an airport, waiting for your delayed flight to get off the ground, you can pass the time and cool off your indignation by reading the fine print on your ticket. A page headed "Conditions of Contract" could serve as a syllabus for a course in travel education.

Phrases such as "miss a connection," "blow a hotel reservation," "sitting in an airport," "waiting for your delayed flight," and so on add specifics most readers can relate to. This writer also uses a technique common to introductions: he begins by asking questions that the discussion will answer.

Since no set introduction is suitable for all purposes, a writer may begin an essay in any one of a wide variety of ways as long as it is appropriate, arouses some interest, and leads the reader into the discussion. What follows are some examples of the most common introduction techniques.

1. Sometimes a writer will begin by cleverly using facts and statistics. Or, to put it another way, by dramatizing facts or statistics related to the central point. We want to stress the word *dramatize*. For most readers, wading through murky lists of facts and statistics is dull going. A good writer will dramatize the information so that the reader will want to plunge into the rest of the essay.

Consider how Harry Stein dramatizes statistics in the opening paragraph of "How to Make It in the Water."

First the bad part. It appears that swimming is here to stay. All signs point in that direction. Drop by a public pool on a ninety-five-degree afternoon and see for yourself; there they'll be, by the hundreds, churning through the water like a herd of water bugs. Then there are the statistics. A. C. Nielsen, the television ratings guy, reports that 103,000,000 Americans swim regularly. Which makes swimming by far the nation's most popular leisure activity, ahead of bicycling (with a mere 75,000,000), fishing (63,900,000), camping (58,100,000), bowling (44,400,000), and tennis (29,000,000).

In the following paragraph Eric Lax in "Quick, Make a Mussel!" dramatizes facts to hook the reader.

This is about Mussels, not muscles. Consider: compared with an equal weight of T-bone steak, 3.5 ounces of mussels have the same amount of protein, one quarter the calories, one eighteenth the fat, eleven times the calcium and twice the phosphorus; mussels also pump fifty percent more iron into your body.

2. Often writers will begin by offering definitions. Good writers won't fall back on Webster's dictionary to supply them with ready-made quotes and leave it at that. Instead they will generate some interest that goes beyond the limits of a dictionary definition by casting descriptions in their own language and drawn from their own understanding.

In beginning a section on lions in *The Bestiary,* T. H. White opens by defining *beasts*.

Leo the Lion, mightiest of beasts, will stand up to anybody. The word "beasts" should properly be used about lions, leopards, tigers, wolves, foxes, dogs, monkeys and others which range about with tooth and claw — with the exception of snakes. They are called beasts because of the violence with which they rage, and are known as "wild" because they are accustomed to freedom by nature and are governed by their own wishes. They wander hither and thither, fancy free, and they go wherever they want to go.

Leo Rosten in *The Joys of Yiddish* begins a description of a *shlimozl* with a definition.

Pronounced shli-MOZ-zl, to rhyme with "thin nozzle." A chronically unlucky person; someone for whom nothing seems to go right or turn out well; a born "loser." Let me illustrate by combining four folk sayings: "When a shlimozl winds a clock, it stops; when he kills a chicken, it walks; when he sells umbrellas, the sun comes out; when he manufactures shrouds, people stop dying."

Often an introductive definition will be less formally structured than these just quoted and will seem to be closer to description (of course, definition is a form of description). For instance, in the opening paragraph of a short piece on packing in the Adirondacks, Anna La Bastille defines *lean-to,* a type of shelter available for public use on the trails.

The lean-to is part of the history and tradition of the Adirondacks. A three-sided open shelter, it was originally designed as temporary quarters for hunters and fishermen in the 1800s but soon evolved into a more permanent structure, often used as a base camp by turn-of-the-century vacationers. There are some 200 lean-tos in the Adirondacks.

3. A writer may use a dramatic narrative to plunge the reader into the midst of an incident and then may follow with an exposition of the central point. Peter Eastman begins "Thermal Injury," an article on burns, with this technique.

Robert, 27 years old, a graduate student; his wife, Anne; Frank, just graduated from Torrance High School; and Sue, Frank's best girl, are breaking an overnight camp on the west bank of Jenny Lake in the Sequoia National Forest.

Morning mists move slowly off the little lake. Pine needles scent the air. Packs are ready to be hoisted.

Robert pulls a cartridge from his tiny backpacker's stove. The shut-off valve sticks. Butane hisses for a moment, explodes loudly, and suddenly he is on fire. Knocked to the ground and shocked by the blast, he sits numbly watching his blazing clothes.

George Orwell begins an essay on poverty in Marrakech with this narrative.

As the corpse went past the flies left the restaurant table in a cloud and rushed after it, but they came back a few minutes later.

The little crowd of mourners — all men and boys, no women — threaded their way across the marketplace between the piles of pomegranates and the taxis and the camels, wailing a short chant over and over again. What really appeals to the flies is that the corpses here are never put into coffins, they are merely wrapped in a piece of rag and carried on a rough wooden bier on the shoulders of four friends. When the friends get to the burying-ground they hack an oblong hole a foot or two deep, dump the body in it and fling over it a little of the dried-up, lumpy earth, which is like broken brick.

4. Straw man and reversal are two other effective techniques a writer can use for opening essays. Both should be used with caution because they reverse the train of thought that the opening sentences establish. Joseph Morgenstern in a review of the film *Easy Rider* uses the reversal. It comes in the last sentence.

Time and again I wanted to reach out and shake Peter Fonda and Dennis Hopper, the two motorcyclist heroes of *Easy Rider*, until they stopped their damn-fool pompous poeticizing on the subject of doing your own thing and being your own man. I dislike Fonda as an actor; he lacks humor; affects insufferable sensitivity and always seems to be fulfilling a solemn mission instead of playing a part. I didn't believe in these Honda hoboes as intuitive balladeers of the interstate highways, and I had no intention of accepting them as protagonists in a modern myth about the destruction of innocence. To my astonishment, then, the movie reached out and profoundly shook me.

The straw man device is similar to reversal: a writer will set up someone else's views in the introduction and knock them down in the discussion. This technique usually begins with a direct quotation or summary that represents the position opposing the writer's. William Murray uses this method in the following quote.

A recent issue of the "Calendar" section in the L.A. *Times* listed twelve theater openings, sixteen ongoing major productions, 56 small-theater shows and 46 presentations in community playhouses. We would seem to be in the middle of a theatrical renaissance of unparalleled dimensions. Compared to what's available in L.A. and the immediate surrounding area, London is a backwater and New York a wasteland. Why isn't more being written about this phenomenon? Has L.A. become an Athens in a Periclean golden age of drama? Of course not.

5. A writer may begin by opposing a commonly held opinion about a subject. In the introduction to "The Joy of Maps," William Hjortsberg tries to shock the reader by challenging the general conception that maps are untrustworthy.

"All maps are bad!" This draconian dictum survives from a math course I took as an undergraduate more years ago than I like to remember. The course, Math 1, known as Math for Idiots, covered such everyday matters as maps and calendars, seemingly simple items that grew increasingly complex as their mysteries were revealed.

Richard Reeves in "Equal Credit for Ghosts" attempts to hook the reader by shaking his belief that celebrities write their own books.

In Jeb Magruder's Watergate book, one line of the acknowledgements reads: "I would also like to thank Patrick Anderson for his invaluable advice and assistance on this book." That was one of the three sentences in the book that Magruder wrote himself.

John Dean, on the other hand, actually did write a manuscript. It wasn't, however, *Blind Ambition* — that was written by Taylor Branch. What Dean wrote was a pile of pages, unpublishable according to some sources, incoherent according to others. When last seen, Dean was on the book promotion trail, telling talk show hosts about the lonely agonies he endured as a writer. This is not about Watergate; it is about ghostwriting.

There are more, many more, kinds of introductions. We've offered a few of the most common to give you a sense of the possibilities. But no single method is suitable for all occasions, and none will work on any occasion if used awkwardly or mechanically.

Numbed Language

You're probably familiar with the feeling that comes from sitting for twenty minutes with one of your legs beneath your hips: the leg loses feeling because the flow of blood has been blocked; the leg goes to sleep; it becomes numb. Language, too, becomes numb. Life is sucked from it so it no longer calls to mind an accurate vision of experience. To edit and revise successfully, you need to recognize any numbed language that's slipped into your prose. You'll need to cut it out and insert more accurate words.

Euphemism

One enemy of plain language is euphemism — pleasant words substituted for blunt ones or, in many cases, inaccurate words substituted for accurate ones. Although euphemism riddles every part of our culture, we can best illustrate it with some examples from the funeral industry. The *corpse* has become the *loved one,* the *deceased,* or the *dearly departed.* A *hearse* has become a *coach;* a *grave* has become a *final resting place.* A *coffin* was once a *casket* and is now a *vault* (no doubt for the loved one to be deposited in the ground like a weekly contribution to a savings account). The person in charge of all this used to be called an *undertaker;* now that person is a *mortician,* and a *funeral* is commonly referred to as a *ceremony.*

Euphemism obliterates any imagery that blunt words carry. The word *corpse* may call up mental pictures, while *dearly beloved* creates a mental vacuum. Can you visualize what an undertaker might look like? You probably see a man in a black suit and string tie, maybe wearing a stovepipe hat and sitting on the seat of a buckboard with a pine box in the back — if you've been conditioned by Westerns. Now try to visualize a mortician. Not easy to do, is it? Can you visualize a grave? Probably. How about a final resting place? Probably not. Our point is that euphemism tends to fog the connection between language and experience. Euphemism numbs the mind.

Euphemism is sometimes acceptable but more often it is harmful. In certain situations we feel more comfortable saying "men's room," "women's room," "bathroom," "rest room," even "powder room" for toilet. All well and good. These kinds of daily deceptions are no more harmful than a dangling modifier or a din of "you knows" scattered throughout someone's speech.

But euphemism can be dangerous to clear thought and plain writing. This danger is our main concern. Basically, euphemism is designed to deceive, and deception in language represents a danger to the way we see the world. If we fail to use words accurately, we will not have accurate pictures of experience; therefore, we will not transmit accurate information in our writing. We will be deceiving both ourselves and our readers.

Of course, you wouldn't set out to deceive a reader through the use of euphemism, would you? But merely having been born in contemporary America is to have been set adrift in a verbal sea of euphemism. A quick glance at advertising reveals that soap is called "body cleanser"; toilet paper, "facial quality tissue"; false teeth, "dentures"; used (or secondhand) cars, "preowned."

The government is probably the biggest euphemism offender. It has attempted to eliminate the word *poor* and replace it with *low income*. Slums and ghettoes are now called the *inner city*. Prisons are called *correctional facilities*. Employees are not fired but *selected out* or *terminated*. Old people are *senior citizens*. When officials claim one thing and something else turns out to be true, the first statement isn't a lie, it's *inoperative*.

Euphemism is designed to separate people from experience. If you've been raised in a society smothered in it, then you will be its victim and it will appear in your thought and writing. In fact, you might quite innocently write something like this passage taken from the opening of a student paper:

> Last summer I visited Mexico City's outskirts. The whole area was underdeveloped and swarming with the disadvantaged, who seemed to be living on a marginal diet. Several families often lived together in a small home, sometimes with no more than a single water source to serve them and several other homes together.

Too often beginning writers are trapped into believing that they should try to write like this. They think it sounds intelligent, perhaps official and authoritative. And why shouldn't they; after all, most beginning writers have had similar prose held up to them as representations of clear thought. Don't be deceived. This is the language of bureaucrats and sociologists unable to commit their emotion to what they see or to the language they use to describe what they see. They fluff their prose with euphemistic fuzz. Inhaling it numbs the reader's sensitivity. A revision of this passage with the euphemism cut out and plain language used to express what lurks behind the camouflage might read like this:

Last summer I visited the outskirts of Mexico City. The whole area was a slum, a ghetto swarming with starving people who seemed to have no more to eat than tortillas and water. Sometimes several families crammed themselves into two-room hovels made of cardboard and sticks. The only water they had came from a single tap shared by fifteen or twenty such dwellings.

Now the passage more closely represents what the writer saw. The numbed language has been replaced with vivid description that creates a picture of the experience. Readers don't have to guess what's behind the words. They can see. Whenever you revise a passage, replace any euphemisms you find with plain words. Your writing will become sharper, and you may even free yourself of some corrupt habits of thought.

Jargon and Pompous Language

Just as euphemism is a menace to good writing, so is jargon. It, too, is numbed language, words that have lost their teeth. Jargon comes from the specialized vocabularies of various professions, and for one reason or another has slipped beyond its professional boundaries. There's nothing wrong with technical vocabularies. Technicians such as doctors, lawyers, educators, mechanics, and policemen need technical language to practice their trades. The problem comes about when the technical lingo crops up in places where it doesn't belong. Then the words become confusing, misleading, or downright deceptive. For instance, a student operating under the influence of a psychology course wrote this way about her fear of taking a test.

I felt traumatically impacted when I read the first question on my history midterm. Normally I'm not one who suffers from paranoia, but I did feel my anxiety level elevate and I experienced a curious syndrome I often associate with a phobia toward standing on the top rung of a high ladder.

What does all this mean — "traumatically impacted," "normally," "paranoia," "anxiety," "syndrome," and "phobia"? Is the writer afraid? Is the teacher out to get her? Is she headed for a fall? The sample may be exaggerated, but it makes a point. Language taken from a specialized field and applied to an everyday situation usually sounds like gibberish to a person trained to spot nonsense. To the untrained it often sounds impressive, perhaps even intelligent.

And that's the danger of jargon. We all want to sound intelligent. Consequently, in our beginning work we try to emulate the nonsense that we confuse with thoughtful discourse. We end up writing confused prose. In fact, jargon is so confusing it has been suggested that the Food and Drug Administration compile a dictionary of current jargonese so that its employees can better cope with the babble.

What all this comes down to is that people use jargon to make ordinary comments sound important. Instead of saying "I'm scared," writers schooled in jargonese might say "I feel anxiety." Instead of saying "I haven't learned to read well," they might say "I'm educationally handicapped." Instead of "you make me angry," "I'm experiencing in-depth hostility toward you." Outside specialized fields, *anxiety, educationally handicapped,* and *in-depth hostility* are merely globs of jargon pasted to the page. Use of this kind of language says more about the writers than about the experiences they are trying to describe. It says their brains have been massaged by insensitive bureaucrats, manipulative politicians, misguided educators. We suggest you learn to nail down your thought with concrete words — in this case words such as *scared* or *fear, ignorant,* or *failure,* and *angry* or *mad.*

Pomposity is related to jargon. People who write pompously use words and phrases that sound scientific, technical, or businesslike. Pomposity is nothing more than tortured detours writers send their readers on when they could have pointed out the direct routes. Here are some guidelines written by an air pollution agency for the staff and students of a local college.

Obligations of College Personnel and Students Regarding Air Quality Alerts in Area:

ALERT ACTIONS

STAGE I: REDUCE VEHICULAR USE BY A) UTILIZING BUS SERVICE, B) IMPLEMENTING CAR POOL PLANS, C) POSTPONING UNNECESSARY MEETINGS AND TRIPS.

STAGE II: (IN ADDITION TO STAGE I). A) USE OF ALL CAMPUS MAINTENANCE VEHICLES WILL BE DISCONTINUED EXCEPT FOR EMERGENCIES, B) GREATER EMPHASIS UPON CAR POOLS, BUS SERVICE, BICYCLES, C) ALL ACTIVITIES THAT WOULD ADD POLLUTANTS TO THE AIR WILL BE DISCONTINUED.

STAGE III: NO DRIVING AT ALL EXCEPT FOR EMERGENCIES. THE COLLEGE AND DISTRICT WILL BE CLOSED, BOTH FROM AN INSTRUCTIONAL AND ADMINISTRATIVE POINT OF VIEW.

The agency could have made a more accurate statement in plain English:

Smog alerts come in three stages. Here are some directions for each one:

> Stage 1. Don't do any unnecessary driving. If you must travel, form car pools or use the bus.
> Stage 2. Continue with stage 1. No campus cars or trucks will be driven except for emergencies.
> Stage 3. Don't come to campus; it will be closed.

Writers flushed with pomposity might say

> The educational impact of our new media courses has surpassed our broadest expectations.

instead of

> Students are learning more than we expected from our TV courses.

or

> My paper will deal with the problematic area of the energy crisis.

instead of

> My paper deals with the energy crisis.

or

> When you think in terms of a major, you probably think in terms of future employment.

instead of

> When you think of a major, you probably think of finding a job.

or

> We don't perform at the same thinking level.

instead of

> We don't think alike.

or

> This college gives students more involvement type of experiences in curriculum-making decisions.

instead of

> This college asks students what should be taught and how it should be taught.

or

> I had many meaningful relationships with various members of my psychology class.

instead of

> I like some people in psychology class.

Words and phrases like *impact, broadest expectations, problematic, area of, in terms of, level, involvement, type,* and *meaningful* are often tipoffs that you're reading or writing pompous prose. Slow down. Ask yourself what the words really mean. Can the information be stated more directly? Don't be impressed with the person who writes pompously or with yourself if you are trying to do it.

Jargon and pomposity are wasteful. Although writers who use jargon and pomposity may sound intelligent, the chances are their material has no more substance than the eruptions from a bean-fed baby's rump. Do we exaggerate? Pause for a second and think of the frightening possibility that language of this sort actually does obscure an accurate vision of experience. Then listen to this kind of nonsense bursting from the lips of your elected officials. If you need a lesson in the use of jargon and pomposity, attend a school board or city council meeting. Listen carefully to hear if the language floating around the room connects to any kind of experience you recognize. But be on guard. Don't listen too carefully. Concentrating on official language for twenty to thirty minutes may affect the mind the way Novocain affects the gums.

How do you combat jargon and pomposity in your writing? Use common sense. Reread your work carefully to be sure you have written as plainly as possible. If you must use a technical term, be sure you know its precise meaning and use it precisely.

Paired Words

Paired words are another danger to thoughtful writing. After years of thoughtless use, words that got hitched now trip hand in hand through much of what we hear and read. Some people call them married words or stock phrases, but the name doesn't matter. What matters is that they do little for concrete communication because a writer can quickly dip into the surface of his language pool and come up with a stock description to fill a blank space. Paired words may not be as deceptive as euphemism, jargon, or pomposity (we feel writers use them mainly out of laziness), but they can be just as numbing, often leading readers to believe they're getting solid information when they're really feeding on formula.

To see how available paired words are, read the following passage and mentally fill in the blanks with the first words that come to mind:

> It was a grim- _____ group that gathered at the Huntsville City Hall and contemplated the _____ future. _____ time was slipping away. They had to _____ reality and make _____ judgments about evacuating people who lived near the town's nuclear power plant.

Although the responses may vary, yours probably aren't too different from ours.

> It was a grim-FACED group that gathered at the Huntsville City Hall and contemplated the NEAR/DARK future. PRE-

CIOUS time was slipping away. They had to FACE reality and make MATURE judgments about evacuating people who lived near the town's nuclear power plant.

These are just a few examples of the paired words floating around in our minds. There are more, perhaps thousands. For instance, whenever a man is accurate with a pistol, he's "deadly" accurate. And what kind of aim does he take? "Deadly" aim, of course.

When there's a need, what kind of need is it? A "dire" need — you're catching on. If a person is passionate, what kind of passion does the person exhibit? Easy, you say — a "firelike" passion. And when a person with a firelike passion has a purpose, what kind of purpose is it? A "compelling" purpose, naturally.

Finally, when a woman whose firelike passion drives her to fulfill a compelling purpose to become a brain surgeon, what kind of operation does she do, what kind of endurance does it take, where does the operation take place, and what do the people helping look like? (This is a tough one, but at this point in the brief lesson you should almost be a master of the formula.)

She performs *delicate procedures* which require *marathon endurance* in *operating theaters* while *grim-faced nurses* and *attending physicians* watch.

By the way, there was probably "precious little time" to save the patient's life since it was "hanging in the balance."

Clichés

Like paired words, clichés are also stock phrases that come easily to mind. We see them as being different from paired words because they often carry images. But the image is so blunted from overuse that it seldom pierces readers' imaginations. Once they were original expressions; now they're trite. You should avoid falling back on them when you're stuck for a more accurate description.

To give you an idea of what clichés are like, here are a few of the most exhausted ones:

flat as a
　pancake

like a chicken
　with its
　head cut
　off

quick as a
　flash

quick as
　lightning

old as
　Methuselah

as hard to
　find as a
　needle in a
　haystack

brown as a berry	hard as nails
fog as thick as pea soup	like a child with a new toy
cool as a cucumber	meek as a lamb
silent as the grave	smart as a whip
good as gold	claw to the top
happy as a clam	tumble to the bottom
rooted to the spot	head over heels
a barrel of monkeys	green as grass

Keep in mind that paired words and clichés are merely substitutes for fresh thinking. They spring to mind when you're in a rush, but they will always sound stale and will usually be confusing and inaccurate. It's easy to write something like

> We were so rushed we scurried about the house like a bunch of chickens with their heads cut off.

The image is a stock attempt to communicate rush and confusion, but it does that only for people who are numb to the visual power of language. Whenever you edit and revise your prose and come across clichés and paired words, strike them out and develop more accurate detail.

Parallelism

Parallelism exists when two or more ideas are expressed in the same grammatical form. In a pair or a series you must make the items parallel to avoid awkward shifts in construction.

> I enjoy going to concerts, hiking through the woods, and playing poker.

not

> I enjoy going to concerts, hiking through the woods, and poker.

> He learned to read rapidly, to speak fluently, and to translate easily in the new language.

not

> He learned to read rapidly, to speak fluently, and translating easily in the new language.

You can express a series of words, phrases, clauses, and even whole sentences in parallel form for both clarity and impact.

Words: I plan to read, fish, and loaf.

Phrases: Climbing the hills, dashing down the slopes, and racing through the valley became a daily routine.

Clauses: The light dimmed, the curtains opened, and the play began.

Sentences: We hope for the best. We fear for the worst. We get what we deserve.

Some of our most memorable quotations achieve their impact through parallel structure.

I came. I saw. I conquered.

Give me liberty or give me death!

Ask not what your country can do for you — ask what you can do for your country.

We shall fight on the beaches, we shall fight on the landing grounds, we shall fight in the fields and in the streets, we shall fight in the hills; we shall never surrender.

Parentheses

Keep in mind that of the three marks used to enclose nonessential elements (commas, dashes, and parentheses), parentheses indicate the greatest degree of digression.

1. Use parentheses to enclose numbers and letters marking items in a series within a sentence.

    To begin playing tennis well, you must remember three fundamental points: (1) tennis is a sideways game, (2) the back stroke makes a loop, (3) the follow-through should end high.

    Remember not to use periods with letters or numbers enclosed within parentheses.

2. Use parentheses to enclose nonessential information.

    One year after the war (his family didn't recognize him at first), he brought out the town's buried anger at draft resisters.

    There is nothing to seek and nothing to acquire (according to ancient Zen masters) because within every mind burns the flame of enlightenment.

Nonessential elements enclosed by parentheses take no special punctuation besides the parentheses themselves. At times you may have a punctuation mark following parentheses, but any such mark would be in the sentences even if the parentheses were not.

> At times when I feel my stomach churning from fear (usually the morning of a midterm or final), I do deep-breathing exercises.

> The dedicated detective buff spends hours each week prowling through used-book stores for first editions of the masters (Poe, Chesterton, Hammett, Chandler, and MacDonald).

Remember also to properly punctuate material you enclose in parentheses.

> Arab students (Egyptians, Iraquis, Lebanese, Syrians) make up the majority of the foreign student population on campus.

Period

You probably have few if any problems using periods.

1. Use periods at the ends of sentences that are declarative, that make mild commands, and that ask indirect questions.

> The class starts Wednesday at noon.

> Come to class Wednesday at noon.

> He asked if class began on Wednesday at noon.

2. Use periods with most abbreviations.

P. K. Smith	Mr.	Mrs.	Engl.
Ms.	Ph.D.	M.B.A.	Hist.
U.S.	Mass.	B.A.	Soc. Sci.

Don't use periods in abbreviations of the names of organizations and national and international agencies when more than two words are being abbreviated.

> IBM   (International Business Machines)
>
> NBA   (National Basketball Association)
>
> NCTE (National Council of Teachers of English)

Don't use periods with some abbreviations that are commonly used as words.

TV	VW	OK
5th	exam	lab
gym	memo	math

When in doubt about whether or not to use a period in an abbreviation, check a good dictionary for the acceptable form.

3. Use periods after numbers and letters in an outline.

    I. Subjects taught in the Department of English

        A. Writing
            1. Communicative
            2. Expressive
        B. Reading
            1. Remedial
            2. Developmental

Don't use a period if a digit or letter is enclosed by parentheses.

(a)

(1)

Point of View

By point of view we mean the way you present your material. In the broadest sense you can do it from either a personal or an impersonal stance. A personal point of view places you in the experience and leads you to use first-person pronouns (I, me, my, we, us, our). Or it may lead you to address your readers directly by using second-person pronouns (you, your). An impersonal point of view positions you out of the experience. It places you in an objective stance. When writing impersonally you'll seldom directly address the reader or use personal pronouns. One is the point of view of personal experience and observation; the other, of reports and research.

The material will usually dictate which stance to assume. You wouldn't take a journal entry that deals with childhood experience and rework it in an impersonal way; nor would you write historical, social, or scientific research in a personal way. So when selecting a point of view ask yourself where your material came from. From research? From reports of others? From personal experience? The point of view will follow naturally from the answer to the question.

In order to get a better feel for point of view let's take a look at several examples. Jan Harold Brunvand uses an impersonal point of view in presenting information on folk riddles in *The Study of American Folklore*.

Folk riddles are traditional questions with unexpected answers — verbal puzzles that circulate, mostly by word of mouth, to demonstrate the cleverness of the questioner and challenge the wit of his audience. The practice of riddling can be traced to the dawn of literary expression; it is referred to in the most ancient Oriental and Sanskrit writings, in the Bible, in classical legends and myths, in European folktales and ballads, and in some of the earliest manuscripts of Medieval literature. Compilations of riddles were among the first printed books in the

Middle Ages, and books of literary riddles remained a popular diversion well into the Renaissance. Since the beginning of professional interest in folklore in the nineteenth century, massive collections of folk riddles have been published in most European countries and in many countries outside Europe. Riddles have been found in the native cultures of all peoples, even the American Indians, who until recently were thought to possess only a few that had been borrowed from Europeans.

Dry, isn't it. The passage is cleansed of personal pronouns; it doesn't address the reader. Brunvand is giving us the results of research. He's not giving life experiences.

The impersonal point of view is not always this dry. Many second-hand reports are written from the impersonal stance — by writers presenting the experience of others. Since they weren't part of it, they report as outsiders. Here's an example from *Alive* by Piers Paul Read. He reports the experiences of people who survived an aircrash in the Andes. This paragraph captures the moment the plane crashes.

Several passengers started to pray. Others braced themselves against the seats in front of them, waiting for the impact of the crash. There was a roar of engines and the plane vibrated as the Fairchild tried to climb again; it rose a little but then there came a deafening crash as the right wing hit the side of the mountain. Immediately it broke off, somersaulted over the fuselage, and cut off the tail. Out into the icy air fell the steward, the navigator, and their pack of cards, followed by three of the boys still strapped to their seats. A moment later the left wing broke away and a blade of the propeller ripped into the fuselage before falling to the ground.

Certainly not dry, but not overdramatized, either. Read keeps his distance: he reports the facts objectively and lets them carry the impact.

Sometimes when deciding which stance to take — personal or impersonal — you'll reach a crossroads. Your material hasn't come from research or from other people's reports. It may fall more into the area of personal experience, yet not be exclusively your experience; others may have had it as well. Let's call it common experience — experience that comes from your general background and knowledge.

Common experience goes beyond our individual lives. It tilts toward the communal. It comes from our participation in society. At this moment you probably have sufficient background to write intelligently about limited aspects of TV, politics, education, racism, sexism, parenting, sports, music, books, films, art, advertising, death, and catastrophes. You could write about them by generalizing from the information you've collected over the years. Your readers could follow what you're saying because they have shared in these experiences. You may not be an expert in any of these areas, but to write about them is not to pretend to be an expert. You do have opinions along with enough information to develop them.

So what point of view do you use when writing from common experience? You can use either impersonal or personal. Either way, though, the writing will tend to sound more impersonal than personal — more authoritative.

Robert Paul Dye draws on common experience from radio to start "The Death of Silence." No doubt he's heard these programs and assumes his reader has also heard them or knows of them. His intent is to draw some general conclusions from them, not to reminisce about a mindless childhood spent sprawled in front of a Philco radio. He selects, therefore, an impersonal point of view.

> Radio's funniest moment occurred on the "Jack Benny Program" when a thief demanded from the great tightwad, "Your money or your life." The long silence that followed was more violently hysterical than any of the quick retorts that are the stock in trade of most comedians. Benny's use of silence, his great sense of timing, made him one of the most popular comics of this century. Benny, of course, was not the only radio artist who recognized that silence could be more effective than sound: silence followed the crash of Fibber McGee's closet, preceded McCarthy's responses to Bergen. The chillers became more chilling when there were moments of silence. Silence was used to make the romances erotic and the quiz shows suspenseful.

Contemporary poet Adrienne Rich in "When the Dead Awaken: Writing as Re-Vision" also generalizes about common experience. She expresses the problems women writers face in confronting images of women developed throughout literary history. She writes with authority. The passage seems impersonal. However, Rich begins one sentence with *I think* to clearly indicate her perspective.

> A lot is being said today about the influence that the myths and images of women have on all of us who are products of culture. I think it has been a peculiar confusion to the girl or woman who tries to write, because she is peculiarly susceptible to language. She goes to poetry or fiction looking for *her* way of being in the world, since she too has been putting words and images together; she is looking eagerly for guides, maps, possibilities; and over and over in the "words' masculine persuasive force" of literature she comes up against something that negates everything she is about: she meets the image of Woman in books written by men. She finds a terror and a dream, she finds a

beautiful pale face, she finds La Belle Dame Sans Merci, she finds Juliet or Tess or Salome, but precisely what she does not find is that absorbed, drudging, puzzled, sometimes inspired creature, herself, who sits at a desk trying to put words together.

The following anecdote comes from the *Autobiography of Malcolm X*. Malcolm X talks about his childhood veneration of that time's leading jazzmen. It's his private experience. No one else went through it. It calls for a first-person point of view.

> Some of the bandsmen would come up to the men's room at about eight o'clock and get shoeshines before they went to work. Duke Ellington, Count Basie, Lionel Hampton, Coote Williams, Jimmie Lunceford were just a few of those who sat in my chair. I would really make my shine rag sound like someone had set off Chinese firecrackers. Duke's great alto saxman, Jonny Hodges — he was Shorty's idol — still owes me for a shoeshine I gave him. He was in the chair one night, having a friendly argument with the drummer, Sonny Greer, who was standing there, when I tapped the bottom of his shoes to signal that I was finished. Hodges stepped down, reaching his hand in his pocket to pay me, but then snatched his hand out to gesture, and just forgot me, and walked away. I wouldn't have dared to bother the man who could do what he did with "Daydream" by asking him for fifteen cents.

The first person point of view is right. Notice how the writer avoids dropping the *I* on the reader's mind the way an ancient Oriental jailer might drip water on a victim's head in unrelenting cadences. When you use the first person singular, suppress the *I, my* and *me* by putting them only where you need to. In this passage Malcolm X uses *I* five times, *my* once, and *me* twice. No drip, drip, drip of personal pronouns that might drive a reader daffy.

The first person plural point of view involves the use of *we*. Never use the "royal we" or the "editorial we" — that is for one person trying to elevate personal experience to cosmic heights:

> Yesterday we went to class and found we had been given a C grade on our midterm.

Nor should you use *we* to avoid personal responsibility:

> We do not like the way this class is run. Our midterms, we find, were graded in too strict a manner.

This would be appropriate if the writer were speaking for the entire class, but the chances are the writer is speaking from personal feeling and using the *we* point of view as a shield.

Do use *we* when you are talking for yourself and others, but try to make the general identity of the others clear:

> Six other class members and I got together and agreed that our midterms had been graded too strictly.

Now the *we* fits.

The *we* point of view is often used to address a common group that includes the author. But the material sometimes has less to do with concrete personal experience and more to do with a general condition. Gerald Holton closes an essay titled "Constructing a Theory: Einstein's Model" with this point of view.

> As limited human beings confronting the seemingly endless parts and interlocking puzzles of the universe, we can nevertheless hope to play, as in Newton's metaphor, with pebbles at the shore of a vast ocean. If we do it well, that play can yield the most highly desirable kind of knowledge: a survey or overview of the world of nature that grants us the perception of an order guiding the phenomena in their infinite, individual variety and in their inexhaustible interactions with one another.

That's a mouthful, isn't it? But notice that Holton clearly establishes the members of the *we* group — all "limited human beings" who are "confronting the . . . puzzles of the universe." It's a glob of people, but a somewhat limited glob. When you confront the universe and have some others who are going to join you, talk to them from a *we* stance.

The use of *you* is right in any passage that directly addresses readers, particularly when it encourages or directs them to do something. If, for instance, you are sending readers on a journey or explaining a process, the use of *you* is natural.

Paul Roberts uses it in "How to Say Nothing in Five Hundred Words," an essay that explains how to go about writing college compositions.

> Say the assignment is college football. Say that you've decided to be against it. Begin by putting down the arguments that come to your mind: it is too commercial, it takes the students' minds off their studies, it is hard on the players, it makes the university a kind of circus instead of an intellectual center, for most schools it is financially ruinous. Can you think of any more arguments, just offhand? All right. Now when you write your paper, make sure that you don't use any of the material on this list. If these are the points that leap to your mind, they will leap to everyone else's too, and whether you get a "C" or a "D" may depend on whether the instructor reads your paper early when he is fresh and tolerant or late, when the sentence "In my opinion, college football has become too commercial," inexorably repeated, has brought him to the brink of lunacy.

Beginning writers seldom have problems addressing "you the reader," but sometimes stumble when using the indefinite *you,* which means *anyone:*

> When you travel east along the southern route to Tucson, you'll enjoy stopping at Ajo Drug for a thick malt and hamburger.

The problem here is that the writer has failed to suggest that the reader has any intention of doing what the writer proposes. The writer is talking to an indefinite you. The sentence could have been written more effectively with "anyone."

> Anyone who likes hamburgers and malts and is traveling east along the southern route to Tucson should stop at Ajo Drug for lunch or dinner.

But perhaps the writer wanted to use "you." It does have a certain intimacy. The writer could have done it by using an "if" clause to identify the reader.

> If you're traveling to Tucson along the southern route and you like hamburgers and malts, then stop at Ajo Drug.

Although it works in a situation like this, we suggest you avoid using the indefinite *you.* It causes trouble.

Sometimes writers shift to the *you* once a passage is under way. The use of *you* draws readers in, makes them feel like participants. The shift takes some skill. It must come smoothly and the experience must be one that readers can identify with:

> Last week I walked up to Kings Point and saw a spectacular sight. If you ever get up there at dusk, you'll see the desert stretching toward a deep blue sky mopped with red clouds. You'll see. . . .

When the shift is made awkwardly, it can be jarring.

> The physical threat to a quarterback passing from the "pocket" is intolerable. To stand there to the last millisecond, waiting for your receiver to reach the place the ball is supposed to go while you are being rushed by mammoth defensive linemen, takes sheer courage.

If directed toward potential quarterbacks, this passage would work. It wasn't, however. Writer Arnold J. Mandell directed it toward a general reader. Our guess is that not many general readers can identify with the experience. The shift is clumsy. Mandell would have written a more effective passage by avoiding the indefinite you, perhaps writing it like this:

> The physical threat to a quarterback passing from the "pocket" is intolerable. To stand there to the last millisecond, waiting for

a receiver to reach the place the ball is supposed to go while he is being rushed by mammoth defensive linemen, takes sheer courage.

Now the point of view is impersonal. Don't you feel safer with a little more distance between you and the charging linemen?

Sometimes beginning writers really muddle a passage by shifting to *you*. Often the shift will take a form similar to this:

> At first, students may find enrolling in college confusing, but if they follow the orderly process established by Admissions, it will be easy. First, before your appointment, fill out and return the preregistration forms. Then you must be sure to keep your counseling . . .

Did you catch the awkward shift from "students" to "you"? Don't make these kinds of shifts. If you know your audience you probably won't. For instance, if this writer had intended his directions for students themselves, he might have written it like this:

> At first, you may find enrolling in college confusing, but if you follow the orderly process established by Admissions, it will be easy. First, before your . . .

Or if the directions were for a more general audience — parents, teachers, clerks, and school administrators — he might have written it in this fashion:

> At first, students may find enrolling in college confusing, but if they follow the orderly process established by Admissions, it will be easy. First, before their appointments, they should fill out and return the preregistration forms. Then they must be sure to keep their counseling . . .

There is a way this should not be written. That's with the deadly "one."

> At first, one may find enrolling in college confusing, but if one follows the orderly process established by Admissions, it will be easy. First, before one's appointment, one should fill out and return the preregistration forms. Then one must be sure to keep one's counseling . . .

Our recommendation is that one should avoid the use of "one" when one writes. Its use adds sand to a fluid process.

A last thought about point of view: once you decide whether it will be personal or impersonal, stick to it. Stick to it through the entire essay. Keep in mind, though, that you can shift back and forth within a personal point of view. You may move from first person singular to first person plural and even to second person. But the shift should not come about out of mindlessness. It should be done skillfully. For example, examine the following passage from Jules Henry's *Culture Against Man.*

Henry begins with *I,* swings to *we* (our language, urge us, our culture, we must search), shifts to *you,* then returns to *we.* Notice that he uses the *you* to separate various members of his *we* group: "If you are propelled by drives," "if you are moved mostly by values." Henry has a strong grip on his point of view. It does not slip away.

> Fundamentally, values are different from what I call drives, and it is only a semantic characteristic of our language that keeps the two sets of feelings together. To call both competitiveness and gentleness "values" is as confusing as to call them both "drives." Drives are what urge us blindly into getting bigger, into going further into outer space and into destructive competition; values are the sentiments that work in the opposite direction. Drives belong to the occupational world; values to the world of the family and friendly intimacy. Drives animate the hurly-burly of business, the armed forces, and all those parts of our culture where getting ahead, rising in the social scale, outstripping others, and merely surviving in the struggle are the absorbing functions of life. When values appear in those areas, they act largely as brakes on drivenness. Though the occupational world is, on the whole, antagonistic to values in this sense, it would nevertheless be unable to function without them, and it may use them as veils to conceal its underlying motivations.
>
> In our own culture the outstanding characteristic of promotable executives is drive. It is no problem at all to locate jobs requiring an orientation toward achievement, competition, profit, and mobility, or even toward a higher standard of living. But it is difficult to find one requiring outstanding capacity for love, kindness, quietness, contentment, fun, frankness, and simplicity. If you are propelled by drives, the culture offers innumerable opportunities for you; but if you are moved mostly by values, you really have to search, and if you do find a job in which you can live by values, the pay and prestige are usually low. Thus, the institutional supports — the organizations that help the expression of drives — are everywhere around us, while we must search hard to find institutions other than the family which are dedicated to values.

Question Mark

The question mark has one principal use and three minor ones.

1. The principal use: use a question mark at the end of a direct question.

   How will we solve this problem?

Do you have the address?

Why haven't the answers been distributed?

2. Use a question mark at the end of a question presented in a series even though it may not be a complete sentence.

How many times have you missed? Six? Eleven? Fifteen times?

Another possibility might look like this.

How many times have you missed — six? eleven? fifteen times?

Whether or not to capitalize *six, eleven,* and *fifteen* would be the writer's option. We suggest that if you arrange questions in a series so that they stand alone, as in the first illustration, then you should capitalize them. But if you link them to the lead sentence, as in the second example, you shouldn't.

3. Use a question mark at the end of a question built into a sentence to make it more emphatic.

Will this situation ever end? I often wonder.

How many days will pass before the check comes? I keep hearing in my head.

Of course, if the question is a direct quotation, then the question mark is required.

"Will this situation ever end?" I heard John ask.

"How many days will pass before the check comes?" I asked Chuck.

4. Use a question mark within parentheses to show doubt about the correctness of numbers and dates.

The *Times* said 22,321 (?) marched on the reactor.

In 1945 (?) American English became the unannounced standard for the world's language.

Remember, use only a period after an indirect question.

Not

The police officer asked if there was anything he could do?

or

Taxpayers often wonder if they are getting their dollar's worth of government?

but

The police officer asked if there was anything he could do.

and

Taxpayers often wonder if they are getting their dollar's worth of government.

Quotations

Whenever you use the exact words of a speaker or writer in your own writing, put quotation marks at the beginning and at the end of the quotation. This will show the reader where the quotation begins and stops.

> A cranky type, Turk would shout "What of it" three times in rapid succession whenever anyone challenged his behavior.

> A. R. Orage said, "There is one art — the greatest of all, the art of making a complete human being of oneself."

These are direct quotations — the exact words of the speaker and writer. They could be arranged differently, but the principle of clearly indicating a quotation by placing marks around it holds up:

> "What of it," Turk would shout three times in rapid succession whenever anyone challenged his cranky behavior.

> "There is one art — the greatest of all, the art of making a complete human being of oneself," A. R. Orage said.

Sometimes writers will interrupt direct quotations. When they do, they are still responsible for separating their own words from those they quote.

> "There is one art — the greatest of all," A. R. Orage said, "the art of making a complete human being of oneself."

There will be times, however, when you'll want to give only a general idea of what someone has written or said. This would be an indirect quotation. Since an indirect quotation doesn't represent a person's exact words, you don't put it within quotation marks.

> A. R. Orage said that the greatest art of all is the art of becoming a complete person.

This indirect quotation more or less captures the gist of Orage's thought, but it needn't be set off by quotation marks.

Now that you have a general idea of how to indicate direct quotations, let's look at some particulars involved in punctuating, introducing, and editing quotations.

Punctuating and Capitalizing Quotations

Nothing makes writing easier than a hard and fast rule. We'll start with a couple. Periods and commas following quotations always go inside the marks, just as they are placed in these examples. Study them.

> Bent over and patting the carpet she said, "Finding a contact lens is like looking for a needle in a haystack."

> "A great writer always puts himself face to face with truth," Thomas Miller wrote.

Got it? Commas and periods that follow quotations always go inside the marks.

When you use colons and semicolons with quotations, always put them outside the marks.

> Some of my Aunt Maude's favorite expressions are "He runs around like a chicken without a head"; "Where there's smoke, there's fire"; "Don't count your chickens until they've hatched": expressions from the common pot of American clichés.

Understand? Always place colons and semicolons outside quotation marks.

Now the problem becomes more complex. Put question marks and exclamation points within the marks when they apply to the quotations.

> The child asked, "When are we leaving?"

> The protesters shouted, "Hell no! We won't go!"

But put them outside the quotation marks when they apply to the whole sentence rather than just to the quotation itself.

> What's the meaning of the phrase "collective unconscious"?

> Did they shout, "Hell no! We won't go"?

> Stop demanding, "Let's leave"!

Also notice that you use only one kind of end punctuation. You would not write

> Did they shout, "Hell no! We won't go!"?

> Stop asking, "When are we going?"!

Very bad form. It looks silly.

If the quotation you are using comes after the sentence is under way, you must handle it in one of three ways. First, when leading into a quotation with any word such as *said, says, states, shouts, shouted, maintains, believes, writes,* and so on, you need to put a comma after the leading word but outside the quotation marks.

> Last week Dr. Peters said, "In ten years we won't see one whale off the southern California coastline."

Next, if the quotation is an integral part of your sentence and you do not lead into it with any word such as listed above, you don't need any punctuation before the quotation.

> Mr. Hallfield told us that he is "the world's greatest historian."

Finally, if your sentence is grammatically complete before the quotation comes, then use a colon to set it up.

> Conrad clearly states the theme of his story through Marlowe: "O Youth! The strength of it, the faith of it, the imagination of it!"

Beginning writers sometimes get tied up over capitalizing quotations properly. No need to. These simple guidelines should straighten the problem out. If the quotation is a complete sentence, capitalize the first word.

> Psychologist Jean Piaget writes, "In order to understand we have to invent, because we can't start from the beginning again."

If you identify the source in the middle instead of at the end or beginning of the quotation, it will look like this:

> "In order to understand," psychologist Jean Piaget writes, "we have to invent, because we can't start from the beginning again."

Notice that the interruption is set off by commas. The word *we* is not capitalized because it doesn't begin the sentence, but continues it. If the second part of the quotation begins a new sentence, however, then you would capitalize the first word.

> "In the pursuit of learning, every day something is acquired," writes a Chinese sage. "In the pursuit of Tao, every day something is dropped."

Working Quotations into the Text

If you merely quote a complete sentence, you'll have no problem; just put quotation marks before and after it.

> "A writer is a person who writes."

But you'll seldom merely quote a complete sentence and leave it at that. More often you'll also introduce a quotation by acknowledging its source. You already had a taste of the practice in the above examples. You can acknowledge the source of a quotation by giving just the person's name.

> Clint Linder has said, "A writer is a person who writes."

You may also work in some information about the person.

> Clint Linder, a leading novelist, has said, "A writer is a person who writes."

Or you may work in even more information.

> Leading novelist Clint Linder, best known for *Naked Jackal,* has said, "A writer is a person who writes."

For various reasons you might want to add a little color to the introduction. If you were on the spot when the comment was made and wish to give the reader a feel for the scene, you can add some detail.

> Standing before an audience of college students gathered in a local pub, leading novelist Clint Linder, after countless whiskeys, lifted a fist to pulp writer J. M. Finnegan's nose and screamed, "A writer is a person who writes."

Or your introduction can be muted yet still packed with detail. You can even let your readers know how you wish them to view the quotation.

> Erich Fromm, psychoanalyst and social philosopher, writes of the deeper lessons that come from studying the mind: "Psychoanalysis teaches one to be skeptical of what a man says, because his words usually reveal, at best, only his consciousness."

When a quotation runs beyond four lines, skip two lines before and after and single space and indent the quotation itself. If the quotation begins a paragraph, indent the first line. Also, since block form indicates you are quoting, there will be no need for quotation marks. Block form should look like this:

> In *The Bestiary* T. H. White describes the general eating patterns of lions:
>
>> Lions abstain from over-eating: in the first place, because they only take food and drink on alternate days — frequently, if digestion has not followed, they are even in the habit of putting off the day for dinner. In the second place, they pop their paws carefully into their mouths and pull out the meat of their own accord, when they have eaten too much. Indeed, when they have to run away from somebody, they perform the same action if they are full up.

Ellipses and Brackets in Quotations

Often in order to sharpen the focus and to speed the movement of your paper, you'll want to cut out the parts of a quotation useless to your point. This is done by an ellipsis — three dots indicating you have omitted something from the quotation. If the ellipsis comes at the end of a sentence, then use four dots: one to indicate a period, followed by three to show omission.

You don't need ellipses to show all omissions. For instance, when you are excerpting single words or short phrases, the reader can see they've been taken from context, so you won't need ellipses. An operating guideline: avoid accumulating rows of dots; use them only when you sense a reader needs to know of an omission.

For instance, the example from White's *The Bestiary* might be used more effectively if trimmed and integrated with the writer's text.

> Lions don't live up to all the myths we have created about them. For example, they are not the insatiable eaters that clichés such as "hungry as a lion" suggest. Instead, as T. H. White states in *The Bestiary,* "Lions abstain from over-eating . . . they only take food and drink on alternate days." Moreover, they may even put off "the day for dinner" if the previous meal has not

been digested. They even have been known to "pop their paws carefully into their mouths and pull out the meat."

Brackets enclosing comments within a quotation indicate you are supplying the reader with information that for one reason or another is not within the quotation but is necessary for understanding. For example,

"Indeed, when they [lions] have to run away from somebody, they perform the same action [sticking a paw down the throat] if they are full up."

Semicolon

Some beginning writers see the semicolon as a mysterious squiggle designed by devious grammarians to addle the brain. Actually, the semicolon is easy to master.

1. Use a semicolon between main clauses not linked by a coordinate conjunction (*and, but, or, nor,* and sometimes *for, yet, so*).

   For some retired citizens Miami Beach is a glamorous lure; for others the city is a final dumping ground.

   The President delivered his speech; the protesters chanted and waved placards in the rear of the hall; the FBI took photographs.

   Remember that although the semicolon can take the place of a period between sentences, you should not substitute a semicolon for a period unless the sentences you join are closely related in meaning.

2. Use a semicolon between main clauses joined by a coordinate conjunction when there are several commas in the clauses.

   Today, families can eat at fast-food restaurants, such as Carl's, Kentucky Fried Chicken, Burger King, and McDonald's; but only a few generations ago, before people could hop in their cars and race to the nearest convenience center, families spent a greater part of their lives preparing food and eating it together.

   The semicolon before the coordinate conjunction *but* makes the break between clauses clearer than a comma would.

3. Use a semicolon between main clauses joined by a conjunctive adverb (*therefore, however, indeed, still, moreover, nevertheless, thus,* and *then*).

   Latin culture has its own sense of time; therefore, you should be prepared to wait as long as two hours for a scheduled appointment to start.

   People who want to know the look of the ocean need only walk straight ahead; moreover, by dipping their fingers into the sea they reach and licking off the drops, they will know the taste of the seven seas.

After a night of worry, I saw the sun rise; still, I felt the darkness inside.

Be sure to remember to put a comma after a conjunctive adverb.

4. Use a semicolon to separate items in a series if they are long and contain commas.

The books that stand out in my memory are Jung's *Memories, Dreams, and Reflections,* an autobiography that focuses on the psychologist's spiritual development; Fowles's *The Magus,* a mysterious novel that captures a character's personal growth and understanding of freedom; Lao Tsu's *Tao Te Ching,* a collection of reflections from an ancient Chinese philosopher.

Subordination

Whenever you want to emphasize one idea over another, use subordination. To subordinate, present the less important information in a dependent clause or phrase and attach it to a sentence. Often, arranging your information in this way will eliminate a series of choppy sentences and make your prose read clearly and smoothly. Read the following examples to see how sentences that seem disconnected can be improved through subordination.

1. We must budget carefully. I hope we can rent out the apartment above the garage. I want to buy a new car next year.

   If we budget carefully and if we can rent out the apartment above the garage, we can buy a new car next year.

2. The storm damaged the crop. Strawberries are selling for a dollar a basket.

   Because the storm damaged the crop, strawberries are selling for a dollar a basket.

3. The professor is an expert on weaponry used in the Civil War. He was raised in the South.

   The professor, who was raised in the South, is an expert on weaponry used in the Civil War.

When you subordinate information, be careful not to subordinate the main idea.

1. Before becoming senator, he lived in the state for only one year.

   After living only one year in the state, he became senator.

2. Because good writers are writing them, mysteries, thrillers, romances, and works of science fiction earn huge sums of money.

Because mysteries, thrillers, romances, and works of science fiction earn huge sums of money, good writers are writing them.

Titles

The title will be the first words your reader confronts, so it deserves some attention. Often you'll write the exact title after the paper is polished because it will be only then that you will have a full view of the content of your paper. But we suggest you always begin with a working title, one that fences in the subject's range.

Whatever you do, don't write tricky titles, ones designed to shock an audience into reading your essay; Gentlewomen Prefer Blondes, Plummeting Grades Suggest Brainrot, Thinking Can Land You in Jail, and such. In some eyes they may be cute, but to the steady gaze they are worthless. And never write empty titles: My Summer Vacation, Memories of Youth, A Work in Progress. Useless things seem to announce several paragraphs of boredom and tend to send a reader into depression. The best policy is to use the title to let your reader know what's coming as accurately as you can.

When you write a title at the top of the first page, don't put it in quotation marks. It's your title; you're not quoting someone else's. If by chance your title happens to include a quotation, then put marks around that part. And never underline your own title. Words underlined in handwritten papers indicate that if they were printed, they would be put in italics.

Be sure to capitalize your titles properly. Always capitalize the first letter of the first word and the first letter of the last word. Also capitalize the first letter of all other words that are not articles, prepositions of fewer than five letters, or conjunctions.

High-Rise and Low Income

Tricks of the Ad Trade

Fairy Tales: Paths to a Child's Mind

Tone

"I love your new coat," Bill said, touching the fabric. "It's soft. Where did you find it?"

Obviously, someone is paying someone else a compliment. The statements are straightforward, honest. But with some slight changes, we can get a new meaning from the dialogue.

> Raising his eyebrows, wrinkling his nose, and elevating his voice to a falsetto, Bill said, "I *love* your new coat. It's so . . . soft. Where did you *find* it?"

By making these changes in the descriptive detail, but without altering the dialogue, we've created a different tone. Do you hear the deception behind the words? For *soft,* interpret *floppy* or *shapeless.* And after the question "Where did you *find* it?" add the line "In a trash heap?" The speaker is no longer offering appreciation but snide criticism.

If you overheard these comments the meaning would be carried in the tone the speaker used to say the words. You'd hear it. Most people convey tone in speech without much thought. If they feel pleasant, they sound pleasant. If they feel snotty, they sound snotty. But to achieve tone in writing you have to make more conscious choices.

To keep it simple we want to start off by talking about tone in general terms. First, tone has something to do with the kinds of English you use, and there are many kinds. Should you write in the kind of English a college president might use in reporting the state of the school? The kind a TV news reporter might use to write copy? The kind your favorite thriller or romance writers might use? Or maybe the kind you might use to write letters to friends?

There is no single kind of English to write in for all circumstances. If you're writing a report for educators, then the circumstances might require you to write in the English of the college president. If you're writing for a universal audience, then the English the TV reporter uses might be appropriate. And, obviously, if you're writing to a friend, then you'd use the kind of English closest to the way you talk. What you always need to keep in mind are the situation and the audience.

Let's consider the way we speak to people. Although writing isn't recorded speech — far from it — it may help to understand how we use different kinds of English when speaking in different situations. Different situations force you to adjust your English and the way you use it.

For example, if you were talking to a toddler you might say something like "See the kitty. Pretty kitty. Fuzzy kitty. Touch kitty. Isn't it nice?" — and you'd be smiling a big I-love-you-baby smile. If, however, you were called on to respond spontaneously in psychology, you wouldn't talk as if speaking to a child: "Freud was a great man. He studied dreams. He also thought a lot." You'd address the group in more formal English: "Freud was the father of psychoanalysis, who thought through the concept of the unconscious."

After class with friends, your English would become more relaxed, full of slang, and more than likely stuffed with "ya know's" and "what'd you think's." Talking with an employer or a professor or anyone who might have the power to evaluate your performance, you would probably avoid the casual street English you'd use with friends; your English, like a military recruit facing an officer, might come to attention. English, then, can be looked at as formal and informal. The informal kind is reflected in the everyday way we talk to family and friends; the formal kind in the way we talk to our loan officers, bankers, college deans, and so on. Of course, there are various levels of formal and informal English, but for your immediate uses, these two will serve as touchstones.

In a broad sense, written tone, like spoken tone, can be looked at as formal or informal. It just depends on what kind of English you're writing in at the moment. Now, since most of us have little trouble adjusting our speech to meet the circumstances of a face-to-face situation, we suggest you consciously evaluate the writing situation as you automatically do the speaking one.

For instance, imagine you are going to write a report for consumer economics. Your job is to write objectively — to present the information in an unbiased way by reporting facts, not your opinions. Your topic is truth in labeling. You decide to focus on the cosmetics industry and zero in on hair-dye manufacturers. Since you're limited to writing an objective report, you would write it in a formal tone, perhaps like this paragraph from *Consumer Reports:*

> "Warning: Contains an ingredient that can penetrate your skin and has been determined to cause cancer in laboratory animals."
>
> In January 1978, the U.S. Food and Drug Administration proposed a regulation that would require a warning label with those words to appear on all hair dyes containing a widely used chemical. But none of the estimated 33 million American women — and the unknown number of men — who dye their hair will ever see the warning. For obvious reasons hair-dye companies don't want it on their products. Some companies have therefore "reformulated" their hair dyes so that the cancer-causing chemical is no longer included.

This is no way to write home from summer camp. Much too formal. Much too objective. But this would serve for any unbiased report.

If, however, the situation changed, and you were to use the information to put forth your attitudes about the industry's attempts to avoid accurate labeling, the tone might shift from formal to informal. You might write a paragraph something like this one:

> About two years ago, the Food and Drug people were on their toes. They forced hair-dye makers using a chemical called for short 4-MMPD to warn buyers that it might cause cancer. Cancer! The industry went into shock. Not because of the threat its product posed for 33 million women and an undetermined number of men who use the stuff. But because the hazardous labeling might cut into profits. Many companies, therefore, "reformulated" their dyes. They excluded 4-MMPD. Good, you might be thinking, a blow for truth and better health. Wrong! These companies haven't stopped using dangerous chemicals. They've merely switched to ones that have yet to be tested by the Feds.

In this example the sentences are simpler and shorter, the words are less complex, the details less ponderous, and the whole paragraph moves the reader forward without giving him much time to stop and think. The tone, then, is more casual than the first example, less formal, a little more souped up. Word choice, sentence structure, the way details are used, even the imagery help create the tone.

From these last examples, you've probably come to suspect there is more to tone than the use of formal and informal English. Besides formal or informal, readers often declare a writer's tone to be ironic, snide, wry, scholarly, pompous, dry, sardonic, witty, scathing, gentle, tongue-in-cheek — the labels are endless. Moreover, a writer's tone often implies, but never directly states, an attitude toward a subject.

For example, consider the tone of this opening paragraph from a piece titled "The Ultimate White Sale" published in *Mother Jones.* What do you think the writer's attitude is toward the Ku Klux Klan? How would you label the tone?

> The New Klan came riding in this decade right on the coat tails of the New South. Dry-look Grand Wizard David Duke has been making the talk-show rounds, promoting his Knights of the Ku Klux Klan. Its new face is cool, Madison Avenue, and cleaned up; it no longer claims to murder blacks — although Duke has been known to occasionally dust off his swastika.

The attitude? It would be safe to bet the writer doesn't like Duke's new Klan. And the tone? Well, naming a tone isn't as important as the impression it leaves with the reader. But clearly the tone suggests cynicism, a cynicism over the chances that the Klan would change its way and perhaps even a wider cynicism over the way people and ideas are merchandised.

Notice, for instance, how the writer uses the title, "The Ultimate White Sale." Although we may not know it at first, by the end of the paragraph we can see the title is used cuttingly. The idea of a department store's semiannual sheet and pillow case sale (keeping in mind that both pillow cases and sheets are part of the Klan's costume) links with Duke's attempt to sell white supremacy. The idea of cynical merchandising also connects with words and phrases, such as *dry-look, promoting, Madison Avenue,* and *claims.* The writer wants us to see that this packaging offers nothing more than a new wrapper for the same old garbage — that the Klan's "new face" still fronts the old policies of terror and suppression: "Duke has been known to occasionally dust off his swastika." And Duke, like so many other hucksters, makes the "talk-show rounds."

A writer's tone isn't always as distinguishable as the tone in the above example. Sometimes a writer will deliberately write in a flat style while using humorous details and images. The result is deadpan humor — a kind of humor that results from a comedian delivering jokes while maintaining an absolutely expressionless face. Samuel L. Clemens, who wrote under the name Mark Twain, uses this technique in the following paragraph from *Mark Twain's Autobiography,* in which he describes the church in his birthplace, Florida, Missouri.

> Most of the houses were of logs — all of them, indeed, except three or four; these latter were frame ones. There were none of brick, and none of stone. There was a log church, with a puncheon floor and slab benches. A puncheon floor is made of logs whose upper surfaces have been chipped flat with the adz. The cracks between the logs were not filled; there was no carpet; consequently, if you dropped anything smaller than a peach, it was likely to go through. The church was perched upon short sections of logs, which elevated it two or three feet from the ground. Hogs slept under there, and whenever the dogs got after them during services, the minister had to wait till the disturbance was over. In winter there was always a refreshing breeze up through the puncheon floor; in summer there were fleas enough for all.

The humor is here. Imagine a church floor with cracks so large a peach could almost drop through. Imagine a congregation sitting through Sunday service munching peaches, for that matter. But the incongruity of eating peaches in church with dogs and hogs battling below is humorous. Clemens tells it in a deadpan tone. The tone also reveals an unflappable attitude; Clemens doesn't judge the experience. Snorting hogs and barking dogs chewing on each other was merely a "disturbance." A winter breeze coming up through the floor was "refreshing." And the fleas? Well, at least everyone got a share.

In contrast to Clemens's understated tone, Richard Selzer, writer and M.D., launches this passage with an exaggerated praise: "I sing of skin, layered fine as baklava, whose colors shame the dawn . . ." *Awe* seems to be the most accurate word to describe Selzer's attitude toward skin.

> I sing of skin, layered fine as baklava, whose colors shame the dawn, at once the scabbard upon which is writ our only signature, and the instrument by which we are thrilled, protected, and kept constant in our natural place. Here is each man bagged and trussed in perfect amiability. See how it upholsters the bone and muscle underneath, now accenting the point of an elbow, now rolling over the pectorals to hollow the grotto of an armpit. Nippled and umbilicated, and perforated by the most diverse and marvelous openings, each with its singular rim and curtain. Thus the carven helix of the ear, the rigid nostrils, the puckered

continence of the anus, the moist and sensitive lips of mouth and vagina.

What is it, then, this seamless body-stocking, some two yards square, this our casing, our facade, that flushes, pales, perspires, glistens, glows, furrows, tingles, crawls, itches, pleasures, and pains us all our days, at once keeper of the organs within, and sensitive probe, adventurer into the world outside?

Enough! We could spend a great deal of time giving you examples of various tones. But our mission is more practical. We want to make you aware of tone in your own work. Ask yourself, "What's the appropriate tone for my piece?" "Formal or informal?" "Should it express an attitude?" "What attitude?" And so on.

Let's face it. Tone conveys involvement. How can a writer express an attitude without feeling connected to the subject? Sure, there are scholarly pieces that at first glance seem toneless. But they're rare, and the chances are that a close look will reveal a tone, perhaps a reserved one, the voice of the meticulous explorer.

There are segments of the writing community, however, that attempt to scour away tone. Your college admissions office, for instance:

> We are pleased to inform you of your acceptance to Fairview College. In the upper right-hand corner of this page, you will find a number. This is your identification number. Please use it in any further communication you have with us in the future.
>
> Good luck in the pursuit of your education.
>
> *Office of Admissions*

And good luck to you, buddy!

This kind of tone is dangerous. When enough people who don't know any better read it throughout their lives, it becomes a standard in their minds for good writing. Don't you make that mistake. Unless you are putting someone on — maybe an admissions officer — don't write in this official tone. It's deadly. In fact, it's so deadly we suggest the admissions office would serve you better by writing something like this instead:

> You're in!
>
> Now, because we have so many people with the same last names and because we are swamped with letters, whenever you write to us use the number we've printed in the upper right-hand corner.
>
> Welcome to our campus, #92139.

At least it would be more honest.

One more thought on tone. In Getting Started we suggested you keep your tone consistent. Certainly writers shift their tone now and then, but as a practical practice, you should try to stay consistent. Whatever you do, avoid awkward shifts from an informal tone into a formal one — like this:

> My grandmother used to avoid black cats, ladders, and activity on Friday the thirteenth. Once I saw her stop in a crosswalk and hold up traffic while she bent over to pick up a penny with her arthritic fingers. What did she do with it? What else. She dropped it into her shoe for good luck. I guess she came from the old school of simple cause and effect, the school of superstition.
>
> Superstitions are often thought of as naive, popular beliefs that are logically or scientifically untenable. Hence, the alternate term *folk belief* is often employed, carrying with it the connotations of unsophistication and ignorance that the word *folk* has in popular usage. Well, my grandmother may have been unscientific but she was not illogical. She operated with an ironbound logic . . .

This kind of fractured tone is unacceptable. It usually comes from confusion. In this case the writer has become confused in writing about personal experience while trying to sprinkle in bits and pieces of official information. This kind of effort needs to be rewritten. The writer needs to integrate the formally written information with his informal tone.

Unity

When writing you need to keep your paragraphs unified. Build each one around the main idea expressed in the topic sentence. No supporting sentence in the final draft should wander from that idea. If one does, delete it or risk the chance your readers will stray. A good way to maintain unity is to keep an eye on the topic sentence — a well-written one always points the way. That's why we suggest you begin paragraphs with them.

Notice how the topic sentence points the way in a paragraph from Norman MacKinzie's *Dreams and Dreaming*. He develops it with examples and keeps the paragraph unified by making sure each one relates to the main idea.

> The public interest in dream oddities never flags. Only a few years ago, an English newspaper regularly published the dreams of a man who forecast the results of horse races, and there are frequent press reports of cases in which it is claimed that a lost person or stolen object has been recovered by following the clues given in dreams. There was a famous example of this in 1932, when the small son of Colonel Lindbergh, the famous American flyer, was kidnapped; newspaper readers were asked to submit

any dreams that might help to find the baby. Hundreds were studied, but less than a dozen bore any resemblance at all to the facts. After Goya's portrait of the Duke of Wellington was stolen from the National Gallery in London in 1961, eager dreamers claimed to have "solved" the crime. In 1958, even the American Atomic Energy Commission considered a proposal that it should employ dream clairvoyants to predict where Soviet bombs might fall in the event of war!

To check the unity of a paragraph of this sort is simple. Merely state the main idea and check the supporting statements against it to see if they relate. In brief an evaluation might look like the following:

1. dreams forecasting horserace results run in a newspaper
2. reports of lost persons or objects recovered following dream clues
3. dreams submitted to solve Lindbergh kidnapping
4. dreams claimed to have solved Goya theft
5. use of dreams considered by Atomic Energy Commission to predict bomb targets

Clearly, all these supporting ideas have to do with dream oddities as they have captured public interest. The paragraph is unified. We suggest you use this technique not only for checking paragraph unity but also for planning paragraphs.

Sometimes a writer will cast a topic sentence as a question. Then the unity can be judged by whether or not the supporting statements answer the question. Gail Sheehy in *Hustling* writes a causal pattern that starts with a question.

> People are puzzled: why this boom in prostitution when young America is bursting with sexual freedom? They forget about men over forty, men who learned their sexual fantasies from nudie calendars in the gas station. To be fun, the bedmate must be a no-no. "You can't fantasize about your wife or girl-friend," one man explained. "The woman has to be an unknown." And where is this illicit thrill of forbidden flesh still to be found? On the black market of course. Furthermore, the prostitute makes no emotional demands. She would never call his office the next day. It is her stock in trade to encourage men's sexual fantasies and exploit them. How else can a girl make seventy thousand dollars a year, tax free!

Often a writer who begins a paragraph with a topic sentence will end the paragraph with a clincher — a restatement or summary of the main point. John R. McBride in "Trifles and Treasures for Drinking the Golden Brew" uses this tactic. After the topic sentence McBride develops his main point through a catalogue of details. The details relate. The paragraph is unified.

> As if in tribute to beer's antiquity — and popularity — man through the ages has devised special vessels from which to drink the beverage. In fact, no other beverage has inspired such a wide variety of drinking containers. They range from wood, leather, and pottery to gold, silver, pewter, porcelain, and glass — from beakers, bowls, and tankards to steins, tumblers, fancy goblets, and paper cups. Beer drinking vessels have been utterly crude and supremely ornate. They are beautiful and grotesque, practical and supercilious.

McBride's closing lines — "Beer drinking vessels have been utterly crude and supremely ornate" and "They are beautiful and grotesque, practical and supercilious" — both summarize the details in the discussion while echoing the main idea that man has developed special containers for beer drinking.

Although you'll have a better chance of keeping a paragraph unified if you start with a topic sentence, you don't always have to. Sometimes writers put them at the end. As we said in Getting Started, this is usually true of paragraphs that move from particulars to a general observation. Joyce Maynard in "My Secret Life with the Rolling Stones" shapes a paragraph in this fashion.

> My mother has kept the albums of her youth in the attic. Frank Sinatra, in close-up, wearing a hat, seems to be looking, with blue eyes not yet labeled "old," right into my own. I wouldn't recognize him as the same Frank Sinatra who not so long ago played golf with Spiro Agnew and wears a toupee. It must be strange and sad for a generation that knew Sinatra as a skinny boy with a brush cut to hear him today singing about facing "the final curtain." When the idols of your youth have aged, it's a pretty clear indication that you've aged too.

This paragraph is unified. Maynard has developed it through a single example that helps the reader understand the main idea she's used to end the paragraph.

Let's take a look at another example. Certain kinds of comparisons often end with a topic sentence. A writer will usually devote the major part of a paragraph describing one thing, then close the paragraph by linking it to another in the topic sentence. The technique builds some suspense, but if the link is not clearly made, the writer faces a breakdown in unity. To begin an explanation of bandwagon, a propaganda technique that motivates people to join the crowd, Donna Cross begins with a description of lemming behavior. In the topic sentence at the end of the paragraph she ties up the comparison.

Ever hear of the small, ratlike animal called the lemming? Lemmings are arctic rodents with a very odd habit: periodically, for reasons no one entirely knows, they mass together in a large herd and commit suicide by rushing into deep water and drowning themselves. They all run in together, blindly, and not one of them ever seems to stop to ask, "Why am I doing this? Is this really what I want to do?" and thus save itself from destruction. Obviously, lemmings are driven to perform their strange mass suicide rites by common instinct. People choose to "follow the herd" for more complex reasons, yet we are still all too often unwitting victims of bandwagon appeal.

Sometimes a writer leaves out a topic sentence. This doesn't mean the paragraph isn't unified; it means the main idea can be clearly understood without being stated. A difficult trick, for most paragraphs need topic sentences to pull all the supporting details together. To see what we mean, reread the last two examples. Ask yourself if the main ideas would be clear without having been stated in the final sentences. Then read the following example written by philosopher and author Bertrand Russell. It has no topic sentence, yet Russell's main idea is clear.

Very gradually I have discovered ways of writing with a minimum of worry and anxiety. When I was young each fresh piece of serious work used to seem to me for a time — perhaps a long time — to be beyond my powers. I would fret myself into a nervous state from fear that it was never going to come right. I would make one unsatisfying attempt after another, and in the end have to discard them all. At last I found that such fumbling attempts were a waste of time. It appeared that after first contemplating a book on some subject, and after giving serious preliminary attention to it, I needed a period of subconscious incubation which could not be hurried and was if anything impeded by deliberate thinking. Sometimes I would find, after a time, that I had made a mistake, and that I could not write the book I had had in mind. But often I was more fortunate. Having, by a time of very intense concentration, planted the problem in my subconscious, it would germinate underground until, suddenly, the solution emerged with blinding clarity, so that it only remained to write down what had appeared as if in a revelation.

Although Russell starts off with a general statement that takes us into the paragraph, the main point dealing with the role the subconscious plays in composition emerges from the details. We need to interpret them to get the point.

To keep unity in a paragraph without a topic sentence, you must have clearly established the main idea in your mind and be sure the idea emerges from the details. Once you've mastered the trick, then you'll find well-unified paragraphs without topic sentences have two advantages: they allow you to stop thumping a reader over the head with your message (if, however, your reader is a teacher and your message is expressed in an essay exam, we urge you to thump as often and as hard as you can), and they help you involve a reader in what you have to say. As an example, study the following paragraph taken from Dick Gregory's *The Shadow That Scares Me,* then supply your own topic sentence.

> I came from a family where I was expected to go to church on Sunday. I used to sit next to so many people who *loved* God — until the chips were down. My momma was like that. She was so busy loving God that it never occurred to her to respect Him. If she had respected God and the Bible, things would have been different in our house. Momma used to bring home food which she stole from the pantry of the white folks she was working for. She would cook it, serve it, and then *demand* that we pray over it. One day I took Momma down into the basement where I hid the things I had stolen. I said, "Here, Momma, you pray over what I have stolen and then I'll go back to the table and pray over what you have stolen." Momma didn't know that I was a better thief than she was. I just couldn't justify mine.

No doubt any topic sentence you might shape for this paragraph would have something to do with religious hypocrisy. All the details of Gregory's anecdote lead to that idea.

So you can maintain paragraph unity through a topic sentence (either stated or unstated) that carries a main idea. Of course, keeping unity requires some work. You must clearly understand the main idea and be sure the supporting sentences reflect it. If they don't, revise.

Reread all your paragraphs for unity — check the sentences against the main idea. The revision may only require reworking the topic sentence to more accurately reflect what follows. Or you may find you've included some material that merely nicks the edges of the main idea. This irrelevant stuff must be cut out. Perhaps it can be used in another paragraph; perhaps it's destined for the trash bin. In either case — out. Or you may have a few details that are on target but need to be attached to another sentence. Fine. Go ahead and make the change. The entire time you're rereading keep in mind that treating these unity concerns is much like treating a cold. The congestion, sore throat, and headache are all related. It wouldn't make much sense to treat them separately.

Now read the following paragraph for unity problems. Check the topic sentence against the supporting sentences. Look for irrelevant material that needs cutting. Watch for details that work but need to be subordinated to other sentences.

Attending this college may be dangerous. Last week in the parking lot my friend Bill accidentally bumped the side of a pickup. Just as he was finishing a note to leave on the windshield, the owner came up, scowled at the grapefruit-sized dent, then punched Bill in the nose. He drove off without looking back or taking Bill's name and address. At least Bill didn't have to pay in cash for the damage. Three days ago a bicyclist wearing portable radio earphones plowed into a psychology instructor. Both went sprawling over the walkway. After several minutes and with some help from passing students, the victims stumbled away, bruised and scraped. Yesterday in the zoology lab a four-foot snake slipped from its cage. No one noticed until it struck at one student, sending four others into shock. Then a lab technician came in, snatched up the snake and stuffed it back into the cage. No one plans to sue the college, but those students have a good case if any would press it.

Now study the following example to see what the version revised for unity might look like:

Attending this college may be unexpectedly dangerous. Last week in the parking lot my friend Bill accidentally bumped the side of a pick-up. Just as he was finishing a note to leave on the windshield, the owner came up, scowled at the grapefruit-sized dent, then punched Bill in the nose⁄ ~~He drove~~ before driving off without looking back or taking Bill's name and address. ~~At least Bill didn't have to pay in cash for the damage.~~ Three days ago a bicyclist wearing portable radio earphones plowed into a psychology instructor. Both went sprawling over the walkway. After several minutes and with some help from passing students, the victims stumbled away, bruised and scraped. Yesterday, in the zoology lab, a four-foot snake slipped from its cage. No

Topic sentence refined to more accurately reflect what follows. Clearly these dangerous events are unexpected.

This sentence linked to the preceding one. The one that follows is deleted because it is irrelevant.

one noticed until it struck at one student,

sending four others into shock/ ~~Then~~ *before* a lab   *"Then a lab . . ." can be linked to the*
                                                                 preceding sentence.

technician came in, snatched up the snake, and

stuffed it back into the cage. ~~No one plans~~   *This whole sentence is irrelevant to the*
                                                                 main idea. The college's legal responsibility
~~to sue the college, but those students have a~~   *for these acts may become the main idea of*
                                                                 another paragraph.
~~good case if any would press it.~~

With the corrections integrated, the final draft reads like this:

> Attending this college may be unexpectedly dangerous. Last week in the parking lot my friend Bill accidentally bumped the side of a pickup. Just as he was finishing a note to leave on the windshield, the owner came up, scowled at the grapefruit-sized dent, then punched Bill in the nose before driving off without looking back or taking Bill's name and address. Three days ago a bicyclist wearing portable radio earphones plowed into a psychology instructor. Both went sprawling over the walkway. After several minutes and with some help from passing students, the victims stumbled away, bruised and scraped. Yesterday in the zoology lab a four-foot snake slipped from its cage. No one noticed until it struck at one student, sending four others into shock before a lab technician came in, snatched up the snake, and stuffed it back into the cage.

Remember, an effective topic sentence always points the way. Use your topic sentence to measure the effectiveness of the other sentences.

Word Choice

Accurate Verbs

Much of what we've suggested about sharpening your prose forces you to use active verbs. Verbs serve as the flywheels of your sentences. We suggest you strain very hard to find the most accurate one you can for each sentence. Consider the following example:

> A man walked down the street.

If you wanted to tell how the man walked, you might write,

> The man walked quickly down the street.

Or you might say he walked rapidly. Okay, but a single verb could do it better:

> A man scurried down the street.
>
> A man strode down the street.
>
> A man swaggered down the street.

Now the sentence is sharper; the verb is more accurate. If you stop to think for a moment, you'll realize how many words we have to describe the way a person might walk — *strut, stumble, promenade, saunter, stride, clump, tramp, tread, pace, step, ramble, march, toddle, waddle, file, glide, straggle, shuffle, scuff, meander, stroll, creep, stalk, wander, trudge, stamp, limp, stagger, ambulate,* and even *perambulate.*

So, whenever you reread a rough draft, check to see if you can sharpen your verbs. But remember to select verbs that fit what you're saying; don't pick them because they may sound fancy. For instance, you wouldn't be helping your prose much if you wrote, "A drunk perambulated down the street" — unless you wanted to get a laugh. Instead of *perambulate,* you would probably write *staggered.*

Sometimes selecting the right verb can change a fairly good passage into a stronger one. Here's a student's fanciful description of an experience in a bookstore:

> The crowd wandered through the bookstore. Some couples talked softly with each other and others walked in silence, stopping at various stands to read a page or two. One woman looked up and called out, "OHMYGOD!" as a rider on a white stallion came through the door.

Now read the revised version to see how more active and accurate verbs create a better passage:

> The crowd browsed through the bookstore. Some couples whispered to each other and some strolled in silence, pausing at various stands to read a page or two. One woman glanced up and blurted, "OHMYGOD!" as a rider on a white stallion clip-clopped through the door.

Browsed, whispered, strolled, and *pausing* help to create a casual atmosphere one might find in a bookstore. Using *glanced* in place of *looked* is more effective because it seems more abrupt. *Blurted* works better than *called* because it conveys shock or surprise. *Clip-clopped* works better than *came* because it generates the sound of hooves and fractures the casual mood established in the opening sentences. By substituting active and accurate verbs the writer has sharpened the passage.

You might say that finding active verbs is easy to do for description, but what about using them in information-centered passages? Well, it can be done. Read the following passage from C. M. Bowra's *Classical Greece:*

> The Greeks won their war with a famous ruse that military men and statesmen often try to repeat in other ways. They gave Troy a gift — a wooden horse with Greeks hidden inside. While the Trojans slept, the Greeks crept out and opened the city's gates to the rest of their army. Masters at last, the Greek soldiers

saw Helen reunited with Menelaus, and everyone started for home. But one among them, the ingenious Odysseus who had devised the wooden horse trick, found the route 10 years long.

Verbs like *won, gave, crept, opened* and *saw* make this passage active. Whenever you can, use active verbs to generate life in any writing you do.

A warning: we don't want to leave you with the impression that you should write hyperactive prose:

The Greeks annihilated the Trojans by using a famous ruse that military men and statesmen often try to repeat in other ways.

They thrust a gift before Troy — a wooden horse with Greeks stuffed inside.

Hyperactive prose usually rings false and sounds silly. It's best left to cheap thriller and romance writers:

An ominous pall crushed the city as agent X slammed the turbo Mustang into second and jammed down the accelerator as he swept into the turn, fish-tailed, and then skidded onto Broadway.

Laura, panting breathlessly, the freezing night air thrusting into her lungs like an ice pick, huddled against the castle wall where fear had paralyzed her.

Hmmmmm! Maybe there is money in it. Anyway, we suggest you sharpen your work by using accurate and active verbs. Whatever you do, don't stretch for the exotic when doing college assignments.

Hidden Verbs

Sometimes you may spend hours tinkering with verbs. You'll rummage through your vocabulary and browse through a thesaurus for the most active and accurate ones you can use. You'll end up with some finished sentences like these:

My research leads me to the solution of Travanian's identity.

Since John Simmons quit the committee, we must search for a replacement.

The P.E. department encourages utilization of the pool during lunch hours.

To understand *The Deer Hunter* we must perform an analysis of its imagery.

Good verbs in these sentences, right?

Yes . . . but . . . And here the "but" is important. *Leads, search, encourages,* and *perform* are not the real verbs in these sentences. *Solve, replace, use,* and *analyze* are the real verbs, but they are hidden because they are disguised to look like nouns. These sentences would be more accurately cast if revised in this fashion:

> My research solves the question of Travanian's identity.

> Since John Simmons quit, we must replace him.

> Students can use the pool during lunch hours.

> To understand *The Deer Hunter,* we must analyze its imagery.

When you edit and revise a rough draft watch out for verbs that have been turned into nouns. Often they can be recast as verbs and used to make your writing more concise.

Concrete Language

Definite, specific, and concrete language pulls the reader to the page. General, vague, and abstract language pushes the reader from the page. As an ad writer might phrase this thought: vivid language gives an "up close" feeling; obscure language gives a "far back" feeling.

Far Back	*Up Close*
He was old when he gained success.	He had turned gray and seen his seventy-first birthday when he won the Nobel Prize.
The police arrested him in an alley.	Six police officers with drawn pistols captured him in an alley.
At Bernard's the sales staff greets customers courteously.	At Bernard's the sales staff greets customers with a smile.
Phil likes independence in his job.	Phil likes being his own boss.
For me to write an essay takes patience.	For me to write an essay takes hours of pacing and pencil chewing, at least a hundred pages covered with useless scribbling, and several pots of black coffee.

Although most writing assignments required in such courses as history, geology, sociology, and psychology will lead you into making general observations, you should never lose your grip on vivid language. Sometimes a line or two of vivid language mixed with the most general of observations will bring the reader up close to the page.

> *Far Back*

> No student of human experience can deny one fact: once we were all children. We still carry that child inside. The childhood

experience has shaped our world view. It has influenced the way we relate to others and created our approach to problem solving. When we find ourselves quarreling over petty issues instead of negotiating reasonable solutions, more than likely our inner child is behind the behavior.

Up Close

No student of human experience can deny one fact: once we were all children. We still carry that child inside. The childhood experience has shaped our world view. It has influenced the way we relate to others and created our approach to problem solving. When we find ourselves quarreling over petty issues instead of negotiating reasonable solutions, more than likely we have activated the tiny tyrant who used to toss himself to the floor, kick his feet, pound his fists, and scream and cry to get his wishes met.

The revised version ends with vivid language that brings the reader closer to the experience. When you find yourself writing general observations, always work in a line or two of vivid language.

INDEX

212 – 217.
293 → 295
3.6 – 311

354

To the Student

Please help us make *One to One* an even better book. To improve our textbooks, we revise them every few years, taking into account the experiences of both instructors and students with the previous edition. At some time, your instructor will most likely be asked to comment extensively on *One to One*. Now we would like to hear from you.

Complete this questionnaire and return it to:

College English Developmental Group
Little, Brown and Company
34 Beacon Street
Boston, MA 02106

School_____

City, State, Zip Code _____

Course title_____

Was this a conference-centered course? _____

Instructor's full name _____

Other books required _____

_____

1. Did you and your instructor regularly hold conferences to discuss your writing? ____

2. Did you like *One to One*? _____

3. Was it easy to read? _____ Difficult to read?_____

4. In what ways did *One to One* improve or fail to improve your writing? _____

   _____

   _____

5. Which sections were the most useful to you? _____

   _____

   Why were they useful? _____

   _____

6. Did you find the examples with parallel comments useful? _____

   How could they be improved? _____

   _____

7. Did you use the Index for Writers? _____ How was it helpful?

   _____

8. Did you find that the tasks in Part Three, Daily Writing, helped your writing

   skills?_____ In what ways?_____

   _____

   Did the tasks in Daily Writing help you in ways not related to writing?_____

   What ways? _____

   _____

9. Did you like the way *One to One* was organized?_____

10. Did you like the physical appearance of *One to One?* _____

11. Should the instructor continue to assign *One to One* next term?_____

    _____

12. Please add any comments or suggestions. _____

    _____ _____

    _____

    _____

    _____

    _____

    Signature _____ Date_____

    Mailing address _____

    _____

    _____